NO ONE'S WORLD

# NO ONE'S WORLD

## THE WEST, THE RISING REST, AND THE COMING GLOBAL TURN

CHARLES A. KUPCHAN

A Council on Foreign Relations Book

OXFORD
UNIVERSITY PRESS

# OXFORD
UNIVERSITY PRESS

Oxford University Press, Inc., publishes works that further
Oxford University's objective of excellence
in research, scholarship, and education.

Oxford  New York
Auckland  Cape Town  Dar es Salaam  Hong Kong  Karachi
Kuala Lumpur  Madrid  Melbourne  Mexico City  Nairobi
New Delhi  Shanghai  Taipei  Toronto

With offices in
Argentina  Austria  Brazil  Chile  Czech Republic  France  Greece
Guatemala  Hungary  Italy  Japan  Poland  Portugal  Singapore
South Korea  Switzerland  Thailand  Turkey  Ukraine  Vietnam

Published by Oxford University Press, Inc.
198 Madison Avenue, New York, NY 10016
www.oup.com

Oxford is a registered trademark of Oxford University Press

CIP record is available from the Library of Congress.

ISBN-13: 978-0-19-973939-4

9 8 7 6 5 4 3 2 1
Printed in the United States of America
on acid-free paper

*To my family; past, present, and future*

# CONTENTS

# ACKNOWLEDGMENTS

For the last two hundred years, Europe and the United States have together shaped the nature of the modern world. Backed by its power as well as its ideas, the West served as both the architect and the steward of the globalized order that began to emerge in the nineteenth century. With the collapse of the Soviet Union late in the twentieth century, the Western way—liberal democracy, capitalism, and secular nationalism—appeared to have finally prevailed against its many challengers.

The West has certainly enjoyed an extended and impressive era of global dominance, but the clock is running out on its primacy. As this new century unfolds, power will become more widely distributed around the globe. Countries that long operated in the shadow of Western hegemony are now entering the top ranks and expecting a level of influence commensurate with their position.

How will the world change as developing regions acquire new wealth, military strength, and sway? Will the West's ideas and conceptions of political order outlast its primacy, or will emerging powers generate their own approaches to governance, commerce, statecraft, and the management of global affairs? The answers to these questions will have a major impact on the nature of the world that emerges as the twenty-first century progresses.

I began to probe these issues over a decade ago. In 2002, I published *The End of the American Era*, a book that foretold the waning of U.S. primacy and the onset of a multipolar world. My last book, *How Enemies Become Friends* (2010), examined how and when nations that are rivals are able to become partners, turning enmity into amity. One of my objectives was to shed light on how to preserve peace as global power shifts and awakens new geopolitical contests. *No One's World* is in many respects the logical sequel to these works. This book explores the struggle over order and ideology that will ensue as China, India, Brazil, and other developing states rise and the dominance of the West gives way to a more equal distribution of global power.

As the title of this book makes clear, I argue that the next world will belong to no one. The Western way is not being universalized, in large part because it emerged from social and economic conditions unique to Europe and the United States. But neither is it being displaced by a new center of gravity or dominant political model. Rather, the coming world will be both multipolar and politically diverse; it will consist of major powers that embrace distinct conceptions of what constitutes a legitimate and just order.

Accordingly, if the emerging global turn is to occur peacefully, the West and the rising rest will have not only to reach agreement on matters of position and prestige, but also to forge a consensus on the ordering rules that define legitimacy and govern matters of commerce, war, and peace. This work seeks to contribute to that goal by exploring the social and economic underpinnings of the Western world, mapping the political landscape that is emerging outside the West, and proposing a set of foundational principles to help anchor the quickening transition in global order.

I would like to thank my two home institutions, Georgetown University and the Council on Foreign Relations, for providing moral and financial support and offering a limitless supply of intellectual stimulation. Wittingly and unwittingly, my colleagues and students have been vital interlocutors as I worked to develop and refine my ideas about the nature of the emerging world and how best to manage global change. Carol Lancaster, the dean of Georgetown's School of Foreign Service, provided steady encouragement and the breaks from teaching obligations needed to complete the manuscript. I would like to thank the president of the Council on Foreign Relations, Richard N. Haass, and its director of studies, James M. Lindsay, for their personal and professional support and for my appointment as the Council's Whitney Shepardson Senior Fellow. I am grateful for the resources and intellectual community provided by the Council's International Institutions and Global Governance Program, directed by Stewart Patrick and funded by the Robina Foundation. I also thank for intellectual stimulation and support the "Europe and Global Challenges" program, funded by Compagnia di San Paolo (Italy), Riksbankens Jubileumsfond (Sweden), and VolkswagenStiftung (Germany).

The Council on Foreign Relations convened three seminars to review the draft manuscript, all of which provided invaluable feedback. I am deeply grateful to the three chairs of these sessions, Jodie Allen, Sebastian Mallaby, and Anne-Marie Slaughter, and to the participants: Abdullah Akyüz, Lawrence Bruser, Aimee Carter, Thomas Christensen, Jean-Marc Coicaud, Heidi Crebo-Rediker, Elizabeth Economy, Amitai Etzioni, Rosemarie Forsythe, Henry Gaffney Jr., Colin Grabow, John Ikenberry, Koichi Imura, Robert Jervis, Peter Kellner, Judith Lee, Aaron Lobel, Paul McQuade, Maurizio Molinari, Adam Mount, William Murray, Daniel Nexon, Stewart Patrick, Stanley Roth, Jack Snyder, Ronald Steel, Paula Stern, Nigel Sutton, David Wargin, Patrick Weil, Allan Wendt, Chris Wood, and Nobuo Yoneyama. I presented an early excerpt from the book at the University of Virginia and thank the seminar participants for their feedback. In addition, I am indebted to the following individuals for their comments on the manuscript: Cliff Kupchan, Simma Kupchan, Jim Lindsay, Hans Maull, John McNeill, John Owen, David Shambaugh, and Julia Sweig. I am fortunate and grateful to have benefitted from the generosity and insight of all these friends and colleagues.

I owe a special debt of gratitude to Adam Mount and Peter Trubowitz, co-authors with whom I recently published a number of essays. A good many of the ideas arising from my intellectual collaboration with these kindred spirits have found their way into this book, especially in chapters six and seven. I also thank *Democracy*, *Foreign Affairs*, and *International Security* for permission to draw on these co-authored essays in this work.[1]

Many individuals helped with research. I am particularly indebted to my research associates at the Council on Foreign Relations,

Isabella Bennett, John Elliott, Connor Mills, and Conor Savoy. They not only backstopped my work, but also made significant intellectual contributions to the book. I also thank Alex Erines, Seth Gainer, Anson Gorga-Highland, Florian Kern, Andrew Pazdon, Hop Wells, Alexandra Wilson, and Stephen Wittels for their time and assistance.

David McBride at Oxford University Press has been a pleasure to work with. His comments on the manuscript were invaluable. I would also like to thank my tireless literary agent, Andrew Wylie, for his wise and steady counsel.

Finally, I am profoundly grateful to my family, Simma Kupchan, Nancy Kupchan Sonis, Clifford Kupchan, Sandy Kupchan, and Nicholas Kupchan for their constant love and support. My father, S. Morris Kupchan, and stepfather, H. Richard Sonis, although no longer with us, have been by my side from start to finish. I would also like to thank Steve and Louie Asher for their support and friendship—and their forbearance as the demands of writing a book on occasion meant my absence from family events. My wife, Simma, provided emotional and material sustenance and pored over the manuscript word by word. She also put up with the inconveniences that accompany an author at work—late dinners, solo outings, a messy desk piled high with books and papers, and an occasionally cranky partner. My family is my world, and I am deeply grateful to all.

Charles A. Kupchan
Washington, DC

NO ONE'S WORLD

# 1 :: The Turn

## Multiple Modernities

In August 1941, Franklin Roosevelt and Winston Churchill held a series of secret talks on the *USS Augusta* and the *HMS Prince of Wales*, both of which were anchored in a secure Newfoundland harbor. As World War II raged in Europe, the two leaders gathered to lay out a blueprint for the world that might come next. The Atlantic Charter they crafted envisaged a global order resting on self-determination, free trade, and disarmament. The United States had not yet entered the war, but the meeting nonetheless marked the moment at which the United States began to assume stewardship of the Western world. After Japan attacked Pearl Harbor later that year, the United States led the Atlantic democracies to victory in World War II. It then went on to anchor the liberal order that ultimately defeated the communist bloc and emerged triumphant from the Cold War.

By the end of the twentieth century, it had become fashionable to argue that history was coming to an end.[1] Following the fall of the Berlin Wall and the collapse of the Soviet Union, democracy and capitalism spread apace; the international order forged by the United States and its European allies at the close of World War II seemed ready to encompass the globe. Although China, Russia, Cuba, and most countries in the Middle East and Africa were stubborn hold-outs, they were expected to soon fall prey to the irresistible allure of the Western way. As the new millennium opened, the

West was not only running the show, but appeared to have finally prevailed against its many antagonists.

Fast forward to December 2009, in Copenhagen. Some one hundred world leaders convene in Denmark to forge an agreement on limiting the emissions that contribute to global warming. Barack Obama arrives on the eleventh day of the conference, which had thus far produced scant progress. That evening, Brazil, China, India, and South Africa hold a closed-door meeting to strengthen emerging-power solidarity. With the summit soon to draw to a close, Obama gambles by barging in. Aides scramble to find chairs for the U.S. president and Secretary of State Hillary Clinton. A breakthrough finally emerges at this impromptu gathering. But the accord falls well short of the binding commitments to curb emissions that most Western countries had hoped for. The rising powers had called the shots. America's European partners were not even in the game. Reflecting on this turn of events, the *Washington Times* pronounced, "The American Century is over."[2]

The Copenhagen Summit is only one of many signs that the twenty-first century marks not the ultimate triumph of the West, but the emergence of a global landscape that is headed toward a turning point rather than an end point. The West is losing not only its material primacy as new powers rise, but also its ideological dominance. The world's autocracies, far from being at their last gasp, are holding their own. China has been enjoying rates of economic growth triple those of the Western democracies, and its surpluses remain critical to underwriting America's pendulous debt. The global downturn took a heavy toll on the Russian economy, but the Kremlin has nonetheless maintained firm control over the state and is pursuing a muscular foreign policy. The oil-rich sheikdoms of the Persian Gulf, although shaken by the contagion of unrest that has recently spread through much of the Arab world, have continued their autocratic ways. Moreover, should participatory government spread in the Middle East, the regimes that emerge may well be much tougher customers than the autocracies they replace. Even rising powers that are democratic, such as India and Brazil, are hardly stalwart supporters of the Western camp. On the contrary, they regularly break with the United States and Europe on geopolitics, trade, the environment, and other issues, preferring to side with ascending states, whether democratic or not. Interests matter more than values.

Meanwhile, the liberal democracies of the West have been stumbling. The problem goes well beyond the Great Recession, which was born and bred in the United States, the West's architect and chief minder. Weak and faltering governance pervades the industrialized world. George W. Bush staggered through his second term with some of the worst popularity ratings on record. Barack Obama entered office committed to the restoration of bipartisanship and national unity, but Democrats and Republicans have been unable to find common ground. No wonder that by 2010, public confidence in Congress had hit an all-time low. The United States is not alone in confronting democracy's discontents. Many industrialized countries—Great Britain, France, Germany, Italy, and Japan among them—have recently been afflicted by divided electorates and enfeebled governments.

The emerging landscape is one in which power is diffusing and politics diversifying, not one in which all countries are converging toward the Western way. Indeed, the world is on the cusp of a global turn. Between 1500 and 1800, the world's center of power moved from Asia and the Mediterranean Basin to Europe and, by the end of the nineteenth century, North America. The West then used its power and purpose to anchor a globalized world—and has been at the leading edge of history ever since. But the West's rise was a function of time and place, and history is now moving on. East Asia has been anointed as the candidate most likely to assume the mantle of leadership. It is doubtful, however, that any country, region, or model will dominate the next world. The twenty-first century will not be America's, China's, Asia's, or anyone else's; it will belong to no one. The emergent international system will be populated by numerous power centers as well as multiple versions of modernity.[3] For the first time in history, an interdependent world will be without a center of gravity or global guardian. A global order, if it emerges, will be an amalgam of diverse political cultures and competing conceptions of domestic and international order.

Failure to foresee this global turn and adjust the West's grand strategy accordingly would be an error of grave consequence. This potential misstep is already in the making. The problem is not a failure to recognize the ongoing diffusion of power. On the contrary, American and European strategists understand that new powers are on the rise and that Western primacy will inevitably wane. Indeed, the United States and its European partners have taken the lead in transforming the G-8, a global directorate dominated by Western nations, into the G-20, a more inclusive grouping of major powers in which the Western democracies are in the minority.

Most strategists are, however, misconstruing the nature of the fundamental challenge posed by the global diffusion of power. The prevailing wisdom holds that the Western powers should capitalize on the twilight hours of their primacy to corral countries into the liberal international order that they have constructed. According to G. John Ikenberry, the West should "sink the roots of this order as deeply as possible," thereby ensuring that "the international system the United States leads can remain the dominant order of the twenty-first century."[4] While it still has the power to do so, the West must complete the process of extending its values and institutions to the rest of the globe. Even Fareed Zakaria, who has recognized that a "post-American world" lies ahead, falls into the same intellectual trap. "The power shift...is good for America, if approached properly," Zakaria writes. "The world is going America's way. Countries are becoming more open, market-friendly, and democratic."[5]

To cast the grand strategic challenge of the era in such terms may be reassuring to Americans and their democratic allies, but it is wishful thinking. The Chinese ship of state will not dock in the Western harbor, obediently taking the berth assigned it. Rather than embracing the rules of the current international system, rising powers will as a matter of course seek to adjust the prevailing order in ways that advantage their own values and interests. They have been doing so since the beginning of time, and the coming era will be no different. The task at hand is not guiding rising powers into the Western harbor. Rather, it is establishing a new order whose fundamental terms will have to be negotiated by Western powers and newcomers alike. The West will have to give as much as it gets as it seeks to fashion a new international order that includes the rest.

The world is barreling toward not just multipolarity, but also multiple versions of modernity—a politically diverse landscape in which the Western model will offer only one of many competing conceptions of domestic and international order. Not only will well-run autocracies hold their own against liberal democracies, but rising powers that are democratic will also regularly part company with the West. Perhaps *the* defining challenge for the West and the rising rest is managing this global turn and peacefully arriving at the next world by design. The alternative is a competitive anarchy arrived at by default as multiple centers of power and the differing conceptions of order they represent vie for primacy.

## The Argument

This book is not the first to foretell the waning of the West's primacy.[6] It is, however, the first to peer into the next world through the lens of the *longue durée*. This account of where the world is headed does draw on current events, but it relies more heavily on deeper historical forces and patterns. It offers a panoramic take on the foundations of the rise of the West and the implications of the rise of the rest. In addition, while previous studies tend to focus on the shifting balance of power in the world, this study focuses principally on what such shifts in power will mean for how the world works. It hones in on how the rise of the rest will affect the ideas and rules that govern politics, statecraft, matters of war and peace, and commerce.[7] Finally, this book is the first to argue that the next world will be dominated by no country or region. Some foresee a global community that will warmly embrace Western values and conceptions of order while others presage the emergence of an Asian century. This book contends that the next world will have no center of gravity. It will be no one's world.

Understanding the nature and implications of the current transition in global power requires unpacking the last global turn—the rise of the West. Accordingly, this book begins by examining the West's ascent to global preeminence between 1500 and 1800. It shows that

the West followed a unique and contingent path that was, paradoxically, a product of its singular political weakness. The main driver of
Europe's rise was socioeconomic ferment. In the midst of the fragmenting political order of medieval Europe, a nascent middle class
of merchants, entrepreneurs, and intellectuals challenged the power
of monarchy, aristocracy, and church. This rising bourgeoisie went
on to serve as the vanguard of the Protestant Reformation, which
fostered religious tolerance and set the stage for the eventual separation of church and state.

The onset of representative government followed; combined with
the emancipatory ideas of the Reformation, the growing costs of the
modern state forced monarchs to share power with their subjects in
order to gain access to their resources and skills. The rising middle
class also provided the economic and intellectual foundations of the
Industrial Revolution, which consolidated market capitalism and
gave birth to secular nationalism via urbanization, public education, mass conscription, and other social developments that were a
by-product of industrialization. Nationalism became the twin sister
of democratization, providing the connective tissue that would hold
together societies by consent rather than coercion.

This pattern of socioeconomic development emerged in Western
Europe and it then spread to North America via the immigrants
who settled the New World in search of economic opportunity and
religious freedom. Thereafter, Europe and North America together
forged a uniquely Western political order defined by three principal attributes: liberal democracy, industrial capitalism, and secular
nationalism.[8] The West thus came to represent both a geographic
zone—the land masses bounding the North Atlantic—and also a
distinctive political community.

The attributes that endowed the West with its singular character also enabled it to sprint ahead of other contenders for primacy.
More rigid and hierarchical orders in the Ottoman Empire, India,
China, and Japan stood in the way of the transformation that
fueled the rise of Europe and North America, enabling the West
to become the globe's center of gravity by the nineteenth century.
Moreover, the concurrent ascent of the Atlantic democracies, coupled with their similar domestic orders, gave rise to a distinctive

Western approach to managing global affairs. The West sought to universalize the values and institutions that its constituent members embraced at home; for reasons of both interest and principle, Europe and North America worked hard to export democracy, secular nationalism, and capitalism. The global spread of the West's founding ideas marked the first time that a single conception of order took hold in most quarters of the world. And the long and expansive run of this order admittedly provides ample reason for confidence that the Western way is here to stay.

Such confidence in the durability of a global order anchored by the West is, however, misplaced. The spread of this order has in large part been a product of the West's material dominance, not the universal appeal of its ideas. Especially since the demise of the Soviet Union, the Western order has been the only game in town. Developing nations, nudged along by the occasional bout of coercion, have had little choice but to play by the West's rules. But now that the West's material primacy is waning, its ideological dominance is very much in question. It is of course plausible that the rest will continue to play by Western rules as they rise. But they are likely to do so only if their socioeconomic orders and domestic values and institutions converge with those of the Western democracies. In other words, the preservation of the Western order requires that the advance of modernization in the developing world produces a homogenous community of nations along Western lines.

The problem is that the defining attributes of the West—liberal democracy, industrial capitalism, and secular nationalism—are not being replicated as developing regions modernize. To be sure, capitalism has demonstrated its universal draw. But most rising powers— China, India, Turkey, and Brazil among them—are not tracking the developmental path followed by the West. They have different cultural and socioeconomic foundations, which give rise to their own domestic orders and ideological orientations. Accordingly, emerging powers will want to revise, not consolidate, the international order erected during the West's watch. They have different views about the foundations of political legitimacy, the nature of sovereignty, the rules of international trade, and the relationship between the state and society. As their material power increases, they will seek to recast the international order in ways that advantage their interests and ideological preferences. The developmental paths followed by the rising rest represent alternatives to the Western way, not temporary detours on the road to global homogeneity.

If the West's rise had been the product of its intrinsic and inevitable advantages, then the rest of the world would likely converge toward the Western model if only because it represents the most efficient way to achieve prosperity and security. But the success of the West was a function of unique conditions, not of a model whose superiority is immutable.[9] Modernization today is occurring in a very different global setting. During the West's rise, the middle class was the main agent of change. Today, China's middle class is a defender of the status quo, not a force of political change. During the early modern era, the international system was sluggish and static; dynamism had to come from below, and the West's more decentralized and pluralistic states were better able to provide it than hierarchical empires. Today, the international system is interdependent and porous; more centralized states are in many respects better able to cope with globalization than more pluralistic ones. Although state-led economies have their own drawbacks when it comes to innovation, the recent economic crisis has made amply clear that the West's approach to financial management is hardly without imperfections. In today's multifaceted global system, different types of states have their advantages and disadvantages. It is for this reason that the twenty-first century will host multiple brands of modernity, not political homogeneity along Western lines.

Even amid such global diversity, it is of course plausible, and perhaps even likely, that liberal democracy will continue to spread. It has done so slowly but surely over the past two centuries, and the human yearning for autonomy and dignity appears to be universal—as demonstrated most recently by the Arab Spring. But even if democracy continues to expand its footprint, the West, for two reasons, still cannot presume that the coming global turn will coincide with the universalization of the Western order.

First, there is a timing problem. The shift in the globe's center of gravity is quickening; the Chinese economy is poised to surpass America's within fifteen years and, as discussed in chapter four, the international pecking order will be completely overhauled over the next three decades. In contrast, the global spread of democracy, if it occurs, will take place much more gradually. Over one hundred countries are still ruled by nondemocratic regimes, and building the social and institutional underpinnings of representative government takes time.[10] It is worth keeping in mind that Britain became a constitutional monarchy late in the seventeenth century, but did not mature into a liberal democracy for another two hundred years. Germany was a constitutional monarchy when it began life as a unified state in 1871, but it took some eight decades and two world wars for democracy to take root. To be sure, today's transitions from autocracy to representative government may occur much more quickly than they did a century or two ago; democracy now has a significant beachhead. But it is a very safe bet that the world will be multipolar long before it is democratic. As Azar Gat observes, "Even if the capitalist nondemocratic great powers eventually democratize, the process could take decades or generations to unfold."[11]

Second, even as democracy spreads, the new regimes that emerge will not necessarily play by the West's rules just because they are democratic. Put differently, democratization does not mean Westernization. Indeed, democratization could well produce states decidedly opposed to adhering to the international order erected by the West. In the Middle East, for example, more democracy may well mean more political Islam and the emergence of Arab states which, precisely because they are representative, will be less willing to cooperate with the West than their autocratic predecessors. In most of the countries that have held democratic elections of one sort or another—Iran, Algeria, the Palestinian Territories, Lebanon, Iraq—Islam has only strengthened its hold on politics. Democratization elsewhere could similarly stoke geopolitical ferment; a more democratic China could well be a more unpredictable and aggressive actor on the global stage.

Moreover, even if emerging powers share the West's values, they will spar with the West over matters of status and prestige; the rising rest are resentful of having long labored under Western hegemony and want more say in managing global affairs whatever the issues at stake. So too will rising states run up against the West when it comes to the pursuit of national interests. The United States and Great Britain shared democratic values and an Anglo-Saxon heritage when America emerged as a great power at the end of the nineteenth century. Nonetheless, the United States pushed Britain out of its neighborhood; America wanted to enjoy uncontested primacy in the Western Hemisphere. Surely China and other emerging powers, whether democratic or not, will aspire to a similar brand of regional hegemony as their resources and ambition rise, leading to a potential confrontation with the United States and its European partners. The assumption that nations will see eye-to-eye with the West as long as they have democratic governments is as illusory as the proposition that the world will soon be populated only by democracies.

 The West and the rising rest are poised to compete over principles, status, and geopolitical interests as the global turn proceeds. The challenge for the West and the rest alike is to forge a new and pluralistic order—one that preserves stability and a rules-based international system amid the multiple versions of modernity that will populate the next world.

## The Plan

This book has two primary goals. The first is analytic: to explore the causes and consequences of the coming global turn. Chapters two and three put the issue of global change in historical relief. Chapter two chronicles the last global turn—Europe's rise and its eclipse of the Middle East and Asia as the world's leading center of power. This tectonic shift stemmed first and foremost from socioeconomic change and the emergence of a middle class with sufficient wealth and power to challenge the political status quo. Chapter three completes the story of the West's ascent by comparing the advances of early modern Europe with the centralized stasis that prevailed in the Middle East and Asia. These regions did not pass through the historic transformations that shaped modernity in the West, holding them back as the West sprinted ahead. The West not only pulled ahead of the rest, but then went on to capitalize on its primacy to "go global"—to export to the developing world its own economic and political principles. First under Europe's leadership, then under America's, the West became the primary supplier of the rules that provided order in the international system.

Chapters four and five explore the next global turn—the rise of the non-West. Chapter four is a prelude to the second half of the book. It briefly chronicles the diffusion of power to new quarters and shows that on many different levels—aggregate wealth, demography, education, manufacturing, military capability—the rest is fast catching up with the West. Even if the United States and Europe reclaim robust rates of economic growth, the West will inevitably lose the global preeminence that it has enjoyed since the nineteenth century. Chapter five then examines the challenges that the rising rest will pose to the Western way. Autocrats in China, Russia, and the Persian Gulf; theocrats in the Middle East; strongmen in Africa; populists in Latin America—these regimes challenge the universality of the Western model and are not just way stations on the path to liberal democracy, industrial capitalism, and secular nationalism. The durability of these non-Western approaches to governance will ensure political diversity as emerging powers rise.

The second goal of this book is prescriptive: to map out how the West should prepare for and adjust to the world of the twenty-first century. Chapter six makes the case that the West must recover its economic and political vitality if it is to anchor the global turn. It first examines the developments that have been sapping the West of its material and ideological strength—the economic downturn on both sides of the Atlantic, the renationalization of political life across the European Union, and an intractable polarization in the United States. The chapter then explores what steps the Atlantic democracies can take to restore economic growth, breathe new life into democratic politics, and reclaim their self-confidence.

The concluding chapter lays out a vision for adapting the international order to the coming global turn. The United States must take the lead in fashioning a new consensus, not insist that the rising rest acquiesce to Western values and institutions. Equating legitimacy with responsible governance rather than liberal democracy, tolerating political and ideological diversity, balancing between global governance and devolution to regional authorities, fashioning a more regulated and state-centric brand of capitalism—these are the types of principles around which a new order is likely to take shape. American deference to a novel set of legitimating and guiding norms would encourage rising powers to respond in kind, offering the most hope of arriving at a bargain that preserves stability in the aftermath of the West's primacy. As Henry Kissinger recently cautioned, "America will have to learn that world order depends on a structure that participants support because they helped bring it about."[12]

# 2 :: The Rise of the West

## History's Arc

For some 1,000 years—from the collapse of the Roman Empire in the fifth century to the stirrings of the Reformation in the fifteenth—Europe was a geopolitical backwater. Power shifted to the east as Rome lost its pride of place to Constantinople, the center of the Byzantine Empire. India and China enjoyed an extended period of economic growth; by 1600, the two empires accounted for almost one-half of global wealth. Meanwhile, Islamic civilization flourished under Arab, Turkic, and Persian leadership, eventually seeking to extend its reach into Europe. Beginning in the eighth century, Moorish invaders from North Africa succeeded in dominating the Iberian Peninsula, by the thirteenth century converting the majority of its inhabitants to Islam. Later, the Ottomans established an Islamic caliphate that spanned the Mediterranean Basin. They eventually ruled much of the Balkan Peninsula and, beginning in 1529, made several unsuccessful attempts to conquer Vienna.

The era of Ottoman domination of the Mediterranean Basin stands in stark contrast to more recent history. Between 1500 and 1800, Europe went from the back to the front of the pack. Europe surpassed in economic and military strength not only the Ottomans, but India and China as well. Indeed, Europeans, accompanied by their offspring in North America, came to dominate global politics over the course of the nineteenth century, extending imperial control to virtually all corners of the globe. Although the age of empire came to an end by the middle of the twentieth century, the West has maintained its military and economic hegemony to this day.

The goal of this chapter is to understand the sources of this last global turn—the West's remarkable rise and its eclipse of other contenders for primacy. Examining the changing of the guard that took place between 1500 and 1800 promises to illuminate the next global turn, which may well change the world as profoundly as the rise of the West did. A historical look at the onset of the modern era will not just deepen understanding of how and why the global distribution of power changes, but also shed light on whether today's emerging powers will follow in the West's footsteps. Did the rise of the West follow a generic path that is being replicated elsewhere, suggesting that the rest of the world will be gravitating toward political homogeneity as modernization proceeds? Or did the West follow a unique trajectory—one that was the product of political, socioeconomic, and religious factors not found elsewhere? If so, then the world should be headed toward multiple versions of modernity and an international order that is not just multipolar, but also politically diverse.

The story line of this chapter is that Europe's stunning rise was the product of its own political weakness. Although the Holy Roman Empire existed in name from 962 until the early nineteenth century, imperial rule was fragmented from the start, with authority widely distributed among the king, the pope, local religious leaders, noble families, and relatively autonomous fiefdoms. The emperor, church, and nobility all vied for power, with competition among them opening up political space for new actors. Those new actors were merchants, artisans, and other members of a nascent middle class who founded independent towns in order to ply their trades and accumulate wealth beyond the reach of manorial and ecclesiastical authority.

The emerging bourgeoisie and the towns they founded were the engines behind Europe's gradual ascent as the globe's center of gravity. European towns, most of which had no more than ten to twenty thousand residents—small by comparison with cities in the Middle East—became centers of commerce. The rapid expansion of trade in turn gave rise to banks and the development of contracts, loans, and modern financial instruments. With the wealth that accompanied commerce and finance came education and literacy, research and innovation, and the rise of a class of individuals able and willing to challenge enduring traditions of dynastic and religious rule. Trade guilds, commercial leagues, and defensive pacts among towns provided horizontal alignments that reinforced the ability of townsmen to stand against the vertical lines of authority defended by empire and church.

Urban populations became the primary supporters of the teachings of Martin Luther, Huldrych Zwingli, John Calvin, and others who, in the sixteenth century, challenged the theology and practices of the Catholic Church. They brought to an end the papacy's exclusive hold on matters of faith and cleared the way for the spread of religious pluralism. After taking hold in the heartland of Germany and then spreading rapidly—primarily to the north and west— the Reformation drove forward not just the remaking of Western Christendom but also the political transformation of Europe. The Habsburg dynasty that ruled the Holy Roman Empire did team up with the papacy to defeat the Protestant challenge to Catholicism; indeed, the wars of the Counter-Reformation succeeded in reclaiming Bohemia, Moravia, and portions of Austria. But the widespread embrace of Protestantism proved irreversible across much of northern Europe. As a consequence, religious tolerance came to Europe by default rather than design; religious diversity had to be accommodated if the different branches of Christianity were to live side by side. After all, the Thirty Years' War, which pitted Protestants against Catholics, killed some forty percent of Germany's population.[1]

Conflict born of confessional difference advanced the fortunes not only of religious tolerance, but also political pluralism. The wars spawned by the clash of faiths led to stronger and more expensive states; war-making was state-making.[2] In the first instance, the exertions of the state strengthened the hand of monarchs, who had lost power to the nobility during the medieval era. But monarchs faced with costly conflicts had to make increasing demands on their subjects, asking them to pay higher taxes and, in some instances, to risk their lives in battle. In the bargain that emerged, dynasts exchanged some of their power for the resources of their subjects—a deal that over time led to the institutionalization of constitutional monarchy.

At the outset, it was only the landed nobility and wealthy bourgeoisie that enjoyed the expansion of political rights. But as the Industrial Revolution led to the education, mobilization, and empowerment of the commoner, rule by lineage and wealth gradually gave way to liberal democracy.

Nationalism was the logical accompaniment to consensual politics; it served as the democratic state's binding ideological glue. Nationalism was also a natural outgrowth of the homogeneity and social intermixing fostered by industrialization, state education systems, and mass conscription. Urbanization, the formation of a middle class that demanded political power commensurate with its wealth, the tolerance engendered by irreversible religious diversity, industrialization and the rise of the democratic nation-state—these were the underlying socioeconomic developments that fueled the rise of the West and its economic and military primacy.

To what extent modernization in the Middle East and the rest of the world will soon follow the Western model is the subject of chapter five. But this chapter's account of the rise of the West lays the groundwork for the argument that Europe's ascendance followed a unique path. Its fragmented and competing centers of authority, its demography and topography, the Protestant Reformation's contribution to both religious and political pluralism—these distinctive characteristics of the West played a defining role in equipping it to eventually eclipse the Middle East and Asia. These underlying social and religious differences between the West and the rest also go a long way in explaining why Western efforts to export liberal democracy, the separation of church and state, and secular nationalism have thus far stumbled so regularly.

This chapter begins by explaining how Europe's political weakness became the main source of its economic advance. Merchants and artisans populated new towns that proved capable of challenging imperial and ecclesiastical power, in turn becoming sites of entrepreneurship that embraced the progressive message of the Reformation. The chapter next examines how the Reformation altered the political map of Europe, creating novel alignments within and among strengthening states and advancing the cause of both religious tolerance and political pluralism. The account focuses primarily on Germany and England. Germany was the birthplace of the Reformation, while England, after its civil wars in the seventeenth century—arguably the last of Europe's successive wars of religion—led the march to modernity as it advanced the causes of religious tolerance, liberal politics, and industrial capitalism.

## The Changing Political Map of Medieval Europe

Three developments during the early phases of the Holy Roman Empire (962–1806) set the stage for Europe's rise. First, the collapse of the Carolingian Empire in 888 cleared the way for the onset of feudalism and the more fragmented political landscape that accompanied the spread of autonomous manors. Second, competition between the emperor and pope and divisions within the church itself weakened both imperial and ecclesiastical authority. Third, the growth of trade led to the rise of a nascent bourgeoisie that established new towns and capitalized on the diminished strength of state and church to expand its own influence. Taken together, these three developments led to the proliferation of fiefdoms, princely states, duchies, counties, and towns, many of which fashioned commercial, political, and military ties to each other, often at the expense of their fidelity to imperial and ecclesiastical authority.[3]

### The Sources of Political Fragmentation

During the Carolingian era, which ran from the coronation of Charlemagne in 800 to the death of Charles the Fat in 888, rotating administrators and cavalry, both of which owed direct allegiance to the monarch, enforced imperial order. After the collapse of the Carolingians and contemporaneous with the establishment of the Holy Roman Empire under Otto I, who was crowned in 962, the cavalry effectively became knights as they put down territorial roots and fashioned lord-vassal relationships with local nobility. Land, which had been the exclusive provenance of the monarch, passed into the hands of the nobility; possession became ownership and ownership became hereditary. Knights offered protection to the now-landed nobility, in return receiving rights to a fief and the agricultural revenue it produced.[4]

The effective independence of feudal manors was reinforced by topography. Empire and church alike found it difficult to exercise authority over manors buffered by rivers, forests, and mountains. Rain and rivers also made such control unnecessary; nature's supply of water meant that Europe did not need the centralized, state-led irrigation projects required to sustain agricultural production in more arid locations in the Middle East and Asia.[5]

Power struggles between emperor and pope further contributed to the political fragmentation of Europe. During the tenth century, imperial authorities had the upper hand. The emperor appointed the pope, imperial courts selected bishops and abbots, and monasteries and other church properties were feudalized and dependent upon knights for their protection. During the eleventh century, the papacy began to push back. In 1059, the church established the College of Cardinals to select the pope. The Holy Roman Emperor, Henry IV, soon thereafter invaded Italy and drove Pope Gregory VII from Rome in an effort to restore imperial control of the church. But his efforts fell short; the pope excommunicated Henry and convinced church officials in Germany to rebel against imperial authority. The emperor consequently replaced churchmen in positions of political responsibility with secular officials—most of whom were German princes or nobles with military experience. These laymen, however, soon asserted their independence. By the early thirteenth century, the struggle between church and state, coupled with the growing autonomy of local officials, had led to "the almost total dissipation of central power."[6]

Tensions between church and state intensified during the late thirteenth century, when the kings of England and France both began to tax members of the clergy. Pope Boniface resisted the encroachment on the immunities of the church, but to no avail— marking the clear subjugation of papal power to secular authority. The influence of the French monarchy over the church increased in 1305, when the College of Cardinals elected a French pope, Clement V. Clement decided in 1309 to take up residence in Avignon, further strengthening the sway of the French monarch over the church and denying the papacy the traditions and prestige associated with residence in Rome.

Strife within the church itself also contributed to the erosion of ecclesiastical authority. In 1054, the Christian world broke into its Roman Catholic and Greek Orthodox variants. The schism was long in coming. In the fourth century, the Roman Empire was divided into administrative halves; the Western Empire was governed from Rome and the Eastern Empire from Constantinople. Soon thereafter, the papacy in Rome and the patriarchate in Constantinople began to jostle over doctrinal questions and status. The church stayed nominally unified until the eleventh century. But the schism of 1054 and the formal separation of the Orthodox Church from Catholicism dealt a sharp blow to the power of the papacy and the unity of Christendom.

Power struggles within the Catholic Church expedited the weakening of the papacy. After the death in 1378 of Pope Gregory XI—a Frenchman who had returned the papacy to Rome—the College of Cardinals elected an Italian, Urban VI. Under pressure from France, the cardinals then voided their selection, instead choosing a Frenchmen. Urban VI refused to step down, leading to a divided papacy, with one pope based in Rome and the other in Avignon. The so-called "Great Schism" deepened with the appointment of a third pope in 1409. Not until Emperor Sigismund selected a new pope in 1417 would the crisis abate, clearing the way for Rome to be restored as the sole site of the papacy in 1446. Amid the turmoil within the papacy, local churchmen demanded a say in the governance of ecclesiastical matters—a practice known as conciliarism—adding to the decentralization of authority within the church.

Meanwhile, initial stirrings of theological dissent emerged in England and rapidly spread to Central Europe. In the late 1300s, John Wyclif and his followers challenged the temporal power of the church and translated the Bible into English. Jan Hus brought dissent to Prague, where he founded a church independent of Rome. Although Hus was burned at the stake as a heretic and Wyclif's followers suppressed in England, the emergence of public movements of dissent added to the church's woes.[7] Over the course of the late fourteenth and early fifteenth centuries, these developments irreversibly diminished papal influence and increasingly subjected clergymen to the authority of secular governments.[8]

The weakening of both imperial and church authority was expedited by the expansion of trade and the accompanying proliferation of towns, which occurred at a particularly rapid pace during the tenth through thirteenth centuries. The growth of trade was in part the product of technological advance. The increasing use of the heavy plough and new irrigation techniques increased agricultural productivity and led to unprecedented food surpluses. The sternpost rudder allowed merchants to link the growing river trade with coastal, and eventually long-distance, shipping. Improvements in navigation and shipbuilding—many of which came from the Portuguese—further advantaged seaborne transport. One of the Ottoman Empire's main economic advantages over Europe—its relatively unobstructed overland transportation network—was eclipsed by the growth of oceanic shipping. According to Craig Lockard, "the growing European role in Asian trade weakened Anatolia's historic position as a middleman…ultimately reducing the Ottomans, once a hub of international commerce, to a secondary power in the emerging global trade system."[9]

Prior to the economic expansion of the late medieval period, Europe's towns were in locations that afforded military advantage. In contrast, the new towns that began to spring up during the eleventh century were located with trade as well as military matters in mind—along rivers, ports, and commercial routes. As a consequence, merchants, who had previously been semi-vagrant, found the new towns suitable for settlement. So too did smiths, metal workers, and other artisans prefer towns to manors because of the much larger markets afforded by a commercial hub.[10]

Especially in Germany, towns were relatively small (a few thousand residents) and, in comparison with urban centers in the Middle East, separated by only small distances.[11] Both conditions favored the establishment of novel political compacts: "The growth of trade and corresponding increase in urban centers," according to Hendrik Spruyt, "gave birth to new sets of arrangements between kings, aristocracy, burghers, and church."[12] Urban residents turned to one another to pursue common interests in expanding markets, protecting shipping, and strengthening their political autonomy. These efforts resulted in commercial and defensive networks that enhanced the ability of townsmen to challenge the hierarchical control exercised by traditional institutions of authority.

## Town versus Countryside

The growth of towns and the rise of a nascent bourgeoisie propelled Europe toward the modern era.[13] The weakening of imperial and church authority created the permissive space for new political and economic actors. The upwardly mobile residents of towns then took advantage of this space, serving as the main segment of society that would ultimately drive Europe's rise. The divide between town and countryside was perhaps the defining cleavage of Europe's early modern era, creating the religious and political fault lines that would eventually bring religious tolerance and political pluralism to the West.[14]

Towns emerged as the engine of progressive change in no small part because of the types of individuals they attracted. Merchants and artisans helped establish new commercial hubs not just to capitalize on economic opportunities, but also to escape the reach of the lords and clergy that dominated manorial life.[15] Peasants followed in order to escape serfdom. Towns thus became magnets for individuals seeking greater autonomy. Local nobility often succeeded in extending the reach of their tax collectors into urban areas, but the sizable revenue generated also gave nobles a vested interest in otherwise letting towns govern themselves.[16] The church too had significantly less influence in urban areas than in the countryside. The church's dioceses and parishes were organized to serve rural populations, and additional priests were unavailable to cover the new towns.[17] As J. R. Hale notes, "towns had bargained and fought their way to some measure of self-government against church, noble and monarch and had thrown off the taint of servility that still clung to the countryside."[18]

Towns and the growth of trade transformed Europe's economy as well as its political landscape. The instruments of modern finance began to evolve, including banks, loans, insurance, and commercial contracts. These innovations further strained relations between townsmen and the church, which was opposed to usury and the practice of pricing commodities for profit.[19] Nonetheless, Europe's commercial class developed quickly and soon extended its reach to distant markets. By the middle of the 1300s, the Dutch city of Bruges was home to some seventeen private banking firms.[20] By the 1400s, European merchants and financiers were already coming to dominate trading posts within the Ottoman Empire.[21]

Towns became centers of not only wealth, but also learning, printing, and innovation. The accumulation of wealth enabled some urban dwellers to focus on intellectual pursuits rather than manual labor. Innovation was driven in large part by the practical demands of commerce. In the countryside, time was marked by nature—seasons, festivals, light, and dark—and trade was based on personal relationships. Towns meanwhile embraced clocked time and developed legal and financial instruments that impersonalized commerce.[22] New technologies were developed to increase productivity and profits. Over time, the expansion of literacy and learning led to progress not only on matters of business. Towns opened up unprecedented opportunities for scholarship, contributing to the humanist movement and advancing study of the arts, literature, law, and medicine.[23]

The advent of the printing press led to a revolutionary advance in literacy and scholarship. The first typeset book was the Gutenberg Bible, which appeared in 1456. By the end of the fifteenth century, Europe was home to some one thousand publishing houses, which had printed roughly thirty thousand titles and six million books.[24] The literacy gap between town and countryside widened dramatically. In towns, some sixty percent of residents could read, whereas less than one percent of the rural population was literate.[25]

Towns were further differentiated from the countryside by the horizontal alignments that emerged within and among them, magnifying the political clout of the emerging bourgeoisie. Guided by the assumption of strength in numbers, town dwellers formed workers' guilds, which were trade unions of sorts. These associations of artisans and craftsmen afforded their members the advantages of collective action—such as defying the efforts of feudal lords to impose tolls and regulations on river traffic. Guilds not only brought economic benefits but also organized entertainment and religious activities, fashioning their members into a coherent social group better equipped to resist the influence of the nobility and church. The economic and political benefits of these business associations prompted their rapid proliferation. Between 1400 and 1500, for example, the number of guilds in the French town of Amiens grew from twelve to forty-two.[26]

Townsmen were empowered by one other set of horizontal linkages: commercial leagues among cities. These trading blocs were initially formed when individual merchants from different cities cooperated with each other to expand trade. Thereafter, towns formed pacts with each other, securing preferential treatment from third parties, thwarting the nobility's attempts to regulate commerce, and providing for the common defense of members and their ships. In 1385, the Swabian-Rhenisch League consisted of eighty-nine towns and fielded a defense force of some 10,000 soldiers. The Hanseatic League, which lasted in various forms from the thirteenth century until the seventeenth, and stretched from the North Sea to the Baltic Sea, at its height consisted of some 200 towns. Such pacts dramatically enhanced the power of urban areas and advanced the economic and political interests of the rising bourgeoisie. Indeed, imperial authorities were fully aware of the political threat posed by such leagues; the emperor in the mid-1300s sought to prohibit their formation—but to no avail.[27]

The leading role of towns in altering Europe's commercial and political landscape was particularly pronounced in Germany, where the breakdown of imperial and ecclesiastical institutions most directly coincided with—and was expedited by—the growth of urban areas and the rise of the bourgeoisie.[28] As discussed below, German townsmen also became central players in the spread of the Protestant Reformation. England followed a quite similar trajectory inasmuch as the proliferation of towns and the ascent of the bourgeoisie were the engines of change. But in England, the landed nobility and the merchants often cooperated with one another; indeed, noblemen not infrequently became businessmen.[29] Economic ties turned into political ones, producing a gentry-burgher alliance that led to a relatively harmonious incorporation of the rising middle class into politics. Accordingly, England experienced an earlier and less turbulent transition toward political liberalization than did Germany.

France had fewer towns than either Germany or England and they were further apart, impairing the formation of commercial leagues. Moreover, the bourgeoisie often allied with the monarchy, which regularly turned to literate and skilled burghers to staff the bureaucracy. Wealthy townsmen could also buy their way into the French nobility.[30] The co-optation of burghers and their incorporation into the existing social hierarchy contained the bourgeoisie's reformist fervor, in the end setting up France for a popular revolution rather than graduated change mediated by a rising middle class.

Italy represented yet another variant. Many Italian cities dated back to Roman times and, by European standards, had quite large populations that included nobility, merchants, and laborers. Accordingly, Italian cities generally remained under noble rule and did not emerge as gathering places for those seeking to challenge traditional patterns of authority. Moreover, the size of Italian cities made them largely self-sufficient in terms of commerce and defense. The urban leagues that emerged in northern Europe did not form in Italy, denying Italian merchants the advantages that came with commercial and strategic alliances.[31] As discussed later, these distinguishing features of Italy's landscape help explain why the Protestant Reformation did not take root there and why Italy followed a comparatively conservative and incremental path toward political liberalization.

Despite the contrasting patterns of development in different countries, the growth of trade and the rise of towns were the principal drivers of Europe's ascent. The emerging bourgeoisie served as the vanguard of change as it proved willing and able to challenge the traditional authority of the monarchy, nobility, and church. Towns and the literacy and learning that came with them also set the stage for the seminal event that was to put Europe on the path to religious tolerance and political pluralism: the Reformation.

## The Reformation

Socioeconomic ferment, religious dissent, and political liberalization worked hand-in-hand to fuel Europe's ascent. The Reformation piggybacked on the social impact of commercialization and urbanization. Religious dissent caught on most readily among the more educated urban bourgeoisie, who welcomed the challenge it posed to the influence of the Catholic Church and were attracted by Protestantism's focus on a personal form of devotion unmediated by the clergy. As the Reformation gained momentum, it became the leading edge of progressive change in Europe. Religious dissent ultimately cleared the way for political liberalization; temporal reforms emerged from the openings afforded by the gradual spread of religious pluralism.

The Protestant movement and its clash with Catholicism had three irreversible effects of fundamental importance. First, the Reformation set the stage for the intellectual advances of the Enlightenment by exposing religion, and ultimately politics, to theological, moral, and rationalist inquiry. The intellectual ferment that made possible Europe's eclipse of other regions was, at least initially, unleashed by religious dissent. Second, Protestantism proved to be a new source of common cause. Protestant communities formed strategic alliances within and across territorial boundaries to enhance their ability to challenge the status quo. New horizontal networks—both religious and geopolitical—furthered the fortunes of those seeking to cut back the hierarchical power of monarchy, nobility, and church.[32] Third, decades of religious war produced both religious tolerance and political pluralism. Tolerance was born of conflict; Catholics, Lutherans, Calvinists, Puritans, Presbyterians— these and other Christian denominations had to accept each other if the bloodshed was to cease.[33] Meanwhile, the costs of armed conflict forced states to increase taxation and make greater demands on their populations. Monarchs extracted more resources and sacrifices from their subjects, but in return had to grant them more political influence. This bargain translated the growing wealth of the bourgeoisie into political power, and ultimately edged Europe's strengthening states toward representative government.

*Theological and Doctrinal Dissent*

The Reformation emerged from the same social awakening that spawned the struggle against the political power of empire and nobility: the desire for greater human autonomy. Medieval Catholicism was very much a top-down affair. The pope was the ultimate religious authority on earth, exercising his power through a rigid hierarchy of bishops, abbots, and priests. Man's relationship with the divine was mediated by the clergy, who conducted mass, performed the sacraments, and involved themselves in the conduct of everyday life through the exercise of canon law.[34]

The medieval church was well aware that it faced challenges to its monopoly over matters of theology and doctrine. Wyclif, Hus, and other dissenters developed followings that made amply clear the yearning for a more accessible and demystified variant of Christianity. Although the Catholic Church readily branded these movements as heretical and repressed them, it did make some accommodations. For example, the concept of purgatory—a holding station on the way to the afterlife—was a medieval innovation intended in part to provide parishioners a say in their own destiny. Good deeds, attendance at mass, and indulgences (contributions to the church to compensate for sins) could shorten one's time in the way station. Purgatory offered the faithful at least a measure of personal control over their afterlife.[35]

Martin Luther, a priest and theologian born in 1483, contested the notion that individuals could buy their way out of purgatory and mounted a broader challenge to Catholic theology and practice. The son of a leaseholder of mines and smelters, Luther was raised in the towns of northern Germany and exposed to the progressive ambitions of urban life. He objected to Catholicism's insistence that the church was an essential intermediary between the individual and the divine, and maintained that through personal devotion and prayer the faithful could sustain a direct relationship with the almighty. "Every faithful Christian was a priest," he avowed, posing a direct challenge to the church's monopoly on doctrine, practice, and prayer.[36] Luther also questioned the authority of church institutions by asserting that the Bible, not the pope, was the only source of divinely revealed knowledge. He proceeded to translate the Bible into German, making it accessible to literate commoners and further compromising the role of the clergy as necessary mediators between God and man.[37]

Luther went public with his ninety-five theses in 1517. The advent of the printing press made possible the rapid dissemination of his message; his ideas spread throughout Europe within a matter of months. In 1521, Luther was excommunicated by the pope and declared a "notorious heretic" by the emperor, forcing him to go into hiding. Nonetheless, the Protestant movement could not be contained. Luther's message was particularly well received among wealthy burghers who saw religious dissent as a justification and vehicle for breaking away from the power of ecclesiastical authority.[38] His teachings also had considerable appeal among commoners, many of whom preferred personal devotion to reliance on the clergy, and favored the religion of the book to the religion of the pope.[39] Indeed, the first bout of bloodshed associated with the Reformation stemmed from revolts among workers and peasants, which broke out in Germany in 1524. Religious conflicts then multiplied quickly, spreading in step with the Protestant faith. By the end of the sixteenth century, roughly half of Europe, in territorial terms, had embraced Protestantism.[40]

Encouraged by the appeal of Luther's teachings, his contemporaries offered variations, from the start giving the Protestant movement a pluralism that further distinguished it from the tighter uniformity of Catholicism. Zurich-based Huldrych Zwingli differed with Luther over the meaning of the Eucharist and other doctrinal issues. John Calvin, a Frenchman, supported the abolishment of bishops in favor of a more egalitarian approach to the governance of the church, calling for each congregation to elect a board of its members—presbyters—to oversee matters of faith and practice.

Germany and Scandinavia embraced what came to be called Lutheranism, while the teachings of Zwingli and Calvin (often referred to as the Reformed Church) predominated in the Swiss Confederation and other parts of continental Europe. In England, the Anglican Church (a cross between Catholicism and Calvinism) prevailed after years of pitched rivalry with Puritanism (an austere variant of Calvinism), other Protestant sects, and Catholicism. In France, Calvinism had widespread appeal, but the monarchy, after repeated attempts at embracing religious pluralism, ultimately sided with Catholicism and expelled most of the country's Protestants.

Such dissent among the dissenters helped ensure that the Reformation was not confined to matters of religion, but ultimately contributed to a broader intellectual pluralism. In the first instance, the debates that swirled between Catholics and Protestants, and among the multiple Protestant camps, were about differing approaches to religious devotion and practice. But they then broadened into a scholarly exploration of the relationship between religion and rationalism, eventually calling into question not just Catholic doctrine, but also the notion of divine right. Hobbes, Montesquieu, Spinoza, Rousseau, Voltaire—these and many other intellectuals addressed how to build legitimate governments and moral societies amid the challenge to dynastic and ecclesiastical authority born of the Reformation. Such questioning also spread from matters of religion and politics to philosophy, the arts, science, and medicine. The theological and doctrinal pluralism of the Reformation in many respects cleared the way for the intellectual fertility of the Enlightenment.[41]

## The Footprint of the Reformation

The spread of the Protestant Reformation generally tracked the socioeconomic divide between town and countryside. The north and west of Europe—Germany, the Netherlands, Scandinavia, and England—which were the most commercialized and urbanized regions, embraced Protestantism in one of its various forms. The south and east—Eastern Europe, Italy, France, and Spain—which had, with the exception of Italy, more agrarian economies and rural populations, tended to remain Orthodox or Catholic.[42] By 1600, of the roughly 620 surviving Catholic bishoprics in Europe, only about sixty remained in northern Europe—less than one-fifth of the number in Italy alone.[43]

Within individual countries, religious divides similarly followed socioeconomic cleavages. The north of Germany—host to the
dozens of trading towns that emerged after 1000—became Lutheran,
while the rural south ended up loyal to the pope. In the Swiss
Confederation, most of the urban cantons became Protestant while
the rural ones stayed Catholic; the resulting religious divide was
to plague the confederation from the sixteenth century until the
middle of the 1800s. Within the Polish-Lithuanian Empire, urban
areas and commercial ports along the coast became hotbeds of
Protestantism, while the rural interior remained Catholic.[44]

Merchants, artisans, intellectuals, and professionals—the emerging bourgeoisie—were the foot soldiers of the Reformation. They
were drawn both to the religious message of Protestantism and to
the economic and political autonomy from traditional institutions
of authority afforded by religious rebellion.[45] Not surprisingly, the
church, monarchy, and nobility generally allied with each other to
suppress the Reformation and preserve the religious and political
status quo.[46] Nonetheless, monarchs and nobles alike on occasion
joined the Protestant movement—primarily when it was in their
political interests to do so.

During the 1520s, a significant number of German princes
came to support local Protestant churches as a means of resisting ecclesiastical power as well as the authority of the Habsburg
monarchy, which tightly allied itself with the Catholic Church.[47]
In England, Henry VIII parted ways with Rome in 1533. The cause
was the pope's excommunication of Henry for the annulment of
his first marriage, which had not produced a male heir. The English
Reformation soon grew into much more than a dispute between
Henry and the pope; it marked the beginning of the political transformation that would eventually erode the power of the monarchy and lead to the creation of parliamentary government. In
the Netherlands, Habsburg Spain used a heavy hand to maintain
political control and enforce adherence to Catholicism. In a revolt
that began in 1568, many Dutchmen—nobility and bourgeoisie
alike—responded by embracing Protestantism as part of a broader
effort to resist Spanish hegemony.[48] They succeeded, and the Dutch
Republic was founded in 1581.

That most of southern Europe, including France, remained Catholic was the product of a number of idiosyncratic factors—only one of which was that it was less commercialized and urbanized. Italy, after all, was home to some of Europe's largest cities and most affluent merchants. As in other regions of Europe, Protestantism in Italy caught on primarily in urban areas and among merchants, professionals, and intellectuals. But Protestants were unable to become a majority in a single Italian city or region, denying them the strong foothold from which dissent could spread.[49]

Italy's history as the seat of Catholicism as well as the sheer density of clergy and church-owned properties certainly provided a natural check against the Reformation.[50] Moreover, "the universities and printing presses, so vital to the Reformation north of the Alps, remained firmly under clerical control in Italy."[51] But the socioeconomic makeup of Italy's urban areas also limited Protestantism's footprint. Italy's cities were older and dominated by the nobility, not by the bourgeoisie. In the commercial towns of northern Europe, the bourgeoisie had the upper hand, and merchants often struggled with local nobility to defend their autonomy. In contrast, Italy's aristocracy and its urban bourgeoisie were allies, not antagonists; they teamed up to fashion "an effective territorial-political community," which in many instances was able to exert considerable influence over local church authorities.[52] As a consequence, Italian cities did not become centers of social and religious dissent as they did to the north. Moreover, Italy's urban areas were large, wealthy, and capable of self-defense, making it unnecessary for them to form the commercial and military pacts that took shape among smaller towns in northern Europe.[53] The horizontal networks that empowered Germany's bourgeoisie did not materialize in Italy.

Catholicism in France, as in Italy, weathered the Reformation. But unlike in Italy, France was host to a major Protestant movement. That the French monarchy ultimately repressed and expelled the country's Protestants in defense of Catholicism was the product primarily of the strength of the state. In France, the state was able to assert effective control over the Catholic Church from the thirteenth century onward. Inasmuch as the French king had control over the church's property rights and taxation levels, ecclesiastical authorities became more beholden to the monarchy than the papacy.[54] Moreover, some members of the upper clergy owned estates that were among the country's largest and most profitable. These holdings gave them, along with the nobility, a vested interest in serving the needs of the crown.[55] With the French church generally loyal to the French state, secular elites—the monarchy and nobility alike— had few political incentives to break with Rome.[56]

Two other factors limited the inroads that the Reformation was able to make in France by forestalling the emergence of the bourgeoisie as an agent of change. First, the French monarchy regularly incorporated burghers into the royal bureaucracy to take advantage of their literacy and professional skills.[57] Merchants also frequently became public servants at the municipal level.[58] Second, the French bourgeoisie was able to buy its way into the nobility. Despite resistance from the landed aristocracy, the crown sold venal offices to avail itself of the revenue provided.[59] In effect, as Spruyt explains, in Italy the nobility became the urban elite, while in France the urban elite became the nobility.[60] France's merchants and professionals were both co-opted by the state and merged into the nobility; their upward mobility denied the Reformation the broad urban vanguard that enabled Protestantism to spread so quickly elsewhere.

On the Iberian Peninsula, Muslim Moors, who had invaded in the eighth century, were finally expelled in 1492. Having fully returned to Catholicism only three decades before the outbreak of the Reformation, the Spanish did not share the spirit of religious revolt that was spreading to their north. Moreover, the Spanish monarchy, like the French, had succeeded in wresting away from Rome control over the church, further limiting the demand for a politically inspired break with the papacy.[61] Indeed, the Catholic Church and Spanish Hapsburgs teamed up to eliminate the small Protestant movement that emerged. Church and crown also kept tight watch on Spain's growing bourgeoisie in order to ward off the temptations of dissent.[62]

Ireland as well remained within the Catholic fold. In many respects, the outcome of religious ferment in Ireland was the opposite of that in the Netherlands. The Dutch revolted against Catholicism as part of an effort to resist Spanish hegemony; the Reformation was an act of political liberation. In contrast, the Irish defended Catholicism as part of their effort to resist English hegemony; turning back the Reformation was their own act of political liberation. The English crown had failed to co-opt the Irish aristocracy and landed gentry. Instead, the Tudors alienated these important constituencies by sending Protestants to settle in Ireland, ensuring that the Irish came to see Protestantism as an instrument of English oppression and usurpation rather than a movement of religious liberation.[63]

## Toward Religious Tolerance and Political Pluralism

The Reformation proved to be the defining development that would bring religious tolerance and political pluralism to Europe. At the outset, the Holy Roman Emperor and the pope responded to the spreading appeal of Protestantism by seeking to eradicate it; the wars of the Counter-Reformation resulted. Although an alliance between empire and church succeeded in substantially reducing the footprint of dissent, the Counter-Reformation failed to eliminate it. Instead, successive bouts of religious war fostered new opportunities for Protestants to cooperate across previous social and political boundaries, deepening the horizontal linkages that checked the power of monarchy, nobility, and church. In addition, the contest between Protestants and Catholics was so destructive that they found their way to mutual accommodation because they had no other choice. Meanwhile, the financial costs of the wars ultimately forced monarchs to extract more resources from their subjects—requiring them to grant broader political rights in return. Accordingly, the bloodshed triggered by the Reformation ultimately promoted not only religious tolerance, but also the beginnings of political pluralism.

### New Networks

The growth of commercial markets gave rise to new networks of traders, merchants, and professionals, which both strengthened the political influence of the bourgeoisie and provided a vehicle for the rapid spread of religious dissent. The Reformation then broadened and deepened these networks; the cause of religious ferment gave rise to new linkages that cut across class, language, region, and state.

In 1531, Protestant communities in Germany formed the Schmalkaldic League to defend themselves against the Habsburgs. The league soon reached out beyond Germany, forging ties with co-religionists in Scandinavia and England.[64] When Dutch Protestants resisted Spanish rule after 1568, English Protestants gave them support. When England's Parliament needed help to depose a Catholic monarch in 1688, the Dutch returned the favor, dispatching forces to England to help defeat the royalists. A Dutch Protestant who was married to the English monarch's daughter consequently took the throne. France's Protestants escaped repression in the late seventeenth century by taking up residence in neighboring countries, thereby establishing new social networks based on religious affinity. As Daniel Nexon points out, "The emergence of...networks centered around religious beliefs and identities undermined the various ways that rulers managed their heterogeneous domains." Disputes over theology and ritual only exacerbated ongoing struggles over political control.[65]

The Reformation also weakened traditional institutions by exposing them to new cleavages—confessional ones. Lines of dynastic descent were broken as families split over matters of faith. James II, England's last Catholic king, was chased off the throne by forces loyal to his Protestant daughter, Mary. Previously united behind the cause of preserving the social and political status quo, Germany's noblemen found themselves at war with each other over religion. And the power of the Catholic Church itself was dramatically diminished as the papacy lost not only a substantial portion of its flock, but also the land and revenues that had accompanied its monopoly on Christianity in Western Europe. In this respect, the Reformation advantaged new political actors and weakened old ones, furthering the opening up of political space that began with the advance of commercialism and urbanization after 1000.

*The Consequences of Religious Conflict:*
*Toleration by Default and War-Making as State-Making*

The Reformation also advanced religious and political pluralism in a less direct way—by spawning religious conflict. The wars of religion that plagued Europe during the sixteenth and seventeenth centuries were destructive enough to make an imperative of religious tolerance and costly enough to compel European monarchs to bargain away political power in return for economic resources.[66]

Religious dissent turned into religious bloodshed relatively quickly. The German peasants that revolted in 1524–1525, although their primary grievances were economic in nature, did demand that religious congregations be self-governing.[67] Charles V responded by deploying imperial troops and crushing the rebellion; as many as 100,000 peasants may have died. The potential for religious cleavage to lead to war increased after numerous Protestant communities formed the Schmalkaldic League in 1531. Initially, Charles agreed to tolerate the Protestant alliance as long as it supported the empire against its external foes; imperial forces had their hands full with ongoing conflicts against the Ottomans and the French.[68] When these conflicts came to an end in 1546, Charles readily turned his attention to the Schmalkaldic League and the rising tide of Protestantism.

In the Schmalkaldic War that resulted, a Habsburg army fighting in alliance with papal forces readily bested the league. Charles promptly made preparations for the reintegration of the defeated communities into the Catholic Church. However, the imperial victory proved pyrrhic. Protestant revolts soon broke out, and fighting between the two camps continued sporadically until 1555. After a decade of war and stalemate, Charles finally concluded that it would be impossible to repress a religious movement that had spread so widely. The emperor had little choice but to embrace religious tolerance and codify its practice through the Peace of Augsburg.[69]

The Peace of Augsburg granted individual German princes the right to determine whether their domains were Lutheran or

Catholic.[70] Individuals whose confessional preference diverged from that of the domain in which they resided were permitted to resettle among co-religionists. Although Augsburg marked the juridical acceptance of Protestantism, it legitimated the practice only of Lutheranism, not of Calvinism and other Protestant variants, which remained illegal and heretical. Such intolerance toward pluralism within the Protestant movement would prove to be a fatal flaw in this first attempt to replace religious conflict with religious tolerance. In addition, mutual accommodation between Protestants and Catholics was easier in theory than in practice, especially when it came to managing shifts in the communal balance of power as principalities changed their religious affiliations due to conversion or succession. Accordingly, Germany later faced another round of religious war—which would be its longest and most destructive.

Following the Peace of Augsburg, the Holy Roman Empire was, with the exception of a few isolated incidents, free of conflicts over faith for the next six decades.[71] Nonetheless, beneath the surface of the quiescence, tensions continued to build among Catholics, Lutherans, and Calvinists. The event that sparked the outbreak of the Thirty Years' War in 1618 was the attempt by Ferdinand II, who was poised to become King of Bohemia and Holy Roman Emperor, to impose Catholicism on predominantly Protestant Bohemia. A Protestant revolt quickly escalated into a wider war. In need of reinforcements, Ferdinand turned to his nephew, King Philip IV of Spain, who promptly dispatched troops to Germany. Thereafter, the Dutch, Danes, Swedish, and French all participated on behalf of the Protestants.[72] By the time the Thirty Years' War eventually came to an end, battles, famine, and disease had ravaged much of Germany.[73]

The Peace of Westphalia (1648) finally brought over a century of religious conflict in Germany to a definitive end. The treaty revived and amended the terms of the Augsburg agreement. The head of each political domain was free to determine the religion of that domain, and Calvinism joined Catholicism and Lutheranism as recognized faiths. Persons living in areas in which their denomination was not the designated faith were nonetheless permitted to practice as they wished. The agreement also included a host of territorial settlements and boundary adjustments.

The Peace of Westphalia marked two transformations that would come to define modern Europe. First, Westphalia codified and legalized the practice of religious pluralism among Christians. Where the Peace of Augsburg failed, the Peace of Westphalia succeeded; after 1648, Catholics, Lutherans, and Calvinists generally lived comfortably alongside each other throughout Germany. Westphalia did *not* separate church and state; most of Germany's many territories still embraced an "official" religion. But dissenters were no longer heretics; they had become minorities. After decades of bloodshed, Germans had finally found their way to religious pluralism.

Second, the Peace of Westphalia formalized the decentralization of political power from monarchy, nobility, and church to territorial states. In many respects, Westphalia marked the de jure recognition of the de facto decentralization of authority, extending to Europe as a whole the system of autonomous states that had been evolving in Germany for several centuries. The European system of states would no longer be controlled by dynasty and church. Rather, the government of each state was to be free from interference by other states and would enjoy territorial sovereignty. Relations among these sovereign states would be a function of interactions among the polities themselves, not a product of institutions of authority that had previously extended political power across territorial boundaries. It is for these reasons that historians view the Peace of Westphalia as laying the foundation for the modern state system. It enshrined the notion of territorial sovereignty and implicitly looked to diplomacy and the balance of power to preserve inter-state order and stability.

The wars spawned by the Reformation advanced the process of building the modern state in one other crucial respect. The financial burden of raising and equipping armies forced rulers who had previously wielded absolute power to grant political rights to gentry and wealthy bourgeoisie in return for their willingness to help cover the costs of war. In England, the civil wars that broke out over religion and the associated struggle between king and Parliament compelled the crown to bargain away absolute power in return for increased taxation—a deal that by the end of the seventeenth century helped give birth to constitutional monarchy. Although Prussia did not adopt a constitution until the middle of the nineteenth century, Germany's growing bourgeoisie began to enjoy a political voice commensurate with its resources well before the formal arrival of constitutional government—in no small part because aristocratic rulers needed their help to pay for war. To be sure, the successive wars that ravaged Europe initially did more to strengthen than weaken monarchical rule. During the eighteenth century, many European monarchs were empowered by expanded bureaucracies and the military arsenals they acquired to turn back challenges to their authority.[74] But over the longer term, war worked to the advantage of pluralism, gradually disseminating power from those who owned land to those who possessed wealth.

## Switzerland, France, and the Netherlands

This basic plotline played out across Europe, even if the details varied widely depending upon the location. The Reformation and the backlash against it spawned conflict that eventually resulted in religious tolerance as the Catholic camp proved unable to prevail. Gradually, the rising bourgeoisie—and eventually an emerging working class—demanded political power in return for the sacrifices put upon them by the increasingly expensive and intrusive state.

In Switzerland, Zwingli's teachings spread quickly; most of the confederation's urban cantons embraced Protestantism over the course of the 1520s. With urban and rural cantons already at odds over political and social issues, the new religious divide promptly contributed to the outbreak of violence. In 1531, Protestant Zurich went to battle against five Catholic cantons. The Peace of Kappel brought the fighting to an end after a matter of weeks—and also secured agreement that each canton would henceforth enjoy autonomy over its own religious affairs. Nonetheless, over the next three centuries, religious divisions would afflict the Swiss Confederation, on successive occasions triggering bloodshed between Catholics and Protestants. Switzerland's last civil war occurred in 1847, when the Catholic cantons effectively attempted to secede, but were quickly defeated by confederate forces. The constitution of 1848 guaranteed religious freedom, political rights, and a bicameral federation, finally consolidating confessional tolerance and inter-cantonal peace.[75]

Protestantism spread to France soon after its birth in Germany. Despite widespread repression, French Protestants (or Huguenots) grew quickly in number; by the 1560s, perhaps two million of some eighteen million Frenchmen were adherents.[76] As elsewhere, the French Reformation was largely an urban movement most popular among the middle class, although it also put down roots among the nobility and peasantry.[77] In addition, the lower clergy were drawn to Protestantism in part as an act of rebellion against their superiors, whom they saw as having been compromised by wealth and allegiance to the crown.[78]

As Protestantism spread, the French crown sought to forestall religious violence through negotiation, initially convincing Catholic prelates to engage in dialogue with Protestant leaders. An interim solution permitted Huguenots to worship publicly outside of towns, and privately inside them. Factional rivalry between noble families became entangled with mounting tension between Catholics and Protestants, however, contributing to the outbreak of violence in 1562.[79] France's successive wars of religion then continued until 1598, when the Edict of Nantes proved relatively successful at enforcing religious tolerance. An uneasy peace between Catholics and Protestants lasted until 1685, when King Louis XIV revoked the terms of Nantes and banned the practice of Protestantism. Huguenots faced the choice of converting or emigrating. Most chose the latter, resettling in neighboring countries as well as in South Africa and North America. France thus resolved the conflicts born of religious dissent by forcibly restoring religious homogeneity.[80]

In the Netherlands, religious conflict was intertwined with resistance to foreign rule. Through a combination of territorial conquest and royal marriage, the Netherlands became part of the Habsburg Empire during the fifteenth century. After the Reformation began in Germany, Protestantism spread broadly throughout the large community of Dutch merchants and artisans. Philip II of Spain, who assumed the Habsburg throne in 1556, was determined to keep the

Dutch within the Catholic fold, and dispatched a Spanish army to the Netherlands in 1567. Not only did the Spanish suppress Protestant worship, but they also executed Catholic noblemen who argued in favor of religious tolerance. Moreover, Philip tightened his grip on power and imposed high taxes on the Dutch to defray the costs of his military exertions—alienating even Catholics who would have otherwise supported his insistence on religious conformity. The struggle against Spanish rule became a fight for political as well as religious independence.[81]

By the end of the 1580s, the northern provinces, which had become the mainstay of the Protestant revolt, attained de facto independence and, absent a reigning monarch, established republican rule. Fighting between the independent north and the Spanish-backed south continued until the 1640s, whereupon the struggle ended with the defeat of Spain. The Peace of Westphalia extended the reach of the Dutch Republic to most of the southern provinces, formalized the practice of religious tolerance, and codified the sovereignty of the Netherlands and its independence from foreign rule. The wars of the Reformation had again advanced the cause of political as well as religious pluralism.

*England*

In England, the Reformation spawned religious conflict more slowly than in other parts of Europe. Nonetheless, the consequences were perhaps the most profound. As elsewhere in northern Europe, the English embraced Protestantism. But the political impact of struggles over religion went further than on the continent. The Reformation combined with ongoing commercialization to give Europe its first constitutional monarchy.

Unlike on the continent, where Protestantism spread at least in part as the result of popular movements, England's Reformation was more of a top-down affair. Henry VIII broke with Rome after the pope excommunicated him in 1533 for annulling his marriage to Catherine of Aragon in order to wed Anne Boleyn. Parliament proceeded to approve the establishment of the Anglican Church (also called the Church of England), which was Catholic in organization—bishops controlled the church hierarchy—but Calvinist in doctrine, liturgy, and ceremony.[82] The monarch was the head of the church and the state, giving the Tudors broad control over matters of faith as well as temporal governance. The English throne thus wielded a level of religious authority not matched by its counterparts on the continent.[83] Nonetheless, English politics was to be defined by religious cleavage for the balance of the sixteenth and seventeenth centuries.[84]

Henry's successor, Edward VI, consolidated the Church of England's embrace of Protestant doctrine and ceremony. After taking the throne in 1553, Queen Mary then attempted to bring England back to Catholicism. But her successor and half-sister, Queen Elizabeth, who ruled from 1558 to 1603, restored the Protestant turn. The relationship of the Church of England with Catholics and with other Protestants—in particular, Presbyterians in Scotland and Puritans in England—would then roil English politics well into the seventeenth century. Indeed, religious disputes, which became intertwined with the confrontation between the monarchy and Parliament, ultimately triggered civil war. England would eventually arrive at the practice of religious tolerance, but, as elsewhere in Europe, only after decades of conflict made clear that there was no viable alternative.

The switch from the Tudor dynasty to the Stuarts in 1603 proved to be a turning point. The Stuarts did not command the authority enjoyed by their predecessors, opening the door to intensifying political and religious dissent. In addition, feudal military obligations had given way to armies consisting of paid volunteers. Since Parliament held the power of the purse, the monarchy was obliged to turn to it to secure the funding needed for war. At the opening of the seventeenth century, Parliament was still an advisory body that was called into session—and dissolved—at the will of the monarch. However, as England became embroiled in wars with other European states and eventually suffered its own civil conflicts, the monarchy's need for revenue provided Parliament the wherewithal to push back against royal power.

During the rule of James I (1603–1625), England was at peace and James promoted religious tolerance by allowing Catholics to practice quietly and encouraging a broad Protestantism that embraced both high-church Anglicans and low-church Puritans.[85] Trouble began when James' son, Charles, took the throne. Charles I was married to a Catholic, raising the possibility of a Catholic heir. Charles also guided England into wars with France and Spain, prompting him to impose new taxes. Parliament granted his request for military funding in 1628, but only after it exacted from the king a "Petition of Right" that protected subjects from arbitrary arrest and extra-parliamentary taxation.[86] Frustrated with Parliament's successful effort to contain his power, Charles did not call it into session for the ensuing decade. Nonetheless, he continued to raise taxes, setting the stage for a clash with Parliament.[87]

Charles' religious inclinations proved to be even more divisive than his struggles with Parliament. He was attracted to a Protestant denomination maintaining that prayer, sacraments, and moral conduct could earn salvation—a direct challenge to the Calvinist notion of predestination. The role of the clergy was elevated accordingly, prompting Anglicans and Puritans alike to worry that Charles was taking England back to the formalism and ceremony of Catholicism.[88] Charles also alienated Presbyterians in Scotland by seeking to restore bishops to the Scottish church and insisting that its prayer book conform to England's version.

## The Onset of Civil War

The Scots rebelled against Charles' encroachments, leading to the outbreak of war between England and Scotland. War costs forced Charles to recall Parliament, which promptly passed a bill making it illegal for the king to impose taxes without its approval and stipulating that the body would henceforth meet in regular session and could be dissolved only with its own consent. Soon thereafter, the Irish revolted against English hegemony. The resurgence of Catholic power in Ireland—rumored to have the support of Charles—prompted Parliament to take further steps to reduce the king's authority. The "Great Remonstrance" stripped the king of his right to raise an army and restored Calvinist practices to the Church of England.[89] The confrontation then escalated, prompting

Charles and Parliament to raise separate armies. The north and west of England, which were more agrarian and still dominated by the aristocracy, backed the king. The south and east, which were more urbanized and commercialized, backed Parliament.[90] Fighting began late in 1642 and continued until the middle of 1645, when Parliament's forces defeated the royalist army.

Despite its victory, Parliament was quickly beset by factional fighting—primarily along religious lines.[91] After an unsuccessful attempt by royalist forces to reclaim power, Parliament's army, flush with victory, disgruntled with its pay and status, and distrustful of quarreling parliamentarians, effectively carried out a military coup. It purged Parliament of alleged royalist sympathizers and allowed only one-third of its members to take their seats. The "Rump Parliament" then established a high court to try Charles as a "tyrant, traitor, murderer and a public enemy."[92] The court found him guilty, and the king was beheaded on January 30, 1649.

Amid the ensuing turmoil, Oliver Cromwell, the commander of Parliament's army, established an effective military dictatorship from 1653 until his death in 1658. Meanwhile, Charles' son, Charles II, took refuge in France. The Rump Parliament returned soon after Cromwell's death, but it was paralyzed by factional quarrels and survived only five months. The prospect of anarchy awakened royalist sentiment, with Charles II returning to England in May 1660 after a new Parliament declared him the lawful monarch. The restoration entailed compromise and balance; Parliament retained a significant measure of the power it had wrested from the monarchy and sought to protect military and political leaders from retribution at the hands of royalists. Charles II proved a willing partner. He appointed former allies of Cromwell to his privy council and supported the broad pardon preferred by Parliament.[93]

Religion again emerged as the main source of discord.[94] The church that accompanied the restoration represented a middle ground in terms of ceremony and doctrine—"the mean between extremes of papists and Puritans."[95] Although the compromise led to a broad tent, it also meant intolerance toward those who strayed too far from the mean. All members of Parliament were required to take the sacrament according to Anglican rites. Parliament passed a statute making it treason to link the king's name with Catholicism. Thousands of Quakers and Baptists were imprisoned. The Act of Uniformity adopted in 1662 required that all members of the clergy conform to Anglican practice; over 1,000 were forced to vacate their posts. The act was so controversial that the king and his advisors opposed it, fearful of a potential alliance between disaffected Catholics and banned Protestant sects.[96]

Religious tensions came to a head when Charles II died in 1685 and was succeeded by his brother James—a Catholic. James II was intent on restoring the rights of his co-religionists. The queen gave birth to a Catholic son in 1688, raising the prospect of a continuing Catholic dynasty. The Anglican Church, members of Parliament, and Protestant nobles promptly conspired to topple James by arranging an invasion of Dutch forces under the command of William of Orange, a Protestant married to James' daughter, Mary. The Dutch-led army easily defeated the royalists in 1688, whereupon James fled to France.

Parliament declared the throne vacant, and installed William and Mary as king and queen. The chamber also passed a Bill of Rights prohibiting a Catholic from occupying the throne, banning the king from raising money without Parliament's consent, and ensuring the rights of free elections and free speech. Following the so-called Glorious Revolution, the monarchy and Parliament alike also embraced greater religious tolerance, with William pressing to end discrimination against Catholics as well as Protestant dissenters. In 1689, Parliament passed the Toleration Act to help ensure that Christians of different denominations would live comfortably intermixed.[97] England had arrived at a form of constitutional monarchy that was pushing the frontiers of both religious and political pluralism.

One of the main beneficiaries of Parliament's expanded power was the bourgeoisie, whose resources had become increasingly vital to fund the modernizing state.[98] The growing commercial class backed and funded the parliamentary cause, helping it prevail against the monarchy. And its wealth ultimately translated into more direct political influence. The regular practice of selling titles meant that by the end of the seventeenth century, according to Mark Kishlansky, "the professional classes of doctors, lawyers, merchants, and financiers could buy the gentry. Their knighthoods came from service rather than genealogy as the locus of power shifted from the arms of the aristocracy to the purses of the professionals."[99] Moreover, as towns grew in population and prosperity, they sent an increasing number of professionals to the House of Commons, further undermining the power of the landed elite. Urbanization was, after all, proceeding at a rapid pace; by the end of the seventeenth century, London had some 600,000 inhabitants, making it Europe's largest city.[100]

England's commercial advance only quickened thereafter. Expanding domestic and international markets, greater reliance on finance capital to foster growth, and the technological breakthroughs made possible by cooperation between entrepreneurs and innovators would combine to fuel the Industrial Revolution. By 1830, some twenty percent of the population had joined the middle class.[101] By 1850, roughly half of the workforce was employed in the industrial and manufacturing sector.[102] This economic ascent was the foundation for Pax Britannica. As Michael Boulton, a nineteenth-century industrialist, remarked to a visitor at his factory, "I sell here, Sir, what all the world desires to have—power."[103]

• • • •

England's early political adjustment to the socioeconomic transformation associated with the commercial revolution would serve the country well. Whereas many other European states would experience domestic convulsion as their political systems adapted to social and economic change, England after the turmoil of the seventeenth century followed a relatively peaceful path to prosperity and liberal democracy. During the eighteenth century, political stability, economic growth, and national power went hand-in-hand. In the words of Paul Kennedy, "commercial interests were well represented in the councils of state, not only because successful merchants entered the ranks of the gentry whilst the great landowners partook in the profits of trade, but also because the political nation as a whole recognized that the encouragement of prosperity was synonymous with the furtherance of national power and prestige."[104]

By 1800, the rise of the West was far from complete. It would take another century for liberal democracy, industrial capitalism, and secular nationalism to be consolidated. Nonetheless, the conditions ensuring that the West would eclipse other contenders for primacy were in place. A growing bourgeoisie had established itself as an indelible feature of Europe's political landscape, leaving monarchs and nobility no choice but to grant this new class a say in matters of governance. In the first instance, merchants, artisans, and professionals served as the rank and file of the Reformation, which had momentous consequences for politics and society as well as religion. As Diarmaid MacCulloch observes, the Reformation endowed Europe with not just "the theory and practice of toleration," but also a new intellectual boldness: "the urge to compare, to assess, rather than to contemplate and acquiesce."[105] Merchants, professionals, and intellectuals would go on to fuel the scientific and industrial revolutions, which dramatically quickened the pace of Europe's economic rise and consolidated its geopolitical primacy.

Finally, it was also the rise of the bourgeoisie that advanced the incremental liberalization of politics. The succession of wars born of religious intolerance led not only to a new spirit of accommodation, but also to the beginnings of the modern state; war-making had become state-making. European states began to "cage" their populations to extract the resources needed for war.[106] In return, those populations—and, in particular, the rising bourgeoisie—earned growing political influence. It was this initial bargain that set the stage for the evolution of representative government, eventually culminating in universal suffrage and institutionalized checks against autocratic power.

# 3 :: The Last Turn

## THE WEST BESTS THE REST

As the story of Europe between 1500 and 1800 makes clear, the West's rise was the product of two main developments. First, the weakness of Europe's political institutions proved to be a latent strength; a rising class of merchants, artisans, and professionals successfully challenged the authority of monarchy, nobility, and church. The relative independence of the bourgeoisie and the horizontal political and social linkages they formed undermined the ability of traditional institutions to preserve exclusively vertical lines of authority. Second, the onset of the Reformation, which was carried forward by this rising bourgeoisie, both further weakened church and monarchy and spawned conflicts along confessional lines. These conflicts initially intensified conflict between Catholics and Protestants, but they ultimately furthered the cause of religious toleration and resulted in the gradual withdrawal of religion from the affairs of state. The wars of the Reformation also advanced the cause of political pluralism as autocratic rulers were forced to grant the bourgeoisie political say in return for the resources needed to prosecute war.

The West's eclipse of other contenders for primacy was the product not just of the socioeconomic, religious, and political conditions that contributed to its rise, but also the absence of similar conditions elsewhere. Otherwise, the Ottoman Empire and other centers of power in Asia might have kept pace with Europe's ascent. This chapter explains why other major states instead fell far behind the West. In broad terms, their centralized and hierarchical institutions of political control engendered more order and stability than in Europe—but at a high cost. Centralization prevented the socioeconomic dynamism that was Europe's greatest asset. The chapter begins by examining the Ottoman Empire—Europe's neighbor and competitor as it ascended—and then turns briefly to China, India, and Japan.

The commercial, political, and technological advances that enabled Europe to leap ahead of alternative centers of power also provided Europeans with the capital, ships, firepower, and other tools needed to extend their reach around the world. Through direct and indirect rule of most quarters of the globe, Europe's seafaring nations were not only able to assert control over the Americas, Asia, the Middle East, and Africa, but also to internationalize the norms and institutions upon which the Western order rested. After World War II, the United States took over from Europe stewardship of the Western order and recast it to reflect U.S. interests and values. The final section of this chapter chronicles when and how the West went global.

## The Ottoman Empire

On matters of both politics and religion, the Ottoman Empire after 1500 followed an altogether different trajectory than did the leading states of Europe. Ottoman rulers maintained centralized control throughout the imperial realm, prohibiting the emergence of the autonomous sites of wealth and power that were the agents of change in Europe. The sultan and his administrators rigidly enforced vertical lines of authority, denying artisans, merchants, traders, and intellectuals the ability to amass the influence and build the horizontal ties needed to serve as a counterweight to the imperial apparatus. Although an asset in terms of enforcing the unity and integrity of imperial rule, this concentration of authority forestalled the dynamism and social mobility that fueled Europe's rise—and was therefore a significant cause of the empire's stagnation. Such centralized control also goes partway in explaining why the Ottoman realm did not experience an Islamic Reformation that could have transformed its religious and political landscape as the Protestant Reformation did for Europe. The split between Sunnis and Shiites had the potential to do just that—but Istanbul drew on its broad authority to repress heterodoxy and enforce conformity to Sunni doctrine and practice.

The centralized and vertical nature of Ottoman rule, however, does not go all the way in explaining the absence of an Islamic Reformation. At least as important is the fundamental difference in how Christianity and Islam approach the relationship between religion and politics. Christianity is a religion of faith, not law and politics. Its central focus on faith is one of the main reasons that doctrinal dissent, once established, led to the proliferation of competing denominations. It is also one of the main reasons that the pope consistently sought alliances with secular rulers; only when wedded to temporal power did the church extend its reach beyond the realm of the sacred. The church had a paramount interest not only in mediating between the secular and sacred, but also in amassing the land and wealth that would augment its political power. Meanwhile, the rising bourgeoisie challenged traditional institutions of authority by consistently playing emperor against pope and state against church.

In contrast, Islam is a religion of faith *and* law in which there is no distinction between the sacred and the secular. The Ottoman sultan was emperor and pope, and the state was the mosque and the mosque the state. This altogether different relationship between religion and politics helps explain why merchants, artisans, and other urban elites with an interest in more autonomy were unable to find the gaps in authority needed to get a firm foothold. Moreover, the very notion of a distancing of religion from state—one of the most important principles to emerge from the Reformation—could not take hold in a political universe in which religion and state were inextricably bound.

## The Political Map of the Ottoman Empire

From the middle of the 1400s, when the Ottoman Turks conquered Constantinople, until the empire began to falter in the

1800s, the Ottoman realm was highly centralized. The sultan wielded absolute power over imperial administration, engendering the loyalty of all appointees—from high-ranking advisers in Istanbul to low-ranking emissaries in the periphery. The state exercised vertical control of political and economic life, deliberately forestalling the emergence of horizontal networks that could challenge imperial rule. According to Karen Barkey, the empire operated as a "hub and spoke network structure, where the rim is absent," a system that "made peripheral elites dependent on the center, communicating only with the center rather than with one another."[1] The contrast with contemporaneous developments in Europe is striking. In the Ottoman Empire, the center rigidly enforced vertical lines of authority, preempting potential threats to unitary control. In Europe, emerging agents of political change—merchants, artisans, Protestant leaders, towns—succeeded in constructing horizontal social linkages that effectively foiled the efforts of monarchy, nobility, and church to maintain top-down rule.

The sultan and his court enforced the vertical exercise of authority by adopting strategies of governance that effectively neutralized alternative sites of wealth and power. Istanbul undercut the potential challenge posed by aristocratic families in Anatolia by expropriating land and converting it to state-owned property. Land and wealth could no longer be passed from one generation to the next. The power of the landed elite was effectively transferred to administrators and cavalry, to whom the sultan assigned the right to draw revenue from farms. In return for their service, imperial appointees could tax agricultural production, keeping some of the income for themselves and sending the rest to the central treasury.[2]

Administrators and cavalry assigned to the provinces were rotated to new areas every three years to ensure that they would not develop strong ties to the local population and organize potential resistance to central authority.[3] The outlying provinces were the only exception. In the far-flung periphery, local elites were co-opted into the imperial apparatus and they functioned as collaborators, enjoying relative autonomy as long as they delivered regular payments to

Istanbul and contributed troops to fight for the imperial cause when asked to do so.[4]

The *millet* system allowed non-Muslim communities to retain their own religious and political institutions—but it then incorporated these institutions into the empire's hierarchical system of control. The leaders of these minority populations functioned as intermediaries between imperial authorities and their local communities. As Barkey describes this system, "Where there was strong community organization and/or strong ecclesiastical hierarchy, the central state adopted these institutions as the representative structures of the community."[5] Armenians, Greek Orthodox, and Jews, for example, maintained their own courts and religious laws.[6] Nonetheless, the *millet* system also fully integrated these institutions into the imperial apparatus; minority leaders directed their allegiance to Istanbul even as they enjoyed significant autonomy on matters of communal governance.

The sultan further strengthened his power by cultivating a personal army—the janissaries—whose ranks were filled by young men from Christian families. Initially, the janissaries consisted primarily of prisoners of war. In the early fifteenth century, a system of conscription (*devsirme*) was put into place. The janissaries were not permitted to come from Muslim families or to marry; these proscriptions ensured that this elite corps could not develop into a warrior class that might pose a threat to the sultan's power. On the contrary, the janissaries' unique privilege and status generally encouraged loyalty to the sultan. Over time, the strict protocols that sustained this trustworthy militia were relaxed; during the later empire, the janissaries were permitted to marry and have children. As the court had initially feared, a loyal imperial guard developed into a hereditary institution that became a potent counterweight to the sultan. This threat to centralized control eventually evoked a harsh reaction. In the early nineteenth century, Mahmud II abolished the janissary system and killed most of its serving members.

Istanbul's tight hold on power also extended to matters of commerce. The prices of goods and the flow of trade were controlled by imperial officials, in no small part to ensure that the government could secure commodities at reasonable cost.[7] Merchants were therefore unable to accumulate substantial wealth, denying them the ability to emerge as a check against state power—as their counterparts did in Europe. Long-distance trade was generally less regulated than commerce within the empire. But it was handled primarily by Greeks, Jews, Armenians, and other non-Muslims; the profits enjoyed by these traders were therefore of minimal political consequence. Some government functionaries were able to amass considerable savings. But they were firmly ensconced within the imperial apparatus, depended upon their posts for their wealth, and could not pass their assets on to their offspring. These restrictions prevented the evolution of powerful and wealthy family lines. Moreover, the Ottomans did not develop a modern banking system—in part due to the constraints imposed by Islamic legal practices—instead relying on informal networks of lending and, eventually, on European financial institutions that did business in Ottoman lands.[8] Accordingly, the financiers that were able to turn wealth into power in cities like London did not emerge in Istanbul or other urban areas within the Ottoman realm.

The pattern of urban settlement in the Ottoman Empire also contributed to the political weakness of its commercial class. By the sixteenth century, hundreds of small cities had sprung up across Europe, many of them home to entrepreneurs and craftsmen seeking to escape imperial and noble power. The relative autonomy of these urban areas was reinforced by topography; rivers, forests, and mountains made overland connections difficult. In contrast, the Ottoman Empire was home to a much smaller number of cities, most of which had been founded centuries earlier and were considerably larger in population than their European counterparts.[9] Accordingly, merchants, artisans, and traders were incorporated into traditional structures of power—just as they were in Italy, where cities were older, larger, and dominated by the traditional elite. Moreover, overland transportation between the main Ottoman cities was relatively efficient and inexpensive, facilitating centralized control and the extension of direct rule to urban areas far from Istanbul.[10]

Political centralization prevented an expanding commercial class not only from evolving into an upwardly mobile and wealthy bourgeoisie, but also from serving as agents of literacy, innovation, and learning. During the 1400s, Ottoman scholars took up a wide range of subjects, including mathematics, astronomy, and medicine. But the influence of religious authorities (*ulema*) increased during the 1500s, dramatically constricting opportunities for the study of subjects other than Islam. Combined with the limited autonomy afforded entrepreneurs, the constraints on secular learning imposed by religious authorities led to a striking intellectual stagnation when compared with contemporaneous developments in Europe.[11]

Printing presses were operating in Istanbul by the late fifteenth century—but they were few in number and owned primarily by Armenians and Jews. It was not until the second half of the nineteenth century that printed matter began to circulate widely. Until that time, according to Donald Quataert, no more than one dozen books were printed annually in Istanbul, and only a small portion of the population was literate. Quataert estimates that literacy rates stood at two to three percent in the early 1800s, and climbed to only fifteen percent by the end of the nineteenth century.[12] By means of comparison, roughly fifty percent of the French population was literate by 1800. The increasingly educated, wealthy, autonomous, and networked bourgeoisie that fueled Europe's rise simply did not exist in the Ottoman realm.

### Religious Diversity without Reformation

Even without the socioeconomic dynamism provided by an empowered bourgeoisie, the divide within Islam between Sunni and Shiite traditions might have brought to the Ottoman realm a religious ferment along the lines of the Protestant Reformation. After all, the split between Sunnis and Shiites dates back to the seventh century, some nine hundred years prior to Luther's excommunication by the pope.

The divide within Islam began in 632, after the death of Mohammed. One group of Mohammed's followers—who came to be called Sunnis—looked to Abu Bakr, the prophet's father-in-law, to assume the mantle of leadership. Others—who came to be called Shiites—saw Ali ibn Abi Talib, Mohammed's son-in-law, as his rightful successor. This rift over leadership of the Islamic community broke into the open in 680 after the followers of Abu Bakr killed Ali's son, Husayn. Although the divide within Islam initially stemmed from a power struggle over leadership, it developed into a broader dispute over doctrine and practice. Sunnis, who dominated the Umayyad caliphate that emerged during the seventh century, became supporters of communal consensus and the unchallenged political and religious authority of the caliphate. Shiites emerged as the more activist sect; they were willing to challenge the political, religious, and moral authority of their leaders and focused less on religious observance than on personal sacrifice and spirituality.[13]

As Vali Nasr observes, the split between Shiites and Sunnis "somewhat parallels the Protestant-Catholic difference in Western Christianity."[14] But even though Islam confronted a sectarian cleavage almost from its outset, it did not experience a reformation of the sort that brought religious tolerance and political pluralism to Europe. Whereas Europe underwent the religious and political transformation wrought by a doctrinal dispute within Christianity, why did an Ottoman realm confronted with a similar divide experience primarily religious and political stasis?

The absence of a wealthier and better-organized bourgeoisie is part of the answer. In Europe, the ideas of the Reformation may well not have spread without the help of merchants, artisans, and professionals who had already won a measure of autonomy—and were seeking more. In Ottoman lands, the commercial class was much less developed and remained firmly under the control of imperial authorities. The relative weakness of the Ottoman Empire's urban elite, however, does not offer a complete explanation of the absence of an Islamic Reformation. Shiism, like Protestantism, had its strongest pull among merchants, artisans, and other kindred spirits looking to distance themselves from traditional institutions of governance. Indeed, the Shiite movement initially took root primarily among craftsmen and other urban dwellers who resented the power of the Arab aristocracy and sought a more egalitarian society. Thereafter, the movement continued to have the strongest support among urban populations. Just as the break between Protestants and Catholics had a strong socioeconomic dimension, so too did the split between Shiites and Sunnis.[15]

The nature of Islam—in particular its integration of the sacred with the secular—helps explain why a sectarian divide within Islam did not produce a European-style reordering of the relationship between religion and politics. As mentioned above, Christianity is a religion of faith rather than law; only through the church's explicit intervention in the affairs of state does the religious become the political. In contrast, Islam is a religion of law; it inextricably intertwines religion and politics, faith and power. It draws no distinction between the state and the mosque because it merges political and religious authority into a single institution: the caliphate. As Bernard Lewis elaborates, Islam "has no words to distinguish between sacred and profane, spiritual and temporal, for it does not accept or even know the dichotomy that these pairs of antonyms express."[16]

The Ottoman Empire was thus founded on a very different conception of the relationship between religion and politics than were European states. In Europe, where the Catholic Church depended upon religious homogeneity and doctrinal conformity to exercise its political sway over the secular state, dissent posed a mortal threat; hence the church's urgent efforts to eliminate alternatives. In the Ottoman realm, where mosque and state were one and the same—and the caliphate employed imperial administrators and *ulema* alike—religious heterodoxy was much less threatening; as long as alternative forms of Islam did not challenge the political status quo, they could be tolerated. After all, Islam had lived with doctrinal pluralism—the split between Sunnis and Shiites—from early on. Accordingly, Ottoman authorities were more accommodating of religious dissent than their European counterparts—provided that it did not upset the established political order.[17] At the same time, they were equally repressive of such dissent when it came at the expense of political stability and the sultan's authority.

The early architects of the Ottoman Empire took a quite flexible stance toward religious diversity. Osman, who founded the empire and ruled from 1299 until 1324, brokered political compacts across religious boundaries, incorporating into the imperial structure not only Muslims who embraced diverse traditions, but also Orthodox Christians from the Byzantine Empire. As Barkey notes, "The foundation of Ottoman power...was the result of brokerage across boundaries, especially religious ones."[18] Grand viziers—who were second in command after the sultan—came from diverse backgrounds. Between 1453 and 1515, only three of fifteen grand viziers were of Muslim and Turkic origin, and non-Muslims regularly staffed the imperial administration.[19] Sunni doctrine and practice were dominant throughout the Ottoman realm, but Shiite practice and other forms of religious heterodoxy were generally accommodated.[20] In this respect, the Ottoman Empire started off more tolerant of religious diversity than did the Holy Roman Empire. Indeed, the Ottomans succeeded in sustaining a much higher level of imperial integrity than their European counterparts—while also permitting a much more significant measure of religious pluralism.

The toleration of religious diversity gradually diminished after the Safavid dynasty came to power in neighboring Persia in the early sixteenth century, putting Shiites in control of a principal geopolitical competitor to the Ottomans. Thereafter, Ottoman authorities no longer viewed Shiites as just religious dissenters, but instead saw them as a direct internal and external threat to the empire. Sultan Beyazid II (1481–1515) expelled many Shiites from Anatolia, relocating them to outlying portions of the empire. Beyazid's son, Selim I (1515–1520), soon thereafter went to war against Safavid Persia, commencing a conflict that lasted most of the sixteenth century.

The Ottoman Empire emerged from its clash with Persia with a much stronger Sunni identity. The sultan placed *ulema* in more powerful positions within the imperial administration, expanding their influence.[21] By the seventeenth century, Istanbul had abandoned its accommodating stance toward Muslim dissent, instead regularizing repression of Shiites. Unlike in Europe, where the church and state lacked the wherewithal to suppress Protestantism, the centralized structure of Ottoman rule enabled Istanbul to enforce religious homogeneity. The divide between Sunni and Shiite did not grow into an irreparable schism because imperial institutions wielded sufficient control to prevent it from doing so. With political, religious, and military power vested in a single authority, the sultan prevailed.

In Europe, the Counter-Reformation aimed at a similar conformity, but the emperor and pope, often divided against each other, did not have the power to enforce homogeneity. Moreover, they confronted not just religious dissent, but religious dissent married to a growing and increasingly restive class of merchants, artisans, and commercial elites. Europe's fragmenting political and religious institutions and its socioeconomic flux, although initially a source of turmoil and conflict, ultimately proved to be significant assets; from chaos emerged dynamism. In contrast, the centralization of authority in Istanbul and the socioeconomic stasis that followed would ultimately deny the Ottoman realm the societal vitality, economic vigor, and political and religious pluralism needed to keep pace with Europe.

## Stasis and Collapse

Despite its highly centralized structure, the Ottoman Empire did prove able to adapt its institutions of governance to changing geopolitical and economic conditions. Frequent and expensive wars—primarily against Persians, Habsburgs, and Venetians—created a pressing need to raise more revenue. As in Europe, extracting more resources from society entailed fashioning new bargains with economic elites. In the case of the Ottomans, that new economic elite first had to be created; the landed nobility had by decree lost most of its wealth during the empire's early decades and Istanbul thereafter prevented the emergence of an affluent bourgeoisie.

The solution, which took place over the course of the 1700s, was to effect a change in the nature of tax farming. Istanbul replaced a system in which rotating cavalry and imperial administrators taxed agricultural production in return for their service with one that assigned property to local notables and granted them life tenure as tax collectors. This new system succeeded in raising additional revenue for the central treasury. And although it effectively re-established a landed gentry of sorts, this propertied class served at the pleasure of the sultan and thus remained loyal to Istanbul.[22]

Over time, however, tax farmers gradually evolved into a new elite capable of pushing back against imperial rule. They capitalized on their growing wealth and autonomy to build local bases of power and political networks that disrupted the vertical lines of authority that had long bound the periphery to the center.[23]

The disciplined centralization of the Ottoman Empire enabled it to survive as long as it did. But by the nineteenth century, local elites posed an increasing challenge to Istanbul's authority. In addition, Europe's eclipse of Ottoman power suggested that such centralization, although it preserved imperial integrity, had also been a source of political and economic stagnation. In response, the so-called *Tanzimat* movement sought to import from Europe a wide range of political and economic reforms. The Ottoman system, however, was too centralized and insufficiently flexible to accommodate such ambitious change. Instead, the empire gradually fragmented as imperial authorities proved unable to maintain control over the periphery.

As the nineteenth century progressed, the provincial elites that emerged from the new system of tax farming grew more powerful and independent. Meanwhile, the *millet* system, which had long served as an effective means of integrating minority communities into the imperial architecture, proved to be a serious vulnerability as the nationalist ideologies exported from Europe awakened centrifugal forces. The Ottoman Empire finally collapsed in the early twentieth century not because the center failed. Rather, the center proved unable to continue exercising centripetal force over the hub-spoke system it had long before erected. As Barkey concludes, "What was left, finally, was a galaxy of nationalisms increasingly floating free from one another."[24]

The centralized strength of the Ottoman Empire's system of governance eventually proved to be a defining source of its weakness. Hierarchical rule long preserved imperial integrity, but it simultaneously denied the imperial realm the socioeconomic ferment that brought to Europe a rising bourgeoisie, religious and political transformation, new financial instruments, and intellectual and technological advance. The Ottomans eventually realized that they were fast falling behind Europe. But they were then stuck in a political no-man's-land—too reliant on traditions of hierarchy to take advantage of the dynamism offered by reform, but too weak for the center to maintain imperial integrity. Political atrophy favored stasis rather than adaptation, ultimately leading to the collapse of the empire in the face of the economic, military, and ideological challenges posed by the rising West.

## China, India, and Japan

The Ottoman Empire was only one of several major states eclipsed by the ascent of the West. China, India, and Japan were all potential competitors for primacy as the modern era took shape. But just as the Ottoman realm fell behind Europe due to its hierarchical imperial structures, so too did the centralization of their political and social orders hold back these other states. As was the case for the Ottomans, the strength of the state became its weakness, standing in the way of the socioeconomic dynamism that ultimately propelled the West ahead of other centers of economic and military power.

### China

According to Kenneth Pomeranz, China during the early modern era was well placed to keep pace with, if not best, Europe's economic performance. The two regions had comparable nutritional levels and agricultural productivity. Life expectancy in the 1700s was between thirty-four and thirty-nine in both Europe and China. China enjoyed distinct advantages over Europe when it came to irrigation and technologies for producing textiles and had a more developed trading system. It also had more advanced commodity, labor, and land markets as well as credit instruments. In addition, much of China's arable land was available for purchase or rent, whereas a substantial portion of Europe's land was still controlled by dynastic families, nobility, and the church.[25]

The main impediments to the economic growth that might have otherwise emerged from China's considerable advantages were its hierarchical institutions of imperial control. According to Fernand

Braudel, "In China, the chief obstacle [to growth] was the state, with its close-knit bureaucracy...[which] lay across the top of Chinese society as a single, virtually unbreachable stratum."[26] The Mandarins had a monopoly on political power, and also hindered the accumulation of wealth outside the state apparatus. Despite this centralized brand of rule, however, China's imperial officials, in contrast with their Ottoman counterparts, wielded power with a light touch. For the most part, farmers and merchants had little interaction with central authorities. Villagers were generally left alone to pursue their livelihoods and did not face the intrusive control over production and trade exercised within the Ottoman realm. Nonetheless, imperial rule was very much a top-down affair.[27]

Despite a measure of autonomy at the local level, not until the twentieth century did Chinese society begin to develop the horizontal societal linkages that emerged much earlier in Europe. Strong allegiances to family, kin, and village stood in the way of the social mobilization that emerged from Europe's system of guilds, city leagues, and, after the Reformation, solidarity among co-religionists. The vast majority of China's population lived in rural areas. Some farmers also became craftsmen. But they continued their agrarian lifestyles, did not migrate to urban areas, and did not develop either the wealth or the political strength to push back against the power of the state.[28] As McNeill observes, "there was nothing to upset the ancient subordination of merchant and artisan to the landowning and official class."[29]

China's relative geopolitical quiescence during the early modern era also meant that it did not bear the fiscal burdens associated with the frequent wars that plagued Europe's states. In Europe, the combination of ongoing battles against the Ottomans, geopolitical competition among rival European monarchs, and the wars of the Reformation forced states to extract increasing resources from their populations, prompting the taxed to exact in return a stronger political voice. After the establishment of the Qing dynasty in 1644, the Chinese faced no peer competitor. Indeed, China was able to "dominate East Asia in a relatively self-enclosed international system."[30] The Qing frequently fought border wars with the Mongols, Russians, and Muslim tribes in Xinjiang. But these tended to be short and contained conflicts, not major wars sustained over decades. Internally, the Qing faced occasional rebellions, particularly in China's south. But such conflicts paled in comparison with the religious bloodshed that wracked Europe's states during the Counter-Reformation. Not until the nineteenth century did the Qing face widespread internal revolts as well as commercial and military competition with Europe's imperial powers.

Accordingly, taxation in China remained relatively low and the state did not "cage" its population as it did in Europe. Moreover, because of a lack of demand for capital as well as the tight grip of the central government, China did not develop the banking system and more advanced debt instruments that contributed to the accumulation of private wealth in Europe. China thus lacked a wealthy middle class that was capable of pushing back against the power of imperial institutions. Stasis in its social order combined with relative geopolitical quiet to deny China the societal and economic dynamism that might have enabled it to keep pace with Europe's rise.

### India

Muslim armies, primarily of Turkic background, began invading India during the early eighth century. Before these invasions, India passed through several centuries of weak and fragmented government. As during previous periods in Indian history, the absence of centralized control contributed to intellectual and economic vitality.[31] As Stanley Wolpert comments, the early centuries of the Common Era were a period of "political fragmentation and economic and cultural enrichment."[32]

Muslim invaders brought this period of fragmentation—and economic dynamism—to an end. The Delhi Sultanate, which was established in 1206 and lasted over 300 years, relied on a highly centralized brand of rule. The sultan deployed spies throughout the empire to detect threats to unity. He kept tight control over not only the imperial administration and army, but also trade.[33] The court set prices for goods and required that all merchants be licensed. Agricultural taxes stood at one-half of output, preventing the accumulation of substantial wealth outside imperial institutions. By the

1400s, a combination of foreign invasion and internal revolt began to weaken the sultanate. The Central Asian armies of Tamerlane, the Tartar leader, first sacked Delhi in 1398. Nonetheless, the sultanate succeeded in holding on until 1526, when Delhi again fell to foreign forces.

The Mughals, a Muslim group originally from Central Asia, were the next to conquer India. The Mughal Empire was consolidated by Akbar, who took the throne in 1556. The administration of the Mughals closely resembled that of the Ottomans. The empire was from the outset tolerant of non-Muslims and incorporated Hindus into the imperial bureaucracy—although mostly at lower levels. The bulk of the imperial staff was comprised of Muslims born outside of India—strengthening their dependence on and loyalty to the sultan. They were charged not only with administration, but also with raising cavalry for the empire. Strict obedience and fealty were mandatory; during the reign of Shah Jahan, top advisers were required to prostrate themselves before the throne twice daily. Imperial bureaucrats were allowed to accumulate wealth, but upon death all their assets became the property of the sultan. To ensure the center's control over the provinces, the influence of the rural aristocracy was cut back and local authority vested in administrators loyal to the sultan. Like the Ottomans, the Mughals maintained exclusively vertical lines of authority.

The Mughal Empire began to stumble late in the rule of Alamgir (1658–1707). He inherited a realm already facing severe economic strains; the lavish expenditures of his predecessors on imperial buildings, monuments, and entertainment had led to an oppressive tax burden on the population. Alamgir was a Muslim zealot who began to oppress Hindus, imposing additional duties on them and prohibiting the construction of new Hindu temples. Mounting taxation and intensifying repression eventually invited widespread revolts against imperial rule. Alamgir succeeded in putting down the rebellions, but not before bankrupting the throne. By the early eighteenth century, the empire was beginning to crumble—and became an easy target for Europe's colonial powers.[34]

As in the Ottoman and Chinese empires, economic and political development in India was arrested by centralized imperial structures that stymied social mobility and prevented the emergence of autonomous centers of wealth and power. India had the resources and human capital needed to emerge as a leading world power. But the rigid political and social hierarchy imposed by imperial rulers ultimately impaired its ability to keep pace with Europe as the modern era unfolded.

## Japan

Japan emerged from the Middle Ages with a socioeconomic order closer to that of Europe than to that of China or India. Feudal estates began to appear in Japan during the 1200s, impairing the ability of imperial authorities to establish exclusively vertical lines of authority. Instead, Japan consisted of a multitude of semi-autonomous polities that were not integrated into a unitary state. As in Europe, topography mattered; mountains, forests, and rivers provided natural resistance to centralized control—and this fragmented landscape contributed to political pluralism and economic entrepreneurship. According to Conrad Totman, "Where higher political authority was fragmented and armies were on the loose—as was the case in much of Japan—residents had a shared interest in defending themselves against outsiders. These shared interests brought neighbors together in assemblies or other communal organizations that drew up and enforced regulations for their villages."[35] "The end result," observes Braudel, "would be a set of quasi-independent provinces, powerful, protecting their own towns, merchants, artisan professions and particular interests." Again paralleling Europe, the establishment of these independent polities also led to the emergence of horizontal linkages among them: "The powerful craft guilds extended their networks and monopolies from one town to another."[36]

The economic and political development that might have been fostered by this combination of political fragmentation and communal cooperation was interrupted by civil war during the 1500s. The fighting spread as local barons who had come to dominate many parts of Japan vied for wealth, territory, and power.[37] During the 1600s, the *samurai*—warrior gentry—capitalized on the chaos to assert control over Japan, rolling back the growing autonomy that had been enjoyed by the emerging economic elite. This military aristocracy effectively ruled the country until the second half of the nineteenth century.

During this era, known as the Tokugawa, Japan was governed from Edo by a *shogun*—the chief warlord. The *shogun* demanded absolute loyalty of the *samurai* leadership (*daimyo*) in the provinces and required them to reside in Edo on a rotating basis. The *daimyo* enjoyed a relatively high degree of autonomy in ruling their respective regions and exercised tight control, enjoying by order of the *shogun* political mastery over artisans, merchants, and farmers. Commerce and urbanization did expand during the Tokugawa era, but economic development was arrested by the hierarchical nature of authority—and a self-imposed seclusion that prohibited almost all foreign trade.

Japan's isolation ended in the mid-1800s with the arrival of European and American traders. The Tokugawa era came to a close soon thereafter, marked by the end of both feudalism and the political ascendance of the *samurai*. The Meiji Restoration of 1868 led to an incremental liberalization of the political order; the power of the aristocracy was tempered by the reemergence of a more independent and influential economic elite. "Although merchants were the low men on the societal totem pole," according to Scott MacDonald and Albert Gastmann "many of them were to emerge richer and more powerful than the samurai."[38] As McNeill observes, "A great burst of economic prosperity followed, which, ironically, permitted the merchant classes to regain much of what they had earlier lost on the battlefield.... Financiers and merchants in turn used their wealth to support a middle-class urban culture, which...stood in self-conscious opposition to the austere code of the *samurai*."[39]

It is no accident that Japan was the first Asian country to industrialize and, by the 1930s, take its place as one of the world's leading economic and military powers. Although its ascent was interrupted by the dominance achieved by the *samurai* in the 1600s, its underlying social order—in particular, the early emergence of a relatively wealthy, autonomous, and urban class of commercial elites—set the stage for a rapid economic rise after the end of the Tokugawa era.

Indeed, the rapidity of that rise and the fact that Japan's modernization was compressed into a few decades may help explain the political dysfunctions that befell the country during the 1930s. Traditions
of conformity, hierarchy, and filial piety at once reinforced but also
clashed with the social and ideological demands of industrialization and nationalism.[40] A political and socioeconomic order stuck
between the pre-modern and the modern produced militarism at
home and excessive ambition abroad.

## The West Goes Global

As Europe ascended, the Ottoman Empire and imperial states in
China, India, and Japan were held back by centralized and hierarchical structures of rule. The strength of these regimes ultimately
proved to be their weakness; centralization stood in the way of the
social mobility conducive to economic dynamism and political
pluralism. The opposite was true for Europe; weakness paradoxically emerged as strength. A nascent bourgeoisie capitalized on the
fragmentation born of competition among monarchy, church, and
nobility to become the vanguard of progressive change. Eventually,
armed with liberal democracy, industrial capitalism, and secular nationalism, the West not only eclipsed the Ottoman Empire,
China, India, and Japan, but also went on to extend its reach into
these and other regions, producing for the first time in world history an integrated international system.

   As Europe began its rise, the world's main centers of power had
little contact with each other. Each imperial sphere of influence had
its own institutions and practices, but such differences had little consequence because the separate imperial zones so rarely interacted.
As Hedley Bull and Adam Watson note, "Contacts among these
regional international systems... were much more limited than contacts within them.... Most importantly, there was no single, agreed
body of rules and institutions operating across the boundaries of
any two regional international systems, let alone throughout the
world as a whole." Instead, each region operated according to "principles that were culturally particular and exclusive."[41] Other scholars
agree that "no constitution of international society was mutually,

explicitly, agreed upon," and that different regions of the world embraced quite different political and commercial practices.[42]

This compartmentalization of the international system eroded in step with Europe's rise. Beginning in the 1400s, oceangoing ships and advances in navigation enabled European explorers, merchants, and immigrants to establish outposts in the Middle East, Africa, Asia, and the New World. As Europe's economic and military advantages increased, these footholds grew in number, size, and influence. By the end of the nineteenth century, Europe's major powers had asserted either direct or indirect control over most of the globe. As they did so, they also exported European conceptions of sovereignty, administration, law, diplomacy, and commerce. In this sense, Europe not only eclipsed and dominated the rest of the world, it also established a global order based on uniquely European values and institutions; Europeans effectively replicated at the global level the founding principles of their own regional order.

The West went global in three phases. Between 1648 and 1815—from the Treaty of Westphalia to the founding of the Concert of Europe—the practices and institutions of a distinctly European order took shape. Europeans exported these practices and institutions as they traded and settled elsewhere, leaving their most notable impact on the New World. Between 1815 and 1914—the era of Pax Britannica—European imperialism expanded in terms of both territorial reach and the scope of political control. A Europe-centered world took shape and Europe's power and principles penetrated most regions of the globe. The era of Pax Americana began after World War II. The United States took over from Europe management of the Western order, adapting it in ways that suited its interests and values. Pax Americana reached its peak during the decade after the end of the Cold War, when the West, absent a countervailing bloc, appeared poised to complete its material and ideological dominance of global affairs.

The West's power and ideals were inseparable as Europe and the United States teamed up to fashion the world's first global order. The West's material superiority enabled it to dominate other centers of power, but it then sought to capitalize on that dominance to ensure that the rest played by the West's rules. Europe and the

United States exported their own values as a means of pursuing their economic and strategic interests, but also as a product of confidence in the universality of their principles. Nonetheless, the Western order was successfully globalized, as C.A. Bayly astutely observes, not because of the intrinsic appeal of the order on offer, but because that order was embedded in the West's global primacy.[43] Confronted with overweening economic and military strength, the rest had little choice but to acquiesce to the West. Remaking the world in its own image was perhaps the ultimate exercise of Western power.

## After Westphalia

The Treaty of Westphalia not only ended the wars of the Reformation, but also codified the founding principles of the evolving European order. In the ensuing decades, core elements of this emerging order were to mature, including: the territorial sovereignty and juridical equality of states; laws and practices governing diplomacy, commerce, the conduct of war, and the making of peace; and reliance on the operation of the balance of power to preserve international stability.[44] With Spain and Portugal leading the way through their pioneering advances in shipbuilding and navigation, European explorers, traders, emigrants, and missionaries took these values and principles with them as they set out for distant lands in the fifteenth century.

Europeans initially exported their ideas about political order primarily to the New World. According to Watson, "The Europeans...incorporated the New World from the beginning into their system of administration and government. It became an extension of Christendom."[45] Elsewhere, Europe's initial impact on the periphery was more limited. During the seventeenth century, European trading posts proliferated in Africa, South Asia, and East Asia. But European traders tended to conform to local commercial practices rather than insisting on their own.[46] And for the most part, Europeans confined their activities to coastal entrepôts, did not penetrate inland, and were politically subordinate to local rulers.[47]

As the eighteenth century opened, the European order had not yet gone global; indeed, the principles of that order were still taking shape. The Treaty of Utrecht (1713), which ended the War of Spanish Succession, the American (1776) and French (1789) revolutions, and the Napoleonic Wars (1799–1815) all played a role in advancing the ordering norms of the West, adding to them a republican element. Nonetheless, the European powers by the early 1700s did have the footholds in many parts of the globe that would soon enable them to rapidly expand their reach and export the Western order to most of the world.

## Pax Britannica

Over the course of the eighteenth century, advances in naval technology—in particular, the development of ocean-going vessels armed with heavy guns—enabled Europe to consolidate its naval dominance over potential rivals. According to Watson, "European maritime technology had made such tremendous strides that no Asian power could even consider matching the British or the French in the Indian Ocean."[48] During the nineteenth century, further advances enabled Europe's imperial powers to more regularly and easily penetrate into the periphery's interior. Steam-driven gunboats armed with mechanized weapons allowed Europe's increasingly professionalized militaries to control river traffic and establish political mastery over much of Africa, India, and East Asia. Quinine and other newly discovered medicines protected Europeans intent on expanding their presence in Africa against malaria and other diseases that had previously decimated the ranks of colonial expeditions. The railway and the submarine telegraphic cable further facilitated imperial expansion and control.[49] By the end of the nineteenth century, Europe had colonized virtually all quarters of the globe (indeed, much of the New World had already decolonized).

Europe's rise to global dominance was made possible not just by these and other technical advances, but also by diplomacy. At the close of the Napoleonic Wars, Europe's great powers formed the Concert of Europe—a more articulated architecture of order.

Under the aegis of the Concert, Great Britain, Russia, Prussia, Austria, and France cooperatively managed the balance of power in Europe and its periphery. Changes to the territorial status quo could be made only through consensus. Congresses were convened as necessary to deal with crises. Buffer zones, neutral zones, spheres of influence, and other diplomatic instruments were used to avert or dampen geopolitical competition. Russia was fully integrated into the Concert, furthering its Westernization. This deepening, codification, and institutionalization of the European order strengthened its hold at home and abroad.

With the Concert preserving stability on the continent, Europe's great powers were free to direct their aspirations and energies outward. Britain, in particular, took advantage of cooperative stability in Europe not only to expand its imperial possessions, but also to build a high-seas fleet that afforded unquestioned naval primacy and control of the world's major strategic arteries.[50] Naval mastery coincided with a shift in British policy from mercantilism to free trade; by the second half of the nineteenth century London was using its naval strength not to defend an exclusive economic zone, but to enforce an open global trading system. The resulting expansion in trade helped fuel Europe's Industrial Revolution, and thereby reinforced its global dominance. By the end of the century, Germany and the United States—both had followed the British model and successfully industrialized—joined the club of imperial powers, further strengthening the West's global presence.

Geopolitical stability, economic growth, and military dominance gave Europeans confidence that "modern civilization was synonymous with European ways and standards, which it was their duty and their interest to spread in order to make the world a better and safer place."[51] The West's projects of imperial expansion had become infused with ideological ambitions—the abolition of slavery, the spread of Christianity, and the realization of the West's civilizing mission. These objectives were pursued through direct rule over much of Asia and Africa, and even states that remained nominally independent "were expected and induced to conform to the rules and institutions of European international society."[52] Legions of missionaries also fanned out into the imperial periphery, ensuring that the West extended the reach of its religion, not just of its commercial and political power. To be sure, Europe's imperial powers were developing the practices of sovereignty and political pluralism at home while imposing hierarchical rule abroad.[53] Nonetheless, through building new states, mapping out new borders, and assigning colonial subjects new identities of nation, ethnicity, religion, and race, the West was remaking the rest in its own image.[54]

British rule in India marked one of the most profound instances of imperial penetration and transformation. Britain extended formal sovereignty to its territories in India in 1813, and thereafter completely revamped its education system, administration, and legal system along British lines. Indian politics had long been dominated by region, religion, and caste. Henceforth, the British nurtured a new English-speaking elite inculcated with Western notions of secularity, administrative efficiency, and justice. According to Percival Spear, author of *The Oxford History of Modern India*, "Britain's supreme function has been that of a cultural germ carrier.... The introduction of the English language provided a vehicle for western ideas, and English law a standard of British practice. Along with English literature came western moral and religious ideas, and the admission of missionaries provided, as it were, a working model of western moral precepts."[55]

The Ottoman Empire also fell under Europe's sway over the course of the 1800s. Although Europeans did not colonize the Ottoman realm during the nineteenth century, they did impose on the empire Western diplomatic and commercial practices. Multiplying political and economic links effectively brought the Ottomans into Europe's sphere of influence, forcing Istanbul to adopt European rules known as "capitulations." "A few decades into the nineteenth century," Thomas Naff affirms, "the Empire's economic subjugation to Europe was well-nigh complete."[56] Moreover, the *Tanzimat* movement explicitly sought to replace Ottoman institutions with Western ones. Although the reformers failed, they clearly saw Europe's political and economic model as the best hope for reviving the empire's fortunes.

The Scramble for Africa, which began in 1881, incorporated most of that continent into Europe's sphere of influence in roughly a decade. China too fell under Western domination in the second half of the nineteenth century as the imperial powers jockeyed for colonial outposts, spheres of influence, and extraterritorial rights. They also invested heavily in Chinese railways, banks, mines, and ports. The colonial powers set up Western-style courts, ran some of China's bureaucracies, and dispatched their troops and warships to treaty ports and stations far up the Yangtze River.[57] Japan preserved its independence from the West—but nonetheless Westernized. As a consequence of the Meiji-era reforms, Japan opened itself up to foreign trade, rapidly industrialized, introduced a parliamentary system of government, and built a European-style empire in East Asia. Japan also established a naval alliance with Great Britain in 1902, a move welcomed by many Japanese as confirmation of its inclusion in the Western club.

The evolution of Europe's political institutions and practices, coupled with the West's imperial expansion, meant that the Western order had gone global by the beginning of the twentieth century. By 1914, European colonies and former colonies represented eighty-four percent of the world's land mass, and the West's substantial footprint was as much ideological as geopolitical.[58] According to Hedley Bull, "By the First World War, then, a universal international society of states clearly existed which covered the whole world."[59] As Bull points out, this society of states not only reflected the West's values and political principles, but also its interests: "The international legal rules...were not only made by the European or Western powers, they were also in substantial measure made *for* them: part, at least, of the content of the then existing international law...served to facilitate the maintenance of European or Western ascendancy."[60] Europe had succeeded in ensuring that its material dominance and its ideological hegemony worked hand-in-hand.

## Pax Americana

World War II brought to a close Europe's long run as the globe's center of gravity. European nations were exhausted as well as devastated by the war, and their dominance had been diminished by the United States' emergence as an industrial and military powerhouse.

Moreover, Europe had been *too* successful in exporting its founding principles. If sovereignty and liberal democracy were integral to the Western way, then the globalization of the Western order ultimately meant that the rest should also enjoy the rights of self-determination and self-rule. Soon after the close of the war, independence movements successfully challenged imperial rule across the globe.

Europe's empires were dismantled as a consequence of not only uprisings in the periphery, but also America's insistence on decolonization. This was not the first time that Washington had tried to wean Europe from colonialism. At the end of World War I, President Woodrow Wilson sought to refashion the Western order. He wanted to end imperial rule in favor of self-determination and democratic governance, do away with the balance of power and turn instead to collective security and disarmament, and replace secret diplomacy with an authoritative and transparent body of international law. The League of Nations was to be the institutional embodiment of this new order.

Wilson's efforts, however, were foiled by political opposition on both sides of the Atlantic. Although many of his ideas played an important role in shaping the liberal order that emerged after World War II, at the close of World War I the U.S. Senate rejected American participation in the League, and Europeans were only slightly more enthusiastic about embracing Wilson's brand of idealism. With the United States opting for isolationism, Europe struggled to maintain its role as the anchor of the Western order during the interwar years. But Europe's democracies suffered from both political and economic weakness, which Nazi Germany and Imperial Japan sought to capitalize upon in their bid to overturn the liberal order. Only as a consequence of the eventual participation of the United States in World War II was the West saved from subjugation by the Axis powers.

Following the close of World War II, the United States not only became the leader of the West, but also revised its ordering norms.[61] Washington insisted on the dismantlement of empire, and Europe's great powers were in no position to resist. Rather than embrace a notion of stability that depended upon the balance of power, the United States favored a more ambitious alternative—combining countervailing power with the export of democracy to the end of transforming enemies, not just checking them. As they took over the mantle of global leadership, Americans "believed that they could use their power to order the world in the direction of democratic capitalism on the American model."[62] The occupation and democratization of Germany and Japan were cases in point; economically and politically, both countries were rebuilt from root to branch.[63] Washington launched the Marshall Plan to rejuvenate Europe's economy and consolidate its political stability.[64] And the United States was determined to eliminate the economic nationalism and protectionism that it saw as having contributed to the onset of World War II, replacing it with an open commercial and financial system that would be managed by international institutions.

Franklin Roosevelt and Harry Truman initially intended the U.S.-led order to be global in scope, with the United Nations providing both great-power tutelage and worldwide representation. But the onset of the Cold War led to a two-bloc order in which democratic capitalism was pitted against autocratic socialism. Thereafter, the Atlantic democracies anchored the Western order and gradually deepened their commercial, political, and institutional ties. In other parts of the globe, the United States established a network of alliances to contain the Soviet Union and, when possible, sought to spread markets and democracy to the developing world.

To be sure, the perceived strategic imperatives of the Cold War regularly prompted the United States to forgo efforts to spread democracy and instead ally with autocratic regimes. But just as Europe sought to export its values and institutions to the periphery during its era of dominance, the United States has capitalized on its period of global hegemony to guide the developing world toward open markets and democratic politics. And just as ideals and interests worked hand-in-hand during Europe's ascendancy, U.S. stewardship of the international system has been shaped by principle as well as the pursuit of security and prosperity. The international order that has been in place since the early nineteenth century has been not just of the West but also for the West.

The collapse of the Soviet Union appeared to herald the ultimate triumph of the West. The main alternative to the Western way had been defeated. The United States and Europe promptly teamed up to integrate their former adversaries into the Western order. The European Union and NATO opened their doors to the new democracies of Central Europe. A panoply of global and regional institutions—the World Trade Organization, the North American Free Trade Area, the Asia Pacific Economic Cooperation forum, NATO's Partnership for Peace, to name a few—were created to promote trade, political liberalization, and geopolitical stability. Such efforts yielded impressive results. During the decade after the fall of the Berlin Wall, the global economy enjoyed robust growth and a wave of democratization swept not only Europe's east, but also Asia, Africa, and Latin America. Not only had the Western way been globalized, but history really did seem to be coming to an end.

# 4 :: The Next Turn

## THE RISE OF THE REST

As the twenty-first century opened, the United States exuded a sense of satisfaction, if not outright hubris, about the triumph of the West. History really did seem to be going the West's way. The confidence, however, did not last long. The attacks of September 11, 2001, the lengthy wars in Iraq and Afghanistan, the global financial crisis, and runaway partisanship cast a gloomy pallor over the United States. The other side of the Atlantic also had its fair share of problems, including sluggish economic growth, a vulnerable euro-zone, and political division within the European Union. By the end of George W. Bush's presidency, talk of the end of history was history. Instead, leading voices were proclaiming the onset of the post-American world and the beginning of the Asian century.[1]

This radical shift in prevailing assessments of the West's prospects was partly the product of a dramatic mood swing—a reaction to a spate of setbacks for the United States and Europe. A more sober view of the durability of Western primacy, however, was not just an ephemeral reaction to temporary conditions. Rather, no longer misled by the triumphalism that accompanied the Cold War's end, analysts and policy makers alike were finally looking at the cold hard facts, which reveal quite conclusively that Western power has peaked.

## Cold Hard Facts

The emergence of a more level global playing field will occur gradually—over the next several decades, not the next several years. But the trend lines are unmistakable and the global turn they indicate unstoppable.

### The Economic Balance

Table 4.1 compares the top five economies in the world in 2010 with the top five projected for 2050. Such projections are, of course, speculative; the conditions on which they are based can and do change. Nonetheless, this "best guess" reveals that a striking change in the pecking order is in the offing.

In 2010, four out of the top five economies in the world were part of the West.[2] In 2050, according to Goldman Sachs, the United States will be the only Western power to make it into the top five. Moreover, as indicated in Figure 4.1, although the United States will be number two in 2050, its economy will be much smaller than China's. Goldman Sachs projects that China's GDP should match America's by 2027, and then steadily pull ahead.[3] As for the West's material primacy at the aggregate level, the collective GDP of the four leading developing countries (the BRICs[4]—Brazil, Russia, India, and China) is likely to match that of today's leading Western nations

**Table 4.1.** Top Five Economies, 2010 vs. 2050

| 2010 | 2050 |
|---|---|
| 1. United States | 1. China |
| 2. China | 2. United States |
| 3. Japan | 3. India |
| 4. Germany | 4. Brazil |
| 5. France | 5. Russia |

*Source*: Jim O'Neill and Anna Stupnytska, "The Long-Term Outlook for the BRICs and N-11 Post Crisis," Goldman Sachs Global Economics Paper no. 192, December 4, 2009, http://www2.goldmansachs.com/our-thinking/brics/brics-reports-pdfs/long-term-outlook.pdf, p. 22; International Monetary Fund, "World Economic Outlook Database: GDP at Constant Prices (USD)," April 2011, http://www.imf.org/external/pubs/ft/weo/2011/01/weodata/weoselco.aspx?g=2001&sg=All+countries.

**Figure 4.1.** GDP of Major Powers, 2010 vs. 2050 (in billions of dollars)

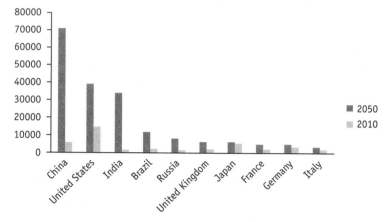

*Source*: Jim O'Neill and Anna Stupnytska, "The Long-Term Outlook for the BRICs and N-11 Post Crisis," Goldman Sachs Global Economics Paper no: 192, December 4, 2009, http://www2.goldmansachs.com/our-thinking/brics/brics-reports-pdfs/long-term-outlook.pdf, p. 22; International Monetary Fund, "World Economic Outlook Database: GDP at Constant Prices (USD)," April 2011, http://www.imf.org/external/pubs/ft/weo/2011/01/weodata/weoselco.aspx?g=2001&sg=All+countries.

by 2032.[5] The World Bank predicts that the U.S. dollar will lose its global dominance by 2025 as the dollar, euro, and China's renminbi become co-equals in a "multi-currency" monetary system.[6]

The scope of this forthcoming shift in the global distribution of power becomes even more arresting when broken into its constituent components. As for economic growth, projections indicate that U.S. GDP will expand at an average annual rate of 2.7 percent between 2009 and 2050, well above the one percent projected for Japan and also higher than the average of 1.7 percent projected for Europe's main economies (Germany, France, Britain, and Italy). During this same period, China is expected to experience average annual growth of 5.6 percent, while India should grow at an average of 5.9 percent.[7] Moreover, the growth differentials are greatest in the earlier decades of this time span, meaning that the gap between the industrialized West and China, India, and other emerging powers will close sooner rather than later.

China has already surpassed Japan to become the world's second-largest economy. Although it will be well into the next decade before China overtakes the United States to become number one, the numbers already speak for themselves. The United States in 2010 posted a current account deficit of $470 billion, contributing to global imbalances that threaten future U.S. growth. Meanwhile, China in 2010 racked up a surplus of $305 billion.[8] America's average rate of consumption over the past decade was seventy percent of GDP and its savings rate roughly 3.5 percent.[9] In contrast, China's average rate of consumption over the past decade was thirty-five percent of GDP and estimates of its savings rate range as high as forty percent.[10] China has funneled some of its accumulating surpluses into sovereign wealth funds, which the government invests strategically around the world. As of the spring of 2010, three of China's largest funds together had approximately $780 billion in assets—a figure roughly equivalent to the GDP of the Netherlands.[11] Meanwhile, public debt in the United States reached $14 trillion in early 2011 (over ninety percent of GDP), with annual deficits at their highest levels since the years following World War II.[12] As American debt has piled up, China has become the leading foreign purchaser of American treasuries, holding some $1.2 trillion in U.S. debt by the end of 2010—over twenty-five percent of U.S. treasury securities held by foreign countries. Indeed, foreigners held over half of all U.S. government debt by 2010, exposing the United States to considerable financial vulnerability.[13]

China's economy will cool off over time; growth rates, savings rates, and budget surpluses normally decline as national economies mature. But the impressive prospects for growth in China, India, and other developing countries are also grounded in immutable demographic realities. The West's population represents less than twenty percent of the globe's total—and is poised to experience both a relative and absolute decline in the years ahead. While the U.S. population and labor force will grow gradually over the coming decades due to both immigration and fertility rates higher than the Western norm, Europe's population is poised to shrink. The EU's aggregate fertility rate falls short of the replacement level and its immigration rate is below that of the United States.[14] Japan's population is also aging rapidly. Meanwhile, although China's population begins to decline around 2025 (due to the one-child policy implemented in 1978),

**Figure 4.2.** Major Power Labor Force Levels, 2010–2050 (in millions)

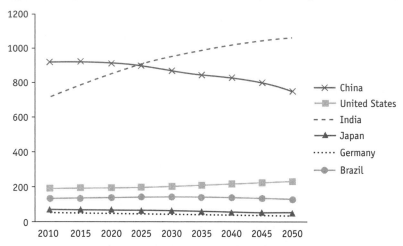

*Source*: Dominic Wilson and Anna Stupnytska, "The N-11: More Than an Acronym," Global Economics Paper no. 153, March 28, 2007, http://www.chicagobooth.edu/alumni/clubs/pakistan/docs/next11dream-march%20%2707-goldmansachs.pdf, p. 19.

as Figure 4.2 shows, China and India both have impressive pools of labor on which to draw for years to come. Many other parts of the developing world will be experiencing significant increases in their labor forces in the years ahead.

Not only will labor pools outside the West be expanding dramatically while those within the West are shrinking, but intellectual capital will also be relocating from the core to the periphery of the global system. The United States still has the best university system in the world. But an increasing number of the students taking advantage of this system are foreigners—and they regularly bring their skills back home.

In 1978 approximately twelve percent of all doctorates awarded in the United States went to foreign students.[15] By 2008, that figure had risen to thirty-three percent for all fields of study. In engineering, foreign students accounted for sixty percent of doctorates awarded, while the share of foreign students receiving doctorates in the physical sciences was forty-eight percent. In 2008, Chinese citizens studying in the United States accounted for nearly thirty percent of all doctorates awarded to foreign students. Students coming

**Figure 4.3.** Science & Engineering Doctorates Conferred, 1997–2007

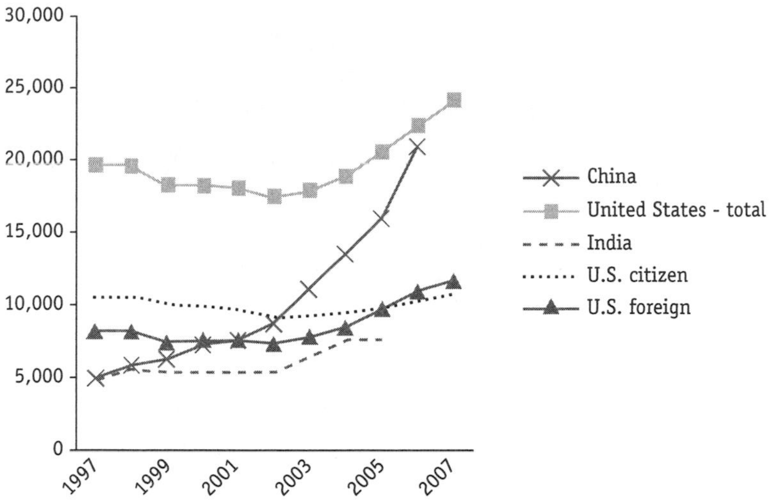

*Note*: Data for India available only to 2005 and for China only to 2006.

*Source*: "Science and Engineering Indicators, 2010," National Science Foundation. January, 2010, http://www.nsf.gov/statistics/seind10/figures.htm, Graph 0.9.

from China, India, and South Korea together received over fifty percent of all doctoral degrees awarded to foreigners. Figure 4.3 charts the steady rise of foreign students receiving science and engineering doctorates in the United States between 1997 and 2007. It also shows the number of science and engineering doctorates awarded in India and China, with the latter showing a dramatic increase. It should be no surprise that Asia's share of published scientific papers rose from sixteen percent in 1990 to twenty-five percent in 2004.[16]

China has also been investing heavily in its own university system. Starting in 1998, Beijing embarked on an ambitious plan to increase the size and quality of the country's institutions of higher learning. Spending on higher education nearly tripled over the ensuing decade. The number of institutions of higher learning grew from 1,022 to 2,263. One million Chinese students enrolled in university in 1997. By 2007, that number had grown to 5.5 million.[17] Over the coming decade, labor pools in the developing world—particularly in China—will not only be expanding in size, but also becoming increasingly educated.

**Figure 4.4.** Global Percentage of Military Spending, 2010

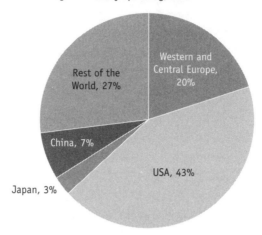

*Source*: "Military Expenditure Data, 2001–10," Stockholm International Peace Research Institute, http://www.sipri.org/yearbook/2011/04/04A.

## The Military Balance

Economic power is evening out much more quickly than military power. On the economic front, the rise of the rest has been gradually chipping away at the West's primacy, and the gap will close quickly in the years ahead. In contrast, the West's military primacy has actually increased of late. Since the sharp rise in expenditure following the terrorist attacks of September 11, 2001, the United States has been spending more on defense than all the world's other major powers combined; the American military will remain second to none for a long time to come. As Figure 4.4 shows, the United States, Europe, and Japan in 2010 accounted for over sixty-five percent of global military spending.

This lopsided balance of military power will not, however, last indefinitely. The foundation of military power is ultimately economic strength. As economic capacity becomes more equally distributed, military capability will eventually follow. Moreover, the development of military capability depends upon the acquisition of certain types of economic infrastructure. A strong manufacturing base, the capacity to produce high-technology goods, output in industries such as steel and shipbuilding, energy consumption and capacity—these are good indicators of the potential for significant

**Figure 4.5.** Global Steel Production, 1980–2010 (in thousands of tons)

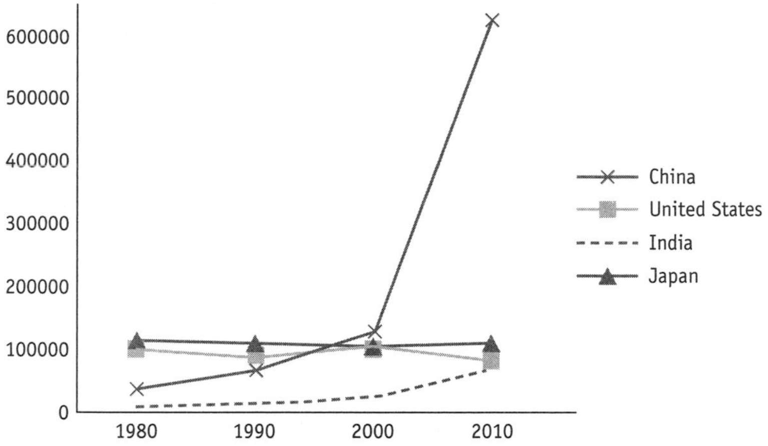

*Source*: "Steel Statistics Archive," World Steel Association, http://www.worldsteel.org/ index.php?action=stats_search; "The Largest Steel Producing Countries," World Steel Association, January 21, 2011, http://www.worldsteel.org/pictures/newsfiles/2010%20 statistics%20tables.pdf. Note: 2010 Statistics are preliminary.

military buildup. Despite the current scope of U.S. military predominance, advances in these core industrial sectors among emerging powers confirm that a global turn is under way.

In 1997, the United States, the EU, and Japan accounted for roughly fifty-five percent of global high-technology exports. By 2008 this figure had declined to roughly thirty-nine percent. China increased its share from about six percent to almost twenty percent over this period.[18] The changing of the guard is even more noticeable when it comes to steel production and shipbuilding, two industries important to the defense sector. In 1980, the United States produced roughly 100 million tons of steel, a figure that would hold relatively stable until 2008, and then drop to eighty million tons by 2010. Over the same period, Chinese steel production rose from roughly 40 million tons per year to over 600 million tons per year. Meanwhile, production in India rose from about ten million tons per year in 1980 to over sixty-five million in 2010 (see Figure 4.5). As for shipbuilding, in 1964 Western Europe was the leading producer at almost five million gross tons annually, followed by Asia at 3.7 million gross tons, and the United States at 250,000 gross tons. By 2009, production in Asia had increased to seventy million

**Figure 4.6.** Global Shipbuilding, 1964–2009 (in thousands of gross tons)

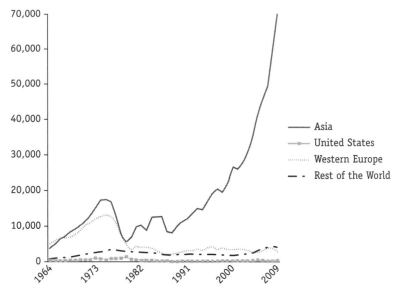

*Source*: "World Shipbuilding Deliveries," Lloyd's Register of Shipping's "World Fleet Statistics," October 11, 2010, http://shipbuildinghistory.com/today/statistics/world.htm.

gross tons, compared with less than seven million gross tons for the rest of world combined (see Figure 4.6). With China leading the way in this vast expansion of industrial output, it is no surprise that in 2010 it surpassed the United States as the world's top consumer of energy.

To be sure, the striking superiority of Asia's output of ships does not have immediate implications for U.S. naval hegemony. The vast majority of the boats produced in Asia are merchant vessels, not warships. When it comes to warships, America's fleet of almost 300 vessels, including eleven carrier battle groups, over seventy submarines, and some 3700 aircraft, puts it far ahead of the competition.[19] Nonetheless, growing shipbuilding capacity in China and elsewhere in East Asia does endow countries with the ability to rapidly expand their fleets of warships if and when they so choose.[20] Moreover, the modernization and expansion of the Chinese fleet is already altering, even if gradually, the balance of naval power in Northeast Asia.

Since World War II, the United States, along with its allies, has maintained pronounced naval superiority in Northeast Asia, relying on a network of bases extending from South Korea through the Japanese mainland and Okinawa to Guam. As of 2011, the U.S. Seventh Fleet, which covers the Western Pacific and Indian Ocean, had under its command up to seventy ships, 300 aircraft, and 40,000 personnel.[21] Nonetheless, China's building program is impressive. The Chinese fleet now contains almost eighty major surface warships. Fleet modernization included delivery of twenty-one conventional attack submarines built in China, ten additional submarines bought from Russia, two nuclear-powered attack submarines, a ballistic missile submarine, eleven destroyers, and sixteen frigates. Operational deployment of aircraft carriers is expected to begin between 2015 and 2020.[22] Although China shows no signs of engaging in a naval buildup sufficiently ambitious to challenge U.S. dominance at the global level, the modernization of its surface and submarine fleets, along with likely advances in anti-ship weaponry, may well challenge America's ability to maintain regional superiority.

This eventuality would constitute a tectonic shift in East Asia's strategic landscape—and it is hardly a remote prospect. Indeed, China's naval doctrine is focused on what its strategists term "near-seas defense." According to a recent study, "This strategy requires the PLAN [People's Liberation Army Navy] to develop credible operational capabilities against potential opponents in China's three 'near seas'—the South China Sea, the East China Sea, and the Yellow Sea—or the space within and slightly beyond the 'first island chain,' which extends from Kurile Islands through the main islands of Japan, the Ryukyu Archipelago, Taiwan, and the Philippines to Borneo."[23] Should China in a decade or two proclaim its own version of the Monroe Doctrine and seek to assert hegemony in its own region, it may well have the naval capability needed to back up its rhetoric.

A similar shift in the regional naval balance is taking place in the Indian Ocean as New Delhi pours resources into its navy. In the late 1990s, the Indian government launched a "maritime strategic drive" intended to dramatically augment its naval power.[24] The Indian navy's budget rose sharply after 1997; the ongoing building program includes over twenty new warships and two new aircraft carriers.[25] With three carriers soon to be operational, it is amply clear that India aspires to be more than just a regional naval power. Indeed, the Indian Navy already engages in exercises in the Atlantic Ocean.[26]

The United States and India are in the midst of fashioning a strategic partnership—in no small part in order to counter the rise of China. Accordingly, at least for now, India's growing naval strength will likely be aligned with, rather than arrayed against, America's regional presence. However, India's geopolitical alignments will be anything but certain as the next two decades unfold. At a minimum, its rising naval role in the Indian Ocean will give New Delhi a growing source of leverage in its dealings with Washington.

• • • •

The economic primacy of the West has already begun to wane—and the global diffusion of wealth will quicken over the course of this decade. The United States is poised to remain the world's premier military power for decades, but its ability to exercise superiority in disparate regional theaters will diminish as emerging powers continue to expand their fleets. And, although with a considerable time lag, a more level playing field economically will ultimately translate into a world in which military power is more equally distributed.

The United States thus appears to be following in the footsteps of Great Britain, the last global hegemon. By the end of the nineteenth century, Britain's economic primacy was being eclipsed by the rise of the United States and Germany. Although the Royal Navy remained second to none at the turn of the century, simultaneous building programs in the United States, Japan, and Germany denied it the wherewithal to maintain naval superiority in all imperial theaters. London relied on astute diplomacy to advance rapprochement with the United States and Japan, enabling it to concentrate its fleet against Germany and ultimately prevail in World War I. All the while, however, Britain's economic and naval hegemony was slipping away. During the 1930s, economic weakness forestalled rearmament, leaving the country woefully unprepared for the threat posed by Nazi Germany and Imperial Japan. With the help of the

United States and other allies, Britain emerged victorious in World War II. But the war revealed just how far Britain had fallen since the days of Pax Britannica.

History never repeats itself verbatim. But its broader trends unmistakably recur. America's military superiority will remain unquestioned well into the next decade. However, the influence that comes with such superiority is already diminishing as the economic playing field evens out. In the coming years, the rising rest will acquire new geopolitical aspirations and the military wherewithal to realize them.

# 5 :: Alternatives to the Western Way

William McNeill ends his magisterial work on the rise of the West by boldly predicting that the West's model of modernity will be replicated on a global basis:

> No matter how it comes, the cosmopolitanism of the future will surely bear a Western imprint. At least in its initial stages, any world state will be an empire of the West. This would be the case even if non-Westerners should happen to hold the supreme controls of world-wide political-military authority, for they could only do so by utilizing such originally Western traits as industrialism, science, and the public palliation of power through advocacy of one or the other of the democratic political faiths. Hence "The Rise of the West" may serve as a shorthand description of the upshot of the history of the human community to date.[1]

Even though McNeill wrote his classic volume in the early 1960s, his view still predominates among Western scholars and policy makers, who maintain that there is only one main path to modernity—the Western one. According to the conventional wisdom, as the non-Western world modernizes, it will follow the West's lead. Just as it did in northern Europe, socioeconomic change and the rise of an urban middle class will spread liberal democracy and secular nationalism throughout the world. As Robert Kagan observes, elites in the West "have operated on the ideological conviction that liberal democracy is the only legitimate form of government and that other forms of government are not only illegitimate but transitory."[2]

Such confidence about the irresistible allure of the Western way has profound geopolitical consequence. As detailed in the previous chapter, the global balance of power is shifting in favor of non-Western newcomers. Another global turn has begun; the pendulum is again swinging, just as it did between 1500 and 1800. If McNeill and fellow travelers are right, then this next global turn will transpire smoothly. As they rise, the newcomers will Westernize and slip comfortably into the berth assigned them in the existing international order. But if McNeill's linear version of history is wrong, then the coming global turn will be far more transformative. It will not just alter the global distribution of power, but also recast the conceptions of political order and the core principles that will define the world that comes next.

This chapter takes on the conventional wisdom and makes the case that the world is headed toward multiple versions of modernity, not political homogeneity. It offers three main arguments as to why rising states, rather than taking the Western way, will follow their own developmental paths and embrace their own views about domestic governance and how best to organize the international system of the twenty-first century.

First, the rise of the West followed a trajectory that was unique to the material conditions of early modern Europe. Political fragmentation, commercial innovation, urbanization, social and economic differentiation between town and countryside—these developments enabled a nascent bourgeoisie to gradually emerge as a counterweight to monarchy, aristocracy, and church, opening up the political space that proved to be fertile ground for the Reformation and the eventual onset of constitutional rule. To be sure, emerging powers such as China, India, and Brazil are experiencing the rise of a middle class that will to some extent play the same role that the bourgeoisie did in Europe between 1500 and 1800. But today's rising powers are each following unique paths toward modernity based on their own political, demographic, topographic, and socioeconomic conditions. Accordingly, they are developing versions of modernity divergent from the West's.

Second, culture matters; it shapes the particular forms of modernity that evolve in different regions. In China, Russia, and other capitalist autocracies, communitarian and paternalistic cultures sharply contrast with the liberal traditions that are a hallmark of the West. In these countries, a mix of illiberal politics and capitalism offers an appealing alternative to the Western model. The Reformation was a seminal event in the rise of the West. But even as a middle class grows in the Middle East, an Islamic Reformation is unlikely to transpire. In a part of the world where religion and politics have been inextricably intertwined since the seventh century, state and mosque are poised to remain inseparable even in the face of widespread socioeconomic change. In much of Africa, where colonial powers drew artificial boundaries that often cut across tribal and linguistic borders, ethnic rivalries continue to spoil even the best attempts to fashion stable democracies. And in Latin America, the legacy of colonial rule combines with economic inequality and racial stratification to produce a unique brand of populism.

Third, today's emerging powers are moving up the pecking order in a very different international setting than the one that hosted the West's rise. In the medieval and early modern eras, imperial powers ruled through centralized institutions of political, economic, and religious authority. Only in Europe, due to the weakness of its governing institutions, were traders, artisans, and professionals able to escape the grasp of states intent on retaining a monopoly on wealth and power. The dynamism unleashed then enabled Europeans to pull ahead of the centralized empires to their east, eventually eclipsing the Ottomans, Indians, Chinese, and Japanese. In a world populated primarily by hierarchical empires, progress had to come from below—from newly autonomous social actors capable of pushing back against the state.

Not so today. Even non-democratic and centralized states like China are intent on enriching and improving the lives of their citizens, not just keeping them down and extracting resources from them. The country's middle class grows by the day and hundreds of millions of Chinese citizens have left behind poverty. Admittedly, the

Chinese government, even though intent on sharing wealth, has yet to share power with its people. But the country has, at least for now, found an effective way of mobilizing the talents and satisfying many of the aspirations of its populace. Traders, artisans, and professionals no longer need to escape the state's grasp to realize their potential. Instead of standing in the way of shopkeepers, entrepreneurs, and bankers, smart autocracies like China are aiding and abetting their prosperity, co-opting the middle class into the state apparatus.

While countries of all stripes have become more responsive and responsible, the global system itself has also changed, becoming much more decentralized, fast, and fluid. Vast quantities of capital, goods, services, and people cross borders on a daily basis. The digital age and globalization have combined to disseminate information and allocate investment with unprecedented rapidity. In a world characterized by speed, porous borders, and interdependence, more centralized states may well regularly outperform their laissez-faire and democratic counterparts. As the recent financial crisis made clear, regulated markets and planned economies can have distinct advantages over the Western alternatives. China emerged relatively unscathed from the Great Recession in no small part due to central planning, ample surpluses, and a high savings rate. Meanwhile, the United States and Europe have struggled to pull off a weak recovery and to fix the inadequate regulatory framework that contributed to the outbreak of the crisis. So too have vested interests, recalcitrant legislatures, and polarized and disaffected electorates made it difficult for Western democracies to reform health care, pensions, taxes, and other programs essential to long-term solvency.

In sum, during the early modern era, hierarchical states defended traditional institutions of authority and enjoyed relative autonomy in a global system that was not yet interdependent; change had to come from below, and Europe's pluralism provided the opening. Today, not only are centralized states more responsive to their peoples than they once were, but they operate in a new global setting— one in which more state control is often an advantage in coping with a fast, interdependent, and porous world.

The upshot is that deviations from the Western way represent not minor diversions along the one-way road to global homogeneity, but credible alternatives to the Western model of modernity. To be sure, liberal democracy has fared well over the past two centuries, and will no doubt continue to spread in the future. But the West's version of modernity is up against alternatives that have both staying power and their own distinct advantages. Under the best of circumstances, democracy will extend its reach slowly and in fits and starts. The coming global turn will occur much more quickly—and is thus destined to produce a world of not only multiple centers of power, but also multiple versions of modernity.

This chapter explores the main alternatives to Westernization by surveying recent political developments across a wide range of countries. In China, Russia, and the sheikdoms of the Persian Gulf, capitalist autocracy is demonstrating an impressive durability. From Iraq to Egypt to Turkey, the advance of modernity and participatory government is consolidating the links between Islam and politics, not fostering the separation of mosque and state. Israel is an embattled outpost of democracy and modernity in the Middle East, but it too faces profound dilemmas when it comes to the relationship between religion and politics. Across most of Africa, strongmen and the systems of patronage they cultivate ensure that elections are little more than a democratic façade. Meanwhile, much of Latin America has been captivated by left-wing populism. These alternatives to the West's brand of liberal democracy are just that— alternatives indicative of the political diversity that will characterize the next world.

The final section of this chapter makes the case that even states that consolidate stable democracy will not embrace the international system erected during the West's watch. Conventional wisdom holds that rising democracies like India and Brazil, due to their democratic institutions and values, will as a matter of course take their seats in the Western tent. Such expectations are, however, as illusory as the notion that China and Russia will obediently follow the West's lead.

India, the world's largest democracy, has only lately warmed up to the idea of alignment with the United States. And even amid the emerging partnership between New Delhi and Washington, the two have recently parted company on Iran, Pakistan, Afghanistan, and trade. Brazil, a stable democracy since 1985, has regularly broken ranks with the United States over policy in the Middle East; Luiz Inácio Lula da Silva, who served as president from 2003 through 2010, took the lead in recognizing Palestine as an independent state and met with the Iranian president, Mahmoud Ahmadinejad, at the same time that Washington was trying to isolate Tehran. Turkey, one of the few democracies in the Muslim world, has of late been steadily drifting from its previous Western orientation. The policies of these rising democracies suggest that a country's place in the international pecking order and its unique national interests will be a much better predictor of its statecraft than the nature of its domestic institutions of governance.

The political landscape poised to emerge as the global turn proceeds is one of striking diversity, not comfortable homogeneity. Indeed, liberal democrats will have to share the stage with leaders of quite different stripes. Autocrats, theocrats, strongmen, and populists will all play a role in ensuring that liberal democracy is only one of the multiple variants of political order that will populate the next international system. Even rising powers that are liberal democracies, for reasons of both prestige and geopolitical interest, will not dutifully take their place in the order on offer from the West.

## The Autocrats

Merchants, artisans, and entrepreneurs—the constituents of an emerging middle class—provided the impetus behind the rise of the West. In Europe, as well as in the Middle East and Asia, states clinging to traditional sources of power and legitimacy resisted the ascent of these new social actors. But it was only in Europe, where states were too weak to prevail, that the rising bourgeoisie succeeded in overturning the status quo. The result was the Reformation, the onset of constitutional monarchy, the Industrial Revolution, and the consolidation of the West's global hegemony.

Since the Cold War's end, Western-style capitalism and entrepreneurship have spread far and wide. But the advance of liberal democracy has not kept pace. One of the main reasons is that today's rising powers, rather than resisting and seeking to keep down their expanding middle classes, are doing exactly the opposite: co-opting entrepreneurs and business elites and incorporating them into state structures. Not only are autocratic states neutralizing the political threat posed by the bourgeoisie, but they are cultivating a professional class invested in preserving the status quo. As a consequence, autocracies are enjoying considerable stability and legitimacy. Even neoconservatives have come to the realization that markets and democracy do not as a matter of course go hand in hand. As Robert Kagan laments, "Growing national wealth and autocracy have proven compatible, after all."[3]

Three main variants of autocracy are exhibiting considerable staying power. *Communal autocracy* entails a mutually reinforcing partnership between the private sector and the state apparatus. The middle class gets what it wants—wealth—while the ruling party gets what it wants—the retention of power. Legitimacy is a function of economic performance and political order; communal autocracy succeeds when it delivers broadly distributed gains to a society that privileges stability and economic progress over individual opportunity and personal liberty. China is a prime example.

*Paternal autocracy* entails a more hierarchical relationship between the state and the bourgeoisie; bureaucrats and other public employees make up much of the middle class, leaving the private sector and civil society small, weak, and under the intimidating eye of state authorities. The broader citizenry sees the state as its caretaker, expecting economic and social benefits in return for political obedience. Legitimacy is a function of authority and predictability; whereas communal autocracies fashion a less than voluntary bargain with a relatively engaged citizenry, paternal autocracies offer a package deal to a more submissive and passive population. A prime example is Russia.

*Tribal autocracy* entails the incorporation of the middle class into a political community defined more by tribe and clan than by the state. Legitimacy stems from lineage and the disbursement of jobs and wealth to powerful families; political order is a function mainly of tribal patronage. The sheikdoms of the Persian Gulf are prime examples.

## Communal Autocracy: China

China is destined to become one of the world's leading powers over the course of the next two decades; its political fate looms large in determining the character of the international order that comes next. China's economic and geopolitical weight will inevitably give it considerable sway over the rules of the post-Western order. Equally important, China promises to be a trend-setter. If Beijing continues to deliver outsized rates of economic growth coupled with sustained political stability, then its brand of capitalist autocracy will enhance its luster as a credible alternative to liberal democracy.

Many Western observers of China contend that the country will democratize in step with its economic advance.[4] This optimism derives in large part from the Western experience as well as the democratic transitions that have taken place in other industrialized states in East Asia. As China's middle class grows, the argument runs, it will play the same role that the emerging bourgeoisie did in Europe, pushing back against the state and translating its economic power into political power. Yet this transition is not occurring. China's middle class is rapidly expanding, but democratization is failing to advance in step. On the contrary, the rise of the middle class appears to be consolidating the political status quo, not fostering liberalization.

This departure from the Western experience is in large part a product of the adaptive nature of the Chinese state. Beginning in 1978, after Deng Xiaoping consolidated his position as Mao's successor, the Chinese Communist Party (CCP) began to transition the country toward a market economy. The results have been stunning. Between 1978 and 2002, the Chinese economy grew by more than eight-fold, per capita income rose more than 600 percent, and the output of the private sector rose from 0.2 to forty-one percent of GDP.[5] Over the course of the past decade China's annual growth rate averaged 10.9 percent, roughly five times that of the West. Such sustained growth has succeeded in lifting over 400 million Chinese citizens out of poverty. It has also dramatically expanded the country's middle class. As of 2005, China was home to some thirty million private businesses.[6]

Were China to have followed the Western model, this pattern of growth should have been accompanied by the advance of political liberalization. The advent of a prosperous and upwardly mobile middle class should have created a counterweight to the state and loosened the grip of the CCP on power. But it has not done so, revealing a historical trajectory that represents a stark departure from the West's.

China's communitarian culture provides a partial explanation for the durability of its autocratic institutions. Chinese society has long privileged stability, solidarity, and communal welfare over personal gain—in contrast with Western traditions of liberalism and the autonomy of the individual. Some scholars trace this cultural disposition to China's early dependence on state-led irrigation projects, which produced a powerful bureaucracy, centrally controlled economy, and embedded social hierarchy.[7] Others focus more on Confucian traditions of loyalty to family and community.[8] The premium that contemporary Chinese society places on order and stability became particularly pronounced after Mao's tumultuous rule, during which the social upheaval and economic hardship produced by the Cultural Revolution and other programs heightened aversion to radical change.

Political culture matters, but the pattern of China's socioeconomic development has played a far more important role in buttressing the staying power of its autocratic institutions. For starters, the economic progress produced by the transition to a market economy has been broadly distributed, not restricted to the rising bourgeoisie. One of the CCP's first moves in liberalizing the economy was to dismantle agricultural communes. The allocation of land to peasants and the resulting accumulation of agricultural surpluses created a strong rural constituency in favor of privatization. Indeed, the earliest cohort of private-sector entrepreneurs came from rural areas, not from the urban population.[9] Peasants in the rural interior also benefited from the industrial boom that took place in major cities along China's eastern seaboard, with millions of farmers migrating to take up jobs in construction and manufacturing. In addition, China's gradualist approach to privatization protected employees in the state sector. As a consequence, China did not confront the high unemployment and large-scale dislocations that accompanied "big-bang" transitions of the sort that took place in the former Soviet bloc.[10] From the outset of the reform era, their rising standard of living meant that peasants and workers, not just aspiring entrepreneurs, had a vested interest in the success of China's economic transition.

Amid China's transition to markets and private ownership, its entrepreneurs have certainly enjoyed greater gains than its peasants and workers, leading to substantial inequalities. Class-based wealth disparities have stoked labor unrest and political protest, prompting China's leadership to identify the reduction of inequality as a top priority. Nonetheless, the widely distributed benefits of economic modernization have done more to bolster rather than undermine the legitimacy of the CCP. An opinion survey conducted in 2010 revealed a high level of public contentment, with eighty-seven percent of Chinese citizens expressing satisfaction with national conditions. (By means of comparison, only thirty percent of Americans in 2010 felt the same way about conditions in the United States.)[11] Such high levels of public satisfaction in China favor the status quo at the expense of political reform. Minxin Pei, a renowned scholar of China—and ardent advocate of democratization—acknowledges that China's rapid economic growth, instead of fueling calls for political liberalization, has consolidated the CCP's rule and forestalled public pressure for greater freedoms.[12]

But the connection between rising incomes, public satisfaction, and the stability of the political status quo is not enough to explain why China's rising bourgeoisie has not challenged the CCP's exclusive hold on political power. After all, Europe's ascending middle class reacted to its economic success by doing just that—chipping away at the power of traditional institutions of authority. A similar process of liberalization has not taken place in China largely because its main institution of authority—the Communist Party—decided to co-opt rather than to repress the middle class. By incorporating into the state the one social sector with sufficient wealth and influence to upset one-party rule, the CCP has succeeded in making the middle class conservative stakeholders in, rather than mobilized opponents to, autocratic rule.

As the private sector has expanded, the core strategy of the CCP has been to build a symbiotic relationship with entrepreneurs, professionals, and intellectuals. The result is that a wide swath of China's upwardly mobile citizenry has either been brought into the state apparatus or lured into a mutually cooperative relationship with it. The rising middle class thus acquired neither the will nor the capacity to develop autonomous power. Indeed, the state has so penetrated the private sector and most quarters of civil society that, in the words of Bruce Dickson, "autonomy is akin to powerlessness."[13] David Shambaugh concurs that the CCP has demonstrated an impressive ability to adapt to changing conditions: "The party remains a nationwide organization of considerable authority and power. It is the only political game in town."[14]

The CCP's strategy of communal incorporation has taken three main forms. First, it formed business associations—effectively private-sector guilds that brought entrepreneurs into regular contact with high-level government and party officials. Influence flowed in both directions; businessmen made known to officials what policy changes they wanted to advance their interests, while the CCP was able to monitor and shape the evolution of the private sector. As Kellee Tsai argues, the most important output of this interaction between the private sector and the state was informal and incremental policy adjustment, which only later would result in changes to laws and institutions.[15] Dickson agrees that business associations generally succeeded in promoting consensus between party cadres and entrepreneurs, who "see themselves as partners, not adversaries, of the state."[16]

The flow of party cadres into the business community constitutes a second means through which the CCP has penetrated commercial enterprise. This cross-fertilization occurs through the appointment of party cadres to managerial positions in state-owned enterprises (SOEs) and through the involvement of party members in the privatization of SOEs. The state sector still produces roughly forty percent of the country's GDP, and the CCP appoints about eighty percent of the managers of SOEs. Since many of these managers are party members, cadres effectively become businessmen.[17] As of 2010, the party had appointed more than one-half of the chairmen and more

than one-third of the CEOs of China's 129 huge state-owned con-
glomerates.[18] It is no accident that China's first billionaire, Rong
Yiren, had Deng Xiaoping to thank for his fortune; Deng tasked him
with founding one of the country's largest state-owned conglomer-
ates, the China International Trust & Investment Corporation.

A good number of party members also directly engage in private enterprise. Some of them leave their government or party posts
to work full-time in the private sector, while others retain their
formal links to the state. Initially, party members—so-called "red
capitalists"—called their privately held firms "collectives" in order
to side-step criticism from ideological purists.[19] But such pretense is
no longer needed. Today, CCP members frequently engage in private enterprise and often take advantage of the patronage system
that accompanies membership to augment their income. This practice gives party members a self-interested stake in creating a political and legal environment conducive to private-sector profits.

A third vehicle for co-optation of the private sector has been the
recruitment of entrepreneurs into the CCP. The key turning point
in this respect came in July 2001, when Jiang Zemin, then the CCP's
head, gave a speech sanctioning the entry of businessmen into
the party. The decision was highly controversial.[20] A party populated primarily by workers and peasants was opening its doors to
capitalists who had for decades been their ideological adversaries;
economic modernization was formally displacing class struggle as
the CCP's defining objective. But despite the formidable resistance
within it ranks, the party had little choice. With China's private sector already booming, the CCP needed the skills of entrepreneurs,
financiers, and technocrats to manage an economy that was increasingly operating according to market principles.

Although the linkages between the party and the private sector
had deepened considerably during the 1990s, the impact of the formal opening of the CCP to the business community had a dramatic
impact. Over 100,000 entrepreneurs reportedly applied for party
membership soon after Jiang's speech.[21] Tsai estimates that over
one-third of entrepreneurs have since become party members.[22]
Moreover, the incorporation of large numbers of businessmen into
the party both made the CCP more favorably disposed toward the

private sector and helped integrate the private sector into the state apparatus.

The CCP pursued a similar strategy of communal incorporation with intellectuals. In the aftermath of the bloody confrontation in Tiananmen Square in 1989, which the leadership blamed in part on activism among students and professors, the party began a vigorous recruitment effort on college campuses. By the mid-1990s, party membership among college students had more than doubled. In 2001, the Chinese press reported that one-third of the country's college students had applied for party membership. According to Dickson, some forty percent of college professors and administrators belong to the CCP.[23] Especially at elite universities in Beijing, many professors maintain strong ties to government and party institutions; the vast majority of the intelligentsia is aligned with, not against, the state.

To be sure, a small cohort of intellectuals and other political activists resists the state's overtures and instead campaigns for democratization and the enlargement of civil liberties. But the effective co-optation of most intellectuals and entrepreneurs makes it relatively easy for the state to repress dissent. The intelligentsia, like the business community, is for the most part invested in the preservation of the political status quo.

China has since 1978 thus followed an evolutionary path that defies the Western model of modernization. The onset of capitalism and the rise of a middle class have not been accompanied by political liberalization. On the contrary, China's entrepreneurs and intellectuals have for the most part been efficiently incorporated into the autocratic state. Dickson concludes that there is scant evidence to support the expectation that entrepreneurs will be agents of political change in China.[24] Tsai agrees that "China's capitalists are pragmatic and creative but they are not budding democrats." "Economic growth," she concludes, "has not created a prodemocratic capitalist class."[25] Moreover, the more prosperous the region, the more satisfied its entrepreneurs—and the more willing they are to work hand-in-hand with the state.[26] At least in China, growing prosperity appears to be inversely related to civic activism and political resistance. Those in the West waiting for economic liberalization to bring democracy to China may be waiting a very long time.

## THE ADVANTAGES OF AUTOCRACY CHINESE-STYLE

China's brand of one-party rule has its distinct advantages. The main one is self-evident: Chinese leaders are able to make policy decisions absent the pulling and hauling of the democratic process. The government must of course manage factional and bureaucratic rivalries, tame corrupt party members and officials, and worry about its popular legitimacy. But it does not have to deal with the constitutional and institutional constraints that are the hallmark of liberal democracy. Deng Xiaoping was notably frank in acknowledging as much: "The Western type of checks and balances must never be practiced. We must not be influenced by that kind of thinking. Efficiency must be guaranteed."[27] The advantages of this top-down approach to governing are especially pronounced at a time when the Western democracies are confronting sluggish economic growth and divided and angry electorates.

During Mao's rule, which was marred by the excesses of ideology and his cult of personality, the absence of checks and balances had clear costs. But the Chinese government is no longer on an ideological crusade. On the contrary, it is now ruthlessly pragmatic, mercantilist, and shrewd in its pursuit of political order, prosperity, and national power. The result has been a remarkable track record of leadership competence, economic growth, domestic stability, and expanding geopolitical reach.

Heady projections of China's continued rise presume sound macroeconomic policy and the investments in infrastructure and intellectual capital made possible by a centralized, autocratic state. China has embarked on a monumental project to build a nationwide highway network linking every city with more than 200,000 residents. The ongoing construction program is producing roughly 4,000 kilometers of roadway per year and will result in a system of some 85,000 kilometers, surpassing the size of the interstate highway network in the United States.[28] High-speed rail, long the exclusive preserve of Japan's bullet train and France's TGV, is fast spreading throughout China. By 2012, China plans to have more high-speed track than the rest of the world combined. The line connecting Beijing and Shanghai opened in 2011, cutting travel time from roughly nine hours to five hours. Moreover, China is incorporating technological improvements into its trains that will enable them to reach top speeds of almost 240 miles per hour, besting the competition. In 2010, China invested $120 billion in high-speed rail, compared with the $8 billion the United States earmarked for the same purpose in its 2009 stimulus package.[29]

Although China has displaced the United States as the globe's top emitter of greenhouse gases, it is also leading efforts to expand green technology. China offers a compelling combination of technological know-how, lower wages for manufacturing than in the United States, Europe, or Japan, and healthy government subsidies. The subsidies are especially important since most green technology is not yet profitable. Chinese production of photovoltaic panels has reduced the price of solar energy by thirty percent, and Chinese firms are at the forefront of developing processes to turn coal into gas.[30] China is also the world's leading producer of wind turbines. The *New York Times* recently commented that China's "efforts to dominate renewable energy technologies raise the prospect that the West may someday trade its dependence on oil from the Mideast for a reliance on solar panels, wind turbines and other gear manufactured in China."[31]

China's rising fortunes on the technological front stem in no small part from sustained investment in its universities, particularly in areas of science and engineering.[32] Beijing has been steadily boosting expenditure on schooling; it plans to spend four percent of GDP on education by 2012, up from less than three percent in 2006.[33] Generous support for scientific research has recently lured back to their homeland some 200,000 Chinese scientists trained abroad, some of whom are leading experts in their fields.[34] Such state-led largess is focused on the humanities as well as science and engineering. Several decades ago, the CCP treated classical music as a symbol of the West's cultural imperialism. Not so today. There has been an explosion in the number of music students, applicants to the top conservatories, and manufacturers of pianos and violins.[35] China also plans to open roughly 1,000 new museums by 2015.[36]

Beijing's handling of the country's foreign policy has been as purposeful and shrewd as its management of the domestic economy. Indeed, China's statecraft is reminiscent of Bismarck's guidance of Germany's foreign policy during its rise. Bismarck succeeded in making Germany Europe's diplomatic pivot; he pursued a muscular brand of statecraft, but knew when to pull back in order to forestall the formation of a balancing coalition. In similar fashion, Beijing is pursuing an ambitious brand of statecraft aimed at making China the diplomatic pivot of East Asia. Even as its regional influence grows, however, China generally treads with care, fully aware that a more assertive approach would prompt its neighbors to form a countervailing coalition.

To be sure, its neighbors in East Asia are nervously watchful of China's rise, prompting a modest uptick in their military preparations. Australia is planning to spend around $10 billion on new warships—its largest naval buildup since World War II. Vietnam recently ordered six new submarines and advanced fighter jets from Russia. And Japan in 2010 released a new national security doctrine that called upon its defense forces to end their focus on threats from the north and instead concentrate on the threat posed by China to its southern islands. Japan has also been seeking to strengthen its military ties with South Korea.[37]

It is also the case that Chinese foreign policy does have its bouts of excess. Until quite recently, the Chinese leadership as a matter of doctrine pursued a foreign policy of limited and modest aims— one that would enable the country to focus on economic growth. China kept a low diplomatic and military profile while it concentrated on building up the resources needed to give it more geopolitical heft and greater stature. China's leadership now believes that the country has reached that threshold and can therefore begin to flex its muscles. As it has begun to pursue this new and more assertive diplomacy, Beijing on occasion overreaches, as was the case during the second half of 2010. Beijing warned that the South China Sea was an area of "core interest," had a run-in with Japan over the disputed Senkaku/Diaoyu islands, and refused to overtly condemn

North Korea's torpedoing of a South Korean naval vessel or its shelling of a South Korean island.

The international response was immediate. The United States embarked on a flurry of diplomacy to elevate its strategic partnership with India, shore up its alliances with Korea and Japan, and deepen its engagement in Southeast Asia.[38] Its overtures were generally welcomed throughout the region. Beijing appears to have received the intended message. By the end of the year, the Chinese had pulled back. Beijing toned down its rhetoric, adopted a noticeably more restrained brand of regional diplomacy, and exerted constructive pressure on Pyongyang to rein in its behavior. At least for now, China seems to be able to curb its foreign ambition whenever it begins to provoke pushback from its neighbors.

China has demonstrated similar shrewdness beyond its neighborhood. Just as Bismarck's Germany took advantage of the stability provided by British hegemony to expand its trade and influence, China is reaping the benefits, but not sharing the costs, of the global public goods provided by the United States. The U.S. Navy guards the world's sea lanes, making it safe for tankers and freighters to circumvent the globe on their way to and from China's ports. The United States has been sacrificing the lives of its soldiers and spending about $100 billion annually to bring stability to Afghanistan; China meanwhile makes strategic purchases of the country's mineral deposits. As Washington organizes sanctions to convince Iran to shut down its nuclear program, China buys its oil. In general, American engagement in troubled parts of the developing world is often in the service of security—combating extremists, preventing civil conflicts, and addressing the socioeconomic causes of instability. In contrast, China heads to the same areas to secure raw materials for its industrial machine. Beijing is also positioning itself strategically in more developed economies; in Brazil, for example, China has invested billions of dollars in ports and infrastructure.[39] China's foreign policy, just like its domestic policy, is guided by an effective, even if cold-blooded, realpolitik.

For skeptics who might claim that China is enjoying these successes in spite of, rather than because of, its autocratic ways, a brief comparison with India suggests otherwise. Over the past two decades, India's annual growth rates have been roughly half of China's. India, with its 1.2 billion citizens, has sufficient population to keep pace with 1.4 billion Chinese. But what India does not have is an autocratic government enabling it to make command decisions about economic policy. Instead, India is a democracy whose political institutions are made all the more unwieldy by the country's striking ethnic and linguistic diversity.[40] As Meghnad Desai observes, "India's bane is the politicization of all aspects of economic life.... This is because of and despite its democratic politics."[41] Decisions about resource allocation depend less on questions of efficiency than on spreading benefits across competing constituencies and servicing multiple political patronage systems. The electoral strength of India's large rural population is especially important in this respect, standing in the way of the state-led industrialization that has fueled China's robust economic growth.

## CHINA'S VULNERABILITIES

China's brand of communal autocracy has plenty of weaknesses. On moral grounds alone, the absence of civil liberties, the violations of human rights, and the repression of dissent are glaring black marks. Moreover, the lack of political pluralism is not only of moral consequence, but also inhibits the country's economic performance. China lacks the mix of venture capital and technological prowess that drives innovation in the United States. Chinese corporations are very good at producing high-quality manufactures at low cost, but they tend to copy Western technology, not to improve upon it. That formula may well mean slower growth as wages rise and manufacturers move elsewhere in search of cheaper labor. In addition, the state, party, and private sector are too intimately connected for their own good—in the words of Carl Walter and Fraser Howie, "China is a family-run business." Corruption thrives in an economy that still depends on patronage. With lending practices often set by party officials rather than financial analysts, the banking sector may well be carrying its fair share of bad loans, making it vulnerable to the same kind of market failure that recently engulfed the United States and Europe.[42]

So too does China face a host of challenges on the political front. Although privatization has led to rising standards of living in rural as well as urban areas, income inequality persists and has the potential to pose a serious challenge to political stability. The socio-economic divide between the coastal cities and the rural interior presents perhaps the greatest risk to the CCP's ability to maintain order and preserve its monopoly on power. China may be the world's leader in green technology, but its rapid economic growth has led to pervasive degradation of the environment.[43] Pollution not only poses long-term health risks, but could foster political instability should, for example, clean water become scare. And although China's new elite has at least for now been co-opted by the state, the continuing growth of the middle class may eventually undermine one-party rule. According to Edward Steinfeld, China will likely fall prey to "self-obsolescing authoritarianism," and ultimately democratize by following the same developmental path as Taiwan and South Korea.[44] Other scholars share the view that China's government is fragile and that ongoing economic growth and integration into global markets mean that autocratic rule can last only so long.[45]

China's political system certainly has its faults. But the central question is not whether it is free of flaws, but whether it is able to deliver sufficiently competent performance on matters of economy and security to hold its own against its democratic competitors. If the country's experience since 1978 is any indication, the answer is definitively in the affirmative. Skeptics such as Minxin Pei contend otherwise, arguing that autocratic regimes of the Chinese variant will inevitably become predatory and focus on extracting resources from their citizens rather than improving their lot.[46] But especially in a globalized world in which performance will ultimately be judged in comparative terms, the CCP fully appreciates that its survival depends upon its ability to deliver to its citizens. China may not be a democracy, but its leaders know well that their legitimacy rides on their ability to promote prosperity and enhance the country's international position. They have thus far been quite mindful of this reality, which is exactly why over eighty percent of Chinese citizens are content with their country's direction. Under these circumstances, there is no logical reason why China's government should shift course any time soon. On the contrary, a winning formula suggests continuity rather than change.

It is of course plausible, perhaps even likely, that China will eventually become a democracy. As its vast rural population continues to transition to the manufacturing sector, a growing working class may eventually demand and succeed in attaining universal suffrage—just as Europe's working class eventually did. But it is worth keeping in mind how long it took for Europe to transition from the constitutionalism associated with the rise of its middle class to the liberal democracy that accompanied the rise of its working class. After the Glorious Revolution of 1688, England granted considerable power to its expanding bourgeoisie, but liberal democracy was not consolidated until the parliamentary reforms of the 1880s. In similar fashion, Germany's ruling class was by the early nineteenth century sharing power with its rising commercial elites. But an alliance between aristocrats and industrialists effectively resisted the power of the growing working class for many decades thereafter. Germany was not a stable democracy until the middle of the twentieth century.

China has a long way to go before it might reach its political tipping point. After all, rural peasants still make up between fifty and sixty percent of its population.[47] By means of comparison, when Britain consolidated liberal democracy in the late nineteenth century, roughly seventy percent of its population lived in cities and towns, the same percentage of urban dwellers today in North America and Europe. By these measures, it will be quite some time, if ever, before socioeconomic change in China makes liberal democracy a safe bet. For at least the foreseeable future, China's communal autocracy is poised to be a durable alternative to liberal democracy, not a fleeting detour on the way to the end of history.

## Paternal Autocracy: Russia

Russia is a paternal autocracy. The heavy hand of the Kremlin, which is for the most part welcomed by a citizenry that looks to the state to provide for them, leaves little room for civil society. In China's brand of communal autocracy, the state has co-opted most of the bourgeoisie; party leaders and the private sector have found their way to a bargain in which the state retains a monopoly of political power in return for meeting the economic needs of the business community. In Russia's brand of paternal autocracy, the state largely controls the bourgeoisie; political leaders have effectively coerced it into playing by the rules of the Kremlin. Russia's private sector has not negotiated its way to a stable equilibrium with the state. Rather, it has been forced into submission.

This difference between Russian and Chinese variants of autocracy has deep historical roots. Tsarist Russia was hierarchical and intrusive; the central government ran the country with a tight grip. The same was true during the Soviet era. Not only did the Kremlin maintain control of political life, but health care, education, and the pension system were all run from Moscow. The Soviet state was at once repressive and expansive; it demanded obedience, and came with all the options included. When the Soviet Union collapsed, many Russians welcomed the freedom to speak their minds, but they longed for the services that had formerly been provided by the state.

As in Russia, China's successive dynasties also wielded hierarchical and absolute control over political life. But Chinese emperors and their Mandarin bureaucrats penetrated much less deeply into daily life; the extended family, not the state, was the provider of last resort. The salience of loyalty to family and local community withstood even Mao's coercive efforts to collectivize agriculture, industry, and much of China's social life. Today, China's health care system is largely privatized. Absent a national pension system, its elder citizens look to their extended families, not to the government, to provide for their needs.

A comparison of residential public spaces offers a revealing window into the differences between communal and paternal autocracy. In China, publicly shared hallways, courtyards, and alleys—even in poor areas—tend to be clean and well-kept; they are cared for collectively by the community that uses them. In Russia, such spaces tend to be unkempt and run-down; residents may have spotless and neat apartments, but their responsibility ends at their front door.

When they cross that threshold, they enter a civic no-man's-land, occupied neither by the state nor by a sense of community that rarely strays beyond the private realm.

## POST-SOVIET RUSSIA: THE CONSOLIDATION OF "SOVEREIGN DEMOCRACY"

Even though the citizens of post-Soviet Russia continued to look to the state to play the role of caretaker, the state often was not up to the task. The dissolution of the Soviet Union in the early 1990s was accompanied by the atrophy of Russia's political and economic infrastructure. Boris Yeltsin, who served as Russia's president from 1991 to 1999, introduced long-anticipated democratic reforms. But liberalization was accompanied by the decay of the country's main political institutions and its economy. Power flowed from Moscow to outlying regions while Moscow itself became a lawless capital, home to mounting crime and corruption. Gun-toting bodyguards and traffic stops by policemen looking only for bribes were signs of the times.

The Soviet Union's command economy was dismantled, but the transition to free markets stalled. Inflation was rampant, reaching almost 900 percent in 1993. As privatization proceeded, Russians with the right connections snapped up assets being sold by the state, often at bargain prices and through shady business deals. By the second half of the 1990s, an exclusive circle of oligarchs had amassed sizable fortunes—and political influence to match. Inflation ensured that the quality of life for the average Russian plunged at the same time that income inequality soared. Moscow's main avenue—Tverskaya—was lined with the world's finest designer stores, yet they were off-limits to all but the wealthiest few. The financial crisis that hit in 1998 transformed a downturn into a freefall. Between 1997 and 1999, Russia's GDP fell by fifty percent, and the ruble, trading at roughly six to the dollar at the end of 1997, was trading at almost twenty-nine to the dollar two years later.

Vladimir Putin, who was elected as Yeltsin's successor in 2000 and then became the prime minister in 2008, dedicated himself to rebuilding the state, recentralizing power, and revitalizing the economy. He succeeded admirably on all fronts. Putin reestablished the Kremlin's authority, brought inflation under control, and, with the help of high energy prices, achieved average annual growth rates of roughly seven percent during his presidency. The return of the state, however, came at the expense of the democratic reforms that had been introduced during the previous decade.

Elections are still held for the parliament and the presidency. They are regularly marred, however, by control of the media, intimidation of the opposition, and irregularities at the ballot box. The Kremlin has recouped its power and reinstated the rule of law—but it is the Kremlin's law, not that of an independent judiciary. The regional governors who had amassed considerable power during the Yeltsin era were elected officials. No longer; under Putin they began to be appointed by, and beholden to, the Kremlin. Putin also cracked down on his political opponents, shuttered independent media outlets, and curtailed the activities of foreign organizations operating in Russia. And he went after the oligarchs. Those who agreed to support the Kremlin or stay out of politics were, for the most part, free to continue conducting business. Those who pushed back, such as Vladimir Gusinsky, Boris Berezovsky, and Mikhail Khodorkovsky, were harassed, coerced into exile, or put in jail.

Russia's economic elites have been cowed, not co-opted. As a consequence, the private sector in Russia has been less politically influential than its counterpart in China. In Russia, the business community has been subordinated to the state; in China, it enjoys a symbiotic relationship with the state. Russia has therefore ended up with a less hospitable and predictable business environment that is still hostage to the whims of the Kremlin—one of the main reasons foreign investors have kept their distance. Doing business in China entails working political connections (and offering the occasional bribe) as well as clearing bureaucratic hurdles—but the result is a reasonably secure investment. Doing business in Russia entails a similar amount of red tape—but the result is an investment more vulnerable to predation by the state. The World Bank's 2010 "Ease of Doing Business Index" ranks China at number seventy-nine, well ahead of Russia at number 123.[48] Foreign investors have responded accordingly. At the end of 2010, direct foreign investment in China stood at roughly $658 billion (seventh in the world), compared with $297 billion in Russia (nineteenth in the world).[49]

Another obstacle facing today's Russia is the questionable competence and limited reach of its governing institutions. The Kremlin has certainly regained authority, but implementing policy requires reliance on bureaucracies stymied by inertia, incompetence, and corruption. Policy issues overseen and implemented by a few key officials—such as macroeconomic policy—are generally well handled. But those that require coordination across different agencies and regions—such as infrastructure—are routinely a mess. Russia has lagged way behind China when it comes to developing roads, railways, and other types of transportation and industrial infrastructure.[50]

The "oil curse" is partly to blame. With the sale of oil and gas representing upwards of fifty percent of the country's exports and of federal revenues, Russia has failed to develop the high-tech knowhow and manufacturing base so crucial to economic growth in many other countries. Energy income is too easy and, by driving up the exchange rate, makes other domestic industries less competitive. Accordingly, energy revenue has both forestalled diversification and, by enriching the Kremlin, advanced its efforts to centralize power. State ownership of huge energy, transportation, and industrial enterprises also means that roughly one-third of the labor force works in the public sector. Officially, Russia's middle class now encompasses some thirty percent of its citizens. But the real number is closer to ten percent. Most of the rest are government bureaucrats and other state employees who are part of the middle class only in terms of their income, not in terms of their mentality or the nature of their economic activity; they are unlikely to rock the boat.[51]

With Russia's true entrepreneurial class so small and its ultra-wealthy elites having been intimidated into political submission, the country lacks an engine of political and economic change. Such change could conceivably come from the top down. President Dmitry Medvedev (a former lawyer) is more liberal in inclination than is Putin (a former KGB agent), and has stressed the importance of economic diversification. But Medvedev has made only incremental changes in policy since taking office in 2008. And Putin, who appears to be headed back to the presidency, will be a power broker for years to come, suggesting plenty of the same for the indefinite future. Moreover, fewer than twenty-five percent of Russian citizens believe that their country needs Western-style democracy, with almost sixty percent preferring either Soviet-style government or a unique form of participatory government in keeping with "national traditions."[52] Most Russians desire the stability of paternalism to the uncertainties of democracy—especially after the experience of the 1990s encouraged them to equate democracy with corruption, chaos, and economic decline. Russians have warmed up to capitalism—but not to liberal democracy.

Due to its sluggish politics, energy-centric economy, and continuing population decline, Russia, in contrast with China, is not poised to offer the world a business model that others will rush to emulate. Nonetheless, Russia's brand of "sovereign democracy"— Moscow's own term for its particular hybrid of democracy and autocracy—may well represent the ill-defined halfway house in which many other countries will find themselves in the coming decades. Indeed, Russia already seems to be setting the standard for its neighborhood. Democratic liberties have been in retreat in most of the former Soviet republics. Freedom House reported in 2010 that according to standard measures of political liberty, eleven of the twelve former Soviet republics (excluding the Baltic states) are worse off than a decade ago.[53] China's "neater" brand of communal autocracy may be the standard bearer, but Russia's muddy mix of autocracy, paternalism, and democracy may well prove to be the more prevalent.

Russia's brand of modernity will challenge the West on matters of foreign policy as well as politics. Putin sought from the outset not only to rebuild the country domestically, but also to reclaim its geopolitical influence. He proved uniquely adept at tapping into Russian nationalism and stoking as well as stroking the nation's great-power aspirations. Putin perfected the art of burnishing his popularity at home and abroad by standing up to the United States and clamoring for a world in which influence is more equitably distributed. In 2007, for example, he referred to U.S. hegemony as a "world in which there is one master, one sovereign." "And at the end of the day," Putin continued, "this is pernicious not only for all those within this system, but also for the sovereign itself because it destroys itself from within."[54]

As on the domestic front, the Kremlin has come up with a hybrid approach to exerting its muscle abroad. On one hand, it casts itself as a member of the great-power club, joining the G-8 and working with the United States and its European allies to reduce nuclear arsenals and rein in Iran's nuclear ambitions. On the other hand, Moscow regularly bolsters its credentials as a counterweight to the West. The Kremlin has crossed swords with Washington over U.S. missile defense and NATO enlargement. Russia invaded Georgia in 2008 and recognized the breakaway regions of Abkhazia and South Ossetia as independent states. Moscow and Beijing teamed up with the nations of Central Asia to form the Shanghai Cooperation Council (SCO)—a body that, like the BRICs summits, serves as an alternative to institutions dominated by the West.

Due to this hybrid approach, Russia may be uniquely poised to help build bridges between the Western order and whatever comes next. Moscow has a long history of diplomacy and engagement with the West, yet also considerable credibility among emerging powers. Moreover, Obama's effort to "reset" relations between Washington and Moscow has yielded fruit, producing new levels of cooperation on Afghanistan, Iran, and arms control. A dialogue has been under way about more fully anchoring Russia in the West, possibly through Russian membership in NATO. Especially if the Atlantic community plays its cards right and succeeds in integrating Russia into its institutions, it may well find Moscow a particularly useful arbiter in negotiating the shape of a post-Western order.[55]

## Tribal Autocracy: The Gulf Sheikdoms

The oil-rich sheikdoms of the Persian Gulf represent a third brand of autocracy—a tribal variant. Rather than drawing on the communal solidarity of China or the paternalism of the Russian state, the conservative regimes of the Arabian Peninsula rely for their legitimacy on tribal traditions of patronage and loyalty. With ample energy revenues filling government coffers, the Gulf's rulers have effectively bought off dissent through the redistribution of wealth among their citizens. The popular unrest of 2011 certainly rocked the boat, but the Gulf's sheikdoms all weathered the storm and acquiesced only to cosmetic political reforms. Despite their distinction as some of the world's most illiberal states, a combination of tribal authority and economic largess gives these autocracies remarkable staying power.

In terms of geopolitical heft, the Gulf states cut small figures when compared to autocracies like China and Russia. The largest state on the peninsula, Saudi Arabia, has a population of some 28 million—less than two percent of China's. The United Arab Emirates (UAE), which is the second largest, has a population of roughly six million, only fifteen percent of whom are citizens; the rest are expatriate workers. Nonetheless, for a number of compelling reasons, these states will continue to punch well above their weight and figure prominently in shaping the emerging global landscape.

For starters, even with growing investment in renewable sources of energy, the world will remain heavily dependent upon fossil fuels for the foreseeable future—especially as China's and India's demand for oil and gas grows. Including Iran and Iraq, the region is home to nearly two-thirds of the world's known crude oil reserves, ensuring that the Persian Gulf will stay center stage. The region's influence is magnified by its sovereign wealth funds, which are generously fed by energy and investment income. The states of the Gulf are also close strategic partners of the United States. They play host to a sizable U.S. military presence, which has been supporting operations in Iraq and Afghanistan, protecting the flow of oil, and warding off the Iranian threat. The winding down of the wars in Iraq and Afghanistan has reduced the U.S. footprint, but not the closeness or the importance of the strategic bonds. Indeed, Washington has of late been building up the defense capabilities of the Gulf states to help them check Iran.

It is also the case that the trajectory of democratic reform in the Persian Gulf is an important litmus test of the global appeal of the Western model—especially in the wake of the U.S.-led invasion of Iraq, a war touted by the Bush administration as a jump-start to liberalization in the region. With the exception of Israel, democracy has had a hard time putting down roots in the Middle East. The Arab Spring may eventually prove to be a turning point, but the Gulf's monarchs have at least for now refused to loosen their tight grip on power. Liberalization in the staunchly autocratic Gulf would therefore mark a particularly notable advance of democracy's fortunes.

This democratic turn, however, does not appear likely any time soon. Bahrain was the only Gulf monarchy to suffer widespread and sustained protests during the Arab Spring. Unlike the other Gulf sheikdoms, which are predominantly Sunni, Bahrain is ruled by a Sunni monarchy despite its Shiite majority; not surprisingly, its Shiites were the ones in the streets.[56] Also not surprisingly, Saudi Arabia, which has a sizable Shiite minority, promptly dispatched forces to Bahrain to help the government snuff out the uprising. The Saudis were keen to nip in the bud the prospect of Shiite unrest coming their way.

The traditions of tribal society run deep in the Gulf, and will act as a powerful brake on political reform for generations to come. Leaders are drawn exclusively from royal families, with succession either hereditary or decided by closed deliberation between the monarch and his inner circle. The Gulf's rulers consolidate their authority by reaching out to powerful clans and family lines, which in turn extend the patronage system through their own tribal and familial networks. In his study of the UAE, a federal state composed of seven different emirates, Ali Mohammed Khalifa observes that, "most of the cabinet ministers appointed were either members of the ruling families of the member emirates or citizens aligned with such families in the configuration of tribal politics in the area."[57] Lower-level appointments are similarly aimed at co-opting influential families. Christopher Davidson notes that the government's careful attention to "kinship loyalties both inside and outside of the immediate ruling family" remains central to satisfying "the ongoing need for powerful tribal support."[58]

The legitimacy and authority of autocratic regimes in the Gulf, as in China and Russia, also depend on their ability to fulfill the economic expectations of their citizens. In the Gulf, the key medium for doing so is wealth redistribution: the government hands out income from energy exports in the form of direct subsidies and jobs. When the UAE was formed in 1971, Abu Dhabi, the emirate with the largest territory and energy income, bankrolled the state, providing roughly ninety percent of the union's budget. The federal government built roads, electricity grids, and telecommunication infrastructure and provided land, housing, and jobs to those in need. It also offered funds to cover the cost of weddings among Emirati nationals. As Davidson observes, "a material pact has emerged throughout the UAE, an unwritten and unspoken contract in which almost all of the population accept the legitimacy of the polity in exchange for the constancy and rewards of their well-paid employment."[59] Since the UAE's citizens, including the more educated and professionally accomplished elite, depend upon the largess of the state for their income, they have little material incentive to alter the political status quo.

If pressure for political change is to mount, it will come primarily from popular frustration about the limited opportunities for upward mobility. It is no accident that a number of Gulf governments unveiled major domestic spending packages early in 2011; they were deeply worried about the building unrest sparked by the Arab Spring. Saudi Arabia committed to social spending of some 100 billion dollars and helped fund stimulus packages for Bahrain and Oman. Although energy revenues provide governments the wherewithal to buy off dissent, the "oil curse" has led to mounting numbers of citizens—especially among the young—without the skills necessary for professional advancement. In Saudi Arabia, almost forty percent of the population is under the age of fifteen; the median age for males is twenty-three, and for females nineteen.[60] The employment prospects for many young Saudis are not encouraging. Women, in particular, generally remain outside the workforce and have limited professional opportunities in male-dominated tribal societies. In the UAE, expatriates dominate the workplace; they represent close to ninety percent of the workforce. Emiratis, even if financially secure, increasingly resent living in a country in which they represent a tiny minority in a sea of foreigners, many of whom are better educated and have far more promising career paths.

Well aware of the need to raise the skills and employment prospects of their citizens, some of the Gulf states are trying hard to diversify their economies and invest in the educational institutions needed to cultivate a more capable workforce. Qatar has opened Education City, a gleaming campus at which Georgetown, Cornell, Texas A&M, Carnegie Mellon, and other U.S. universities offer degree programs. In the UAE, New York University, among other distinguished institutions, has set up shop. Meanwhile, Saudi Arabia is in the midst of building six new cities to serve as centers of commerce and manufacturing, which by 2020 are intended to provide one million new jobs.[61]

Over the next several generations, the investments of the Gulf sheikdoms in the intellectual capital of their citizens promise to yield concrete payoffs—a more educated and gainfully employed citizenry. Even so, as an educated middle class expands, it is poised—as in China and Russia—to be an ally, not an opponent, of the autocratic state that enriches it. And in the meantime, traditions of tribal rule coupled with energy revenues sufficient to sustain adequate standards of living for many will continue to secure the political compliance of the bulk of the population.

Kuwait is the one Gulf sheikdom to have embraced a more democratic form of government; its parliament is elected rather than appointed, and its role is legislative and not, as in other Gulf states, merely advisory. In 2010, prior to the region's uprisings, Freedom House ranked Kuwait the most democratic country in the Arab world. The concrete benefits of its more open political system, however, have been less than apparent. Islamists and tribal conservatives have of late dominated Kuwait's parliament. Stalemate between the ruling family and the parliament has blocked economic reform and diversification, dampening growth. In April 2009, amid disagreements over succession as well as economic and social policy, the Kuwaiti emir dissolved the parliament—not the first time the monarch has done so. This turmoil has hardly gone unnoticed in the region; Kuwait's neighbors frequently reference its political troubles to tout the advantages of autocracy.[62] Moreover, foreign investors have favored the more predictable business environments in absolute monarchies such as Qatar and the UAE.

Kuwait is not the only country in the region giving democracy a questionable name. Iraq's experimentation with electoral rule—in stark contrast to the expectations of the George W. Bush administration—is not making a compelling case for the advantages of participatory government. Iraq's Gulf neighbors do not miss Saddam Hussein. But they do see a deeply dysfunctional country in which flawed elections have produced governments bedeviled by ethnic, sectarian, and factional divides. Iraq's violent repression of the protests that came its way during the Arab Spring hardly spoke well of the government's liberal credentials. And the ongoing confrontation between Iraq's Sunnis and Shiites continues to intensify a schism that extends throughout the region. If anything, the Gulf sheikdoms have interpreted developments in Iraq as a warning against, not an endorsement of, democratic rule.

Change is as unlikely to come from outside the region as within. Although Washington regularly embraces the rhetoric of democratization in the Arab world and did back the intervention in Libya, it is likely to do little to alter the status quo—especially after the sobering experiences of trying to export democracy to Iraq and Afghanistan. The conservative sheikdoms of the Gulf are generally gracious hosts to a U.S. military presence that Washington will want to sustain for years to come. The global economy remains dependent on fossil fuels from the region. Although stability in the Gulf would be enhanced by economic diversification and gradual political reform, the United States has little incentive to undermine the absolutist regimes with which it has a mutually dependent strategic and economic relationship. Tribal autocracy in the Gulf is alive and well, and will remain so for the foreseeable future.

• • • •

China, Russia, and the Gulf sheikdoms are only a handful of over one hundred non-democracies that populate the world. Some of these illiberal states will surely make the transition to democracy in the coming decades. Many will surely not. Whether communal, paternal, or tribal in nature, autocracies are poised to hold their own well into the coming global turn.

## The Theocrats

Secular democracy is a defining feature of the Western world. In contrast, the Middle East is home to theocrats as well as autocrats. The Gulf sheikdoms are notable for not just their tribal brand of autocracy, but also their integration of Islam into politics. Although the region's rulers are tribal heads, not religious leaders, they govern in close alignment with Islamic authorities; state and mosque are intimately intertwined. Religion penetrates virtually all aspects of political and social life, including the legal code, dress and diet, gender roles, and foreign policy. The Gulf Cooperation Council, a regional grouping of six Gulf countries, notes in its founding charter that its members enjoy "mutual bonds of special relations, common characteristics and similar systems founded on the Creed of Islam."[67] While the Gulf sheikdoms link state and mosque only in spirit and practice, Iran links them also in form. In Tehran, religious leaders sit atop the political hierarchy. Although the Iranian president, Mahmoud Ahmadinejad, is a layman, the country is an effective theocracy run by the Supreme Leader, Ayatollah Khamenei. He is supported by the Assembly of Experts, a body composed of eighty-six religious scholars. The mullahs generally call the shots.

Although the influence of Islam on politics and policy is particularly pronounced in the Gulf states, religion plays a prominent role in political life across the Middle East. To be sure, a majority of countries in the region are governed by laymen, not religious authorities. But most of these states have maintained their secular orientation through coercion, not consent. Secular regimes in the Middle East have generally been imposed from above by leaders fearful that Islamic movements will foil their quests for absolute authority. In contrast, secular politics in the West emerged from below—as the product of a popular struggle for religious and political pluralism. Accordingly, secular governments in many parts of the Muslim world rest on contrived and fragile foundations; they are not polities that have emerged naturally from underlying socioeconomic conditions.

Until the uprisings that toppled President Hosni Mubarak early in 2011, Egypt's government had long ruled with an iron hand, in no small part because of concern that the Muslim Brotherhood, a main opposition party, would otherwise take the country in an Islamic direction. Indeed, the Brotherhood's political influence was only strengthened by Mubarak's departure—not a surprising outcome given that some ninety-five percent of Egyptians believe that Islam should play a large role in politics, with nearly two-thirds of the population wanting civil law to adhere strictly to the Koran.[64] Iraq was for decades governed by a secular regime, but Saddam Hussein maintained his grip on power only through the brutal repression of dissent. Now that he is gone, Islam is playing a much greater role in political life. Algeria is governed by a secular regime—but only because the Islamists who won free and fair parliamentary elections in 1991 were blocked from taking power by the military. Even in Turkey, which was run by staunchly secular regimes from its founding as a republic in the 1920s until a decade ago, the military long stood ready to keep the Islamists at bay, on occasion seizing power in order to do so. Moreover, as discussed below, economic growth and the broadening of Turkey's middle class have been deepening, not diminishing, the role of religion in politics—in sharp contrast with the Western experience.

In a further departure from the path followed by the West, the spread of participatory politics in the Middle East has strengthened rather than weakened the political sway of religious parties. In the aftermath of the U.S.-led invasion in 2003, Iraq embraced a truncated form of democracy; Islamist forces have been one of the main beneficiaries. When Palestinians held elections in 2006, Hamas—a militant Islamist party committed to confrontation with Israel—came out on top. After a power struggle with the other main political party among Palestinians, Fatah, Hamas seized control of the Gaza Strip and proceeded to impose its radical brand of Islam on Gazans while carrying out missile attacks against southern Israel. Recent elections in Lebanon have enhanced the influence of Hezbollah, a party wedded to Islamic fundamentalism and hostility toward Israel. Indeed, after the fall of the Lebanese government in January 2011, Hezbollah succeeded in installing its man, Najib Miqati, as the new prime minister. The Arab Spring could have a similar impact elsewhere, strengthening Islamist forces in countries whose regimes have been toppled by popular uprisings.

## An Islamic Reformation?

It should come as no surprise that the Middle East is not tracking the Western experience when it comes to the relationship between religion and politics. The West followed a unique path. After the Protestant Reformation found fertile ground among Europe's emerging bourgeoisie, separating state from church came naturally; secular power was distinct from religious authority, even if the two realms had been in a temporary marriage of convenience from the time of Constantine. Christianity is a religion of faith, not law, giving it direct political consequence only via secular institutions. The break between monarch and pope was thus an irreparable blow to the church's political influence.

The advance of modernity has followed an altogether different path in the Islamic world. The split between Sunnis and Shiites subjected Islam to doctrinal diversity from early on. In contrast to Catholic tradition, which vested unitary authority in the pope and the institutionalized hierarchy of the church, Islamic authorities have long debated theology and practice. Bernard Lewis points to "the notion, deep-rooted in Islam, that a certain measure of diversity of opinion is harmless and even beneficial."[65] Islam thus proved less brittle than Catholicism when opinions diverged. Islam also faced far fewer challenges from social change than did Catholicism. Socioeconomic conditions in the Ottoman realm did not lend themselves to the development of a middle class ready to overturn the status quo; imperial authorities maintained tight control over markets, merchants, and intellectuals. Finally, since Islam is a legal system as well as a faith, politics and religion in Muslim countries have always been intertwined—and will likely remain so for the indefinite future. As Olivier Roy observes, "a theological reformation makes sense only if it turns on cultural, social, and political issues perceived by those involved."[66] In light of underlying trends in the Middle East, an Islamic Reformation is anything but around the corner.

Another fundamental difference between the West and the Muslim Middle East has to do with the concept of nationhood. The nation emerged as the primary political unit in the West late in the game—well after the Protestant Reformation and the embrace of religious pluralism. Most European nation-states thus crystallized with the institutionalized church either outside or at a distance from the realm of politics. In addition, nations in Europe tended to be relatively organic units that consisted of affiliated linguistic and ethnic groupings, facilitating their ability to become the main source of political identity and allegiance.

The nation-state was then exported globally, largely via the imperial projects of Europe's great powers. Since nationalism arrived in a Muslim world in which Islam was still very much a part of political life, nations in the Middle East generally crystallized with religion as part of their core identities. And instead of being organic polities, most nations in the Middle East are contrived entities that cut across pre-existing political, ethnic, and tribal loyalties. Accordingly, the nation-state in the Muslim Middle East has not enjoyed the primacy it has in the West; religious and tribal identities have in many countries remained far more powerful than national allegiances. In the West, secular nationalism has supplanted religion as the primary source of identity. In most of the Muslim world, nationalism is neither secular nor does it trump religion, sect, and tribe as the main anchor of political identity. Indeed, as Lewis points out, the Arabic language had no real equivalent to the Western notions of nation and patriotism—and developed them only after the concepts were imported from the West.[67]

A secularized, Western-style modernity in the Muslim world is thus at best a remote prospect. Across the Middle East, religion and politics are poised to remain inseparable—although Iran, paradoxically enough, may prove to be an exception. Iran is today the leading exemplar of theocracy, but it may well end up being one of the few Muslim countries to eventually push religion out of politics by popular demand.

Despite the long-running confrontation between Iran and the West, significant parallels exist between Iran's political evolution and the Western path of development. The Catholic Church in pre-modern Europe was both highly institutionalized and directly involved in politics. Shiites in Iran, in contrast with traditions elsewhere in the region, have similarly developed an institutionalized mosque that is heavily involved in politics. Since the revolution in 1979, clerics have called the political shots. According to Roy, Iran's Islamic revolution installed a "political-clerical apparatus" that relies on religion to reinforce its position of power.[68] As Iran's citizens tire of the economic duress and social constraints that have accompanied theocratic rule, they may well seek to remove the mosque from politics—just as Europeans did with the Catholic Church. After all, Iran has a broad and educated middle class that yearns for better business conditions and more personal autonomy. And Iran, as the inheritor of centuries of Persian history and culture, enjoys a relatively organic sense of nationhood—despite its ethnic diversity. A secularizing swing of the pendulum in Iran is hardly foreordained, but it is entirely plausible.

Elsewhere in the Muslim world, the linkage between religion and politics, although intimate, is more subtle and less direct; it stems from matters of identity, faith, and political culture, not from the formal penetration of the state by religious institutions. Indeed, clerics in many parts of the Middle East deliberately avoid direct engagement in politics in order to cordon off religion from the temptations and compromises that accompany political ambition. In Iraq, for example, Ayatollah Sistani is one of the country's most influential figures. But he deliberately shuns day-to-day involvement in politics. The same goes for Afghanistan. President Hamid Karzai presides over a secular government that is formally detached from the country's religious institutions. But the Ulema Council, which is composed of some 3,000 mullahs from across the country, exercises considerable influence. In the West, the separation of church and state was about saving politics from religion. The same may one day soon be true of Iran. But in most of the Muslim world, the opposite is the case: clerics keep their distance from the state in order to save religion from politics.[69]

Recent developments in Turkey underscore yet another way in which Muslim countries are taking their own path to modernity. In early modern Europe, the rising middle class was primarily responsible for the secular turn in politics. In Turkey, economic advance and the broadening of the middle class have weakened rather than strengthened the secularization of politics. Following the close of

World War I, Turkey's first president, Kemal Ataturk, enforced a rigid secularism based in part on the presumption that Islam had long held back economic and social progress in the Ottoman Empire. His determination to craft a Turkish version of modernity based on the Western model of secular nationalism was backed by the military, the courts, and, as it developed in strength, a business elite that resided primarily in Istanbul and the country's other main cities. Four times during the second half of the twentieth century the military seized control of the country to defend the secular republic against Islamist alternatives.

This staunchly secular brand of Turkish politics came to an end in 2002, when elections brought to power the Justice and Development Party (AKP). The AKP, a party with Islamist roots, has been in power ever since. Under the leadership of Prime Minister Recep Tayyip Erdogan, the AKP dramatically scaled back the influence of the military and the courts—both of which have long enforced secular rule—in favor of the power of the presidency and parliament. The main vehicle for doing so was a popular referendum passed in 2010, which approved the revision of the constitution that the military had put in place after seizing power in 1980. The AKP has also realigned Turkish foreign policy. The country's economic and geopolitical orientation was for decades almost exclusively westward—toward Europe and the United States. Now Turkey spends much more time and effort looking south and east, keen to deepen its economic and geopolitical engagement with its Muslim neighbors. Turkey's formerly close relationship with Israel has been one of the main casualties of this strategic reorientation.

This shift in Turkish politics has stemmed in large part from the economic and political empowerment of what was formerly the country's urban and rural working class. More conservative and religious than the traditional urban elite, this rising sector of the Turkish population is the AKP's electoral base—and the primary backer of the party's Islamist bent. The emergence of a new middle class committed to Islamic practice and values is not unique to Turkey. As Roy comments, "Conservative in faith and beliefs, but modern in terms of business, a middle class of Islamic puritans with a Weberian work ethic can be seen to be emerging. . . . This

neo-bourgeoisie adheres to traditional values and is eager to per-
petuate them in a modern environment."[70]

Turkey's economic and political trajectory is thus diverging
quite starkly from the Western model. Economic advance and the
broadening of the middle class are bringing religion back into politics, not ensuring the separation of mosque and state. And with
Turkey's economy on the rise, the country is poised to be a trend-
setter for the broader Middle East. As the middle class expands in
the Muslim world, religion may well strengthen, not lose, its influence over political life.

What likely lies ahead is an Islamic brand of modernity, not the
secularization of Islam. As Tariq Ramadan, a devout Muslim intellectual based at Oxford University, has argued, this Muslim version
of modernity will not converge with that of the West, meaning that
the two must learn to coexist comfortably. Ramadan is correct to seek
a synthesis that enables Muslims to preserve their beliefs and traditions while living with and within the Western world.[71] The West
should not be advocating or waiting for an Islamic Reformation; it
is not in the offing. Rather, it should be advocating a tolerant and
moderate brand of Islam that is respected by and respectful of the
political and religious traditions of the West.

## The Arab Spring

The popular uprisings that began sweeping through the Middle
East and North Africa late in 2010 seemingly challenge the asser-
tion that the Muslim Middle East will continue diverging from the
Western version of modernity. As protesters gathered in one country
after another, the region appeared to be on the cusp of embracing
democracy. Policy makers and pundits alike initially compared the
unrest to the French Revolution and the fall of the Berlin Wall—a
historical watershed marking the arrival of participatory politics to
the Arab world. And, indeed, this political awakening was without
question a remarkable and uplifting confirmation of the universality of the human desire for dignity and liberty.

But as the dust settled and the initial euphoria subsided, a more
sobering picture began to emerge. Governments in Bahrain, Iraq,

Libya, Syria, and Yemen, among others, unleashed lethal force to shut down the demonstrations. In the case of Libya, the specter of a massacre in Benghazi, a rebel stronghold, convinced the UN Security Council to authorize armed intervention to protect civilians. The NATO-led mission eventually led to the downfall of the Libyan regime. But the outside help offered to Libya's opposition movement proved to be the exception, not the rule. In many of the other countries beset by popular uprisings, autocratic regimes cracked down as Western governments did little more than urge restraint. Repression—sometimes brutal repression—more often than not effectively extinguished the unrest.

Admittedly, a number of the region's coercive rulers—Tunisia's Zine El Abidine Ben Ali, Egypt's Hosni Mubarak, Libya's Muammar Qaddafi—were forced from office. But the new governments that have been gradually evolving in the aftermath of their departures, although they have been introducing meaningful reforms, are unlikely to cohere as liberal democracies any time soon. Moreover, even though Egypt may be the most populous and influential country in the Arab world, it should not be seen as a trendsetter for the region as a whole; Egypt enjoys political advantages that most of its neighbors do not. The Egyptian military, a professional and disciplined institution with strong ties to the United States, played a central role in facilitating Mubarak's departure and will oversee the reform of the country's constitution and political bodies. Most of Egypt's neighbors lack national institutions capable of mediating political change.

Moreover, Egypt's sense of nationhood dates to ancient times, engendering a social cohesion rare in a region where most of the states are political constructions left behind by retreating colonial powers. In Iraq, Jordan, Lebanon, Syria, and much of the Arabian Peninsula and North Africa, tribal, sectarian, and ethnic divides regularly trump a weak national identity. These cleavages have long been suppressed by coercive rule, and democratization would do more to bring them to the surface than to repair them. If Egypt is on the slow road to democracy, most of its neighbors can be expected to trail considerably further behind.

Even if the tide does turn, and democracy rapidly spreads across the Middle East, the region still would not take its place in the international order on offer from the West. The more democratic the Middle East becomes, the greater the role that Islam—even if a moderate brand—will play in public life. This outcome would be neither good nor bad; it simply would be a reality in a part of the world where politics and religion are intertwined. Nonetheless, Western observers and policy makers had better stop operating under the illusion that the spread of democracy in the Middle East also means the spread of Western values. Moreover, the quest for dignity that is fueling the clamor for democracy is also likely to fuel a strident call to stand up to the United States, Europe, and Israel. In a poll taken during the spring of 2011 (after the fall of Mubarak), for example, over fifty percent of Egyptians favored annulling the country's 1979 peace treaty with Israel.[72] In a region long dominated by outside powers, more democracy in the Middle East may well mean much less strategic cooperation with the West.

## The Israeli Exception?

Israel is commonly seen as a liberal and democratic outpost of the West in the midst of a Muslim world in which both liberalism and democracy are in short supply. But in actuality, Israel is a hybrid; it has imported to the Middle East many of the values and institutions of the West, but then blended them with the values and institutions of the Middle East.

Israel is a liberal democracy that embraces an institutionalized separation of synagogue and state. But unlike Christianity and like Islam, Judaism is a religion of law as well as faith. The five books of the Torah lay out laws covering religious practice and moral conduct as well as mundane matters such as business transactions, farming, and cooking. The Talmud is a lengthy discourse on Jewish law revolving around 613 *mitzvot*—commandments related to virtually every aspect of daily life. Moreover, as in the Muslim world, the Jewish concept of nationhood is intermingled with that of religion. Israel is a nation-state for Jews, a people defined to a significant degree by their religion. The identity of Israelis and Jews living in the Diaspora contains strong religious as well as cultural and historical elements.

It is precisely because Judaism inextricably links faith, law, and nationhood that Israel is in a no-man's-land when it comes to the relationship between religion and politics. In form Israel is a secular democracy, but in substance religion infuses political life. As a consequence of legislation pushed through the Knesset by religious parties, El Al Airlines and other major companies do not operate on the Jewish Sabbath. The ultra-Orthodox are exempt from military service. Civil marriages do not exist—Israelis travel abroad if they want one—and rabbis perform weddings only if bride and groom are both Jewish. Even the basic question of citizenship—who is a Jew and therefore enjoys a legal right of return to Israel—turns on religious law.

Matters of war and peace are similarly affected by the intimate connection between religion and politics. Many Israelis who reside in the West Bank do so for religious reasons—a biblical commitment to Judea and Samaria. Their attachment to the land poses a significant obstacle to a peace deal with the Palestinians, because any such deal would entail the dismantling of at least some of the Jewish settlements in the West Bank. During his first year in office, President Obama sought to advance the peace process by pressing the Israeli government to halt the expansion of settlements. Although he secured from Israel a moratorium on expansion, the moratorium lasted only ten months; it was lifted in no small part due to pressure from the religious right. The Palestinians promptly broke off negotiations with Israel.

Although the Orthodox represent only about twenty-five percent of the population, their political power is magnified by a parliamentary system that regularly makes small religious parties key to the viability of governing coalitions. And the influence of the Orthodox will only grow over time due to their comparably higher rates of birth. The demographic trends suggest an intensification of already tortured struggles within Israeli society between religious and secular Jews. The differences in lifestyle and outlook are so substantial that a physical separation of sorts is emerging. As religious families increasingly populate Jerusalem, secular Jews are moving to Tel Aviv and other cities where they are in the majority. Although a rare exception, these cleavages have the potential to turn violent—as made tragically clear by the 1995 assassination of Prime Minister Yitzhak Rabin by a militant Orthodox Jew opposed to Rabin's pursuit of a peace settlement with the Palestinians. Violence also occurs for far more mundane reasons. During the summer of 2009, for example, Orthodox Jews clashed with police in Jerusalem over a public parking garage that was open for business on the Sabbath.

In important respects, Israel is a microcosm of the complicated interface between a Western version of modernity and an alternative one unique to the Middle East. Most of the main beach in Tel Aviv teems with bikini-clad women and bars blaring rock music. But at its northern end is a walled-off enclosure where Orthodox women can bathe without coming into contact with men. Herzliya, a coastal town just north of Tel Aviv, is one of the world's centers of high-tech innovation. It is a vital node through which Israel's thriving economy plugs into global markets. But in nearby Bnei Brak lives a large ultra-Orthodox community intent on cordoning itself off from globalization and the Western version of modernity it represents. The clash between the different worlds of Herzliya and Bnei Brak will roil politics in Israel for the foreseeable future. And these two towns offer a taste of the competing versions of modernity that the West will face in the broader Middle East as it seeks to manage the global turn.

## The Strongmen

If the Middle East will be distinctive for its intimate connection between religion and politics, Africa is set to be the continent of strongmen.[73] Autocrats routinize their power; they maintain control through bureaucracies and a professionalized security apparatus. In contrast, strongmen concentrate power in their own hands; they maintain control through personal patronage systems and loyal militia. The tradition of strongmen predates the era of African independence; decades of governance by Europe's imperial powers bequeathed to the continent a legacy of top-down rule.[74] Upon independence, local leaders replaced European emissaries, but they too governed with few checks on their power.

As they departed, Europe's colonial powers also left behind political boundaries that cut across ethnic and linguistic boundaries. As mentioned, Europe's nation-states tended to be organic constructs, fashioned among peoples that shared linguistic and cultural ties. In contrast, post-colonial Africa was populated by states with few natural sinews holding them together. As Felix Houphouet-Boigny, president of Côte d'Ivoire from 1960 to 1993, remarked, "We have all inherited from our former masters not nations but states, states that have within them extremely fragile links between ethnic groups."[75] A further legacy of the colonial era was the connection between political loyalty and economic patronage. Colonial governments regularly cultivated local collaborators, who relied on controlling the flow of goods and arms to build political networks and wield influence. Doling out resources was the currency of political power.

Following the transition to independence after World War II, most African states emerged as either autocracies or one-party electoral regimes. Among countries that held elections, outcomes were foregone conclusions; of the 106 presidential contests that took place between independence and 1989, the winner on average received ninety-two percent of the vote.[76] African leaders maintained that authoritarian leadership was needed to bring stability and economic growth to impoverished countries composed of disparate ethnic and linguistic groups—and they were often unabashed about the scope of their powers. As Hastings Banda, the leader of Malawi from 1964 to 1993, put it in 1972, "Everything is my business. Everything. The state of education, the state of our economy, the state of our agriculture, the state of our transport, everything is my business. Anything I say is law. Literally law. It is a fact in this country."[77]

## The Façade of Democratization

During the 1990s, a wave of apparent democratization swept Africa. One-party rule had clearly failed to deliver positive results. Economic conditions in many African countries had actually declined during the decades since independence. Foreign debt had mounted while corruption spread. Meanwhile, the emergence of a more urbanized and educated sector of the population provided a vocal constituency for change.[78] Pressure from foreign donors combined with economic stagnation and domestic discontent to prompt a widespread move to more open electoral competition. Over the course of the 1990s, forty-two of forty-eight African states held multiparty elections. In addition, transitions in power began to occur through constitutional mechanisms. From the 1960s through the 1980s, most African rulers left office through a coup or violent overthrow. Since 1990, a majority have left office in a manner consistent with established laws and procedures.[79]

Most African states, however, have embraced democracy only in form, not substance. Elections serve primarily to consolidate the power of the ruling party while deflecting domestic opposition and earning the approval of Western donors. Nicolas van de Walle observes that in most African countries "the turn to multiparty competition amounted to little more than an erstwhile authoritarian ruler donning the garb of democracy and tolerating regular elections as a successful strategy for holding on to power."[80] H. Kwasi Prempeh concurs: "the modal African presidency has emerged from the recent round of democratic reforms with its extant powers substantially intact."[81] Africa is home to a few success stories— Botswana is one of them—in which reasonable standards of liberal democracy have been upheld. Democratization in South Africa has also made significant advances, even though the dominance of the African National Congress compromises genuine democratic competition.[82] But across most of the continent, the move to multiparty democracy has been little more than a façade.

Rule by strongmen has come to be called neopatrimonialism— patrimonial because power is vested in an individual who governs through prestige and patronage, neo because this type of governance has only recently become consolidated in political institutions.[83] The institutionalization of patrimonialism gives strongman rule exceptional staying power. It has become a system, not just a temporary political order dependent upon the charisma and authority of a specific individual.

The electoral outcomes produced by Africa's recent turn to multiparty democracy reveal just how shallow the political reforms have been. When they stand for reelection, incumbent presidents still win more than eighty-five percent of the time.[84] In the rare instances in which an opposition party is able to win the presidency, it readily gravitates to strongman rule; the new government finds it difficult to resist the advantages that come with a monopoly on power. Nigeria's elections in 2007, although marred by corruption and violence, succeeded in producing the country's first orderly transfer of power from one civilian government to another. But the new president promptly resorted to "the doling out of patronage along ethnographical lines," ensuring that "politics revolves around personal and factional competition for control over the precious oil resource."[85]

The story is the same in most other African countries. Senegal enjoyed a peaceful and rules-based change of power in 2000, but soon slid backwards to "electoral authoritarianism."[86] Kenya held multiparty elections in 2007, but accusations of fraud were widespread and the outcome contested. After the incumbent, Mwai Kibaki, declared victory, violence broke out along ethnic lines, leading to hundreds of deaths. A dysfunctional coalition eventually emerged between Kibaki and his competitor, Raila Odinga. In Tanzania, the ruling party controls the media and resorts to illegal forms of coercion to neutralize the opposition.[87] Ghana held relatively free and fair elections in 2008, but the new president concentrated power in the executive branch and overrode institutional checks on his power.[88]

The legacy of top-down rule certainly contributes to this stunted form of democratic rule, but strongman politics persists in Africa in part because most of the continent has yet to experience the socioeconomic transformations that undermined authoritarian rule elsewhere. Absent a level of economic development able to sustain class formation and nurture a sizable bourgeoisie, politics throughout Africa still runs along ethnic lines.[89] Governance is primarily about distributing resources to one's kin group, and much less about devising and implementing public policy. Meredith elaborates on the degree to which ethnicity anchors Africa's politics, a trend left behind by the establishment of post-colonial borders that cut across ethno-linguistic lines:

In a continent where class formation had hardly begun to alter loyalties, ethnicity provided the strongest political base. Politicians and voters alike came to rely on ethnic solidarity. For politicians it was the route to power. They became, in effect, ethnic entrepreneurs. For voters it was their main hope of getting a slice of government bounty. What they wanted was a local representative at the centre of power—an ethnic patron who could capture a share of the spoils and bring it back to their community. Primary loyalty remained rooted in tribal identity. Kinship, clan and ethnic considerations largely determined the way people voted. The main component of African politics became, in essence, kinship corporations.[90]

Legislatures have been unable to chip away at presidential power and the ethnic patronage on which it relies in part because constitutions deny them the ability to do so.[91] In many Western countries, the executive branch enjoys only those powers expressly assigned to it. In Africa, constitutions tend to grant to the presidency all powers not expressly assigned elsewhere. African presidents often have the sole authority to originate legislation. Ministers and other high-level appointees are regularly picked from the legislature, blurring the significance of a separation of powers. In a recent Kenyan government, over forty percent of legislators also held positions in the executive branch.[92]

Even when legislatures and courts have statutory primacy, their power is often trumped by informal systems of patronage; presidential prerogative regularly makes short shrift of institutional checks and balances.[93] Members of opposition parties do frequently call for constitutional reforms intended to contain the power of the executive branch. But they also work hard to curry favor with the president in order to reap the benefits of patronage. And when the opposition does succeed in winning the presidency, it regularly refuses to implement the reforms it formerly advocated, and instead chooses to partake of the privileges of unchecked power.[94]

## The Weak Middle Class

The informal sway of Africa's presidents stems in no small part from their control over resources and their ability to sustain patronage networks through doling out economic favors and jobs.[95] Kenneth Kaunda, Zambia's president from 1964 to 1991, reportedly controlled 40,000 patronage positions in Lusaka alone.[96] In Kenya, legislators make the equivalent of 150,000 dollars per year, while forty percent of the population lives on less than one dollar per day.[97] A significant portion of government revenue in many countries comes from trade tariffs and foreign assistance, enabling the executive branch to control the purse strings and diminishing the role of legislatures in managing public finances.[98] And in countries fortunate enough to have substantial income from oil revenues, such as Nigeria, the pattern is the same.[99]

The concentration of wealth in the hands of government officials and their patronage networks creates a self-reinforcing cycle. Economic activity, including that of the private sector, is mediated by the state, preventing the emergence of a middle class able to push back against strongman politics. In Uganda, for example, where almost ninety percent of the population lives in rural areas, the business community is "too thoroughly dependent on state patronage ever to challenge the status quo, while those few businesspeople who are independent are too thin on the ground to venture jumping into the political fray."[100] Michael Bratton and Nicolas van de Walle argue that the problem is structural and endemic. Through their reliance on executive power and patronage, neopatrimonial regimes enfeeble independent entrepreneurs and businesses, leaving "the weak national bourgeoisie of Africa...frustrated by state ownership, overregulation, and official corruption."[101]

Neither Africa's democratic activists nor foreign donors have been able to seriously challenge strongman politics. Coercive intimidation has enabled presidents across the continent to either squash or co-opt movements aimed at advancing liberal democracy. Foreign donors have made aid contingent on good governance—and the approach has yielded a few successes, such as Mozambique. But more often than not, governments make changes that are largely cosmetic; they keep donors happy and the aid flowing, but do little to curb presidential power or reliance on patronage. Rather than consolidating democracy, the move to multiparty elections has served primarily to mask the continuation of strongman politics.

And with China steadily augmenting its strategic and economic presence in Africa—Beijing regularly invests in and gives assistance to regimes without regard to their standards of governance—the political status quo looks more robust than ever. Most of Africa will likely be run by strongmen for the foreseeable future.

## The Populists

Among the world's rising regions, Latin America is the one that is most closely following the Western model of development. Central and South America have been steadily urbanizing and democratizing over the past half-century. Since the 1980s, liberal democracy has put down firm roots; as of 2010, Freedom House ranked ten of the region's nineteen countries as "free," eight as "partly free," and only one (Cuba) as "not free." Many of the region's longstanding rivalries have abated, and Mercosur, a South American trade bloc launched in 1991, has advanced economic integration among its members.

Nonetheless, Latin America has followed its own path of socioeconomic development and is forging its own version of modernity. The result is a left-wing populism that caters to an underclass long excluded from wealth and political power and that taps into the undercurrent of anti-American sentiment that has long animated the region's politics. This populism, although not that distant from a European brand of social democracy, leaves much of Latin America uneasy with the prospect of universalizing the Western order, opposed to the free-market ideology of the Washington Consensus, and predisposed to a geopolitical alignment that tilts toward the developing world more than the Atlantic democracies.

Latin America's version of modernity has its origins in the legacies of the colonial era. During Spanish and Portuguese rule, power was regularly concentrated in the hands of an omnipotent imperial governor—a tradition that, after independence, continued in the guise of the *caudillo*, a charismatic and authoritarian figure usually of military background. Europe's imperial powers also left behind gaping inequalities in wealth stemming largely from the concentration of land ownership in the hands of a select few. Social stratification was racial as well as economic, with immigrants from Europe dominating the indigenous Amerindians as well as the population of African origin initially brought to Latin America as slaves.

Imperial rule in much of Latin America came to an end in the early nineteenth century. A good number of the military commanders that led the fights against colonial rule then became the political leaders of the independent states that emerged, beginning a long tradition of direct military involvement in governance. During the early decades of independence, the armed forces that provided order served at the behest of the *caudillo*. In the late nineteenth century, most of the militaries in Latin America professionalized and modernized. But efforts to create an apolitical officer corps under civilian command were largely unsuccessful. Instead, Latin American militaries developed an ethos of loyalty to *la Patria*—the homeland—not to civilian leadership. Especially amid the economic downturns and political instability that arrived after World War II, military leaders cast themselves as guardians of the nation.[102] Coups and military regimes were widespread; every country in Latin America, with the exception of Mexico and Costa Rica, experienced a significant period of military rule between the 1950s and the 1980s. Campaigns against left-wing insurgencies and democratic activists led to the bouts of repression and abuse for which some of Latin America's militaries became infamous.

## Expedited Urbanization

On the socioeconomic front, halting attempts at modernization and industrialization began in the late nineteenth and early twentieth centuries. However, it was not until the second half of the twentieth century that most countries in the region embarked on systematic efforts to industrialize, urbanize, and democratize. The late start led to a rushed transition and a pattern of socioeconomic development that diverged from the Western experience. In 1900, seventy-five percent of Latin America's population was rural, and roughly the same proportion was illiterate.[103] Despite the rapid industrialization taking place in North America and Europe during the first half of the twentieth century, economic change came slowly to Latin America: in 1960, sixty percent of its population still worked the land. Thereafter, urbanization proceeded at a rapid pace. By 2007, over seventy-five percent of Latin America's population lived in urban areas.[104]

Expedited urbanization gave the cities of Latin America a very different political complexion than the urban areas that drove modernization in Europe. Cities in Europe tended to be magnets for entrepreneurs, merchants, and professionals who were intent on breaking away from autocratic institutions of power; the emerging middle class served as the engine of political change. In contrast, Latin America's urban populations, which consisted of a nascent middle class and a burgeoning working class, were captured by autocratic states well aware that socioeconomic development was bringing to an end the era of political dominion by the landed elite. Military dictators or civilian strongmen (many of whom worked closely with the military) effectively co-opted the bourgeoisie and the urban working class by trading economic favors for political obeisance.

The middle class won perks such as subsidies, protective tariffs on manufactured goods, construction contracts, and favorable tax codes. The working class, organized through unions and other labor associations affiliated with the state, reaped the benefits of social protection. During the early decades of urbanization, neither the bourgeoisie nor the working class pressed for democratization; both opted for economic gain rather than political liberalization. Landed elites accepted a similar bargain. They lost their traditional political sway, but in return staved off land reform and succeeded in retaining the bulk of their holdings. In contemporary Brazil, one percent of landholders still own some fifty percent of the country's rural property.[105] The principal social sectors absent from this political compact were the urban poor—laborers in the informal economy who were not members of a union—and the peasantry, which included many families of mixed race, black, and indigenous origin.

As a consequence of these class alignments, cities in Latin America, unlike their forerunners in Europe, began as conservative supporters of authoritarian rule, not agents of political change. This unusual mix of socioeconomic evolution and political stasis yielded a distinct ideological by-product: right-wing populism. The centralization of power in the hands of a charismatic leader tapped into traditions left behind by colonial rule and the *caudillo*. Nationalist ideology helped unite societies divided by class and race. Populist leaders pursued the nationalization of major industries to access the revenue needed to allocate resources to the working class—without raising taxes on the economic elite. State penetration of markets encouraged the corporatism and corruption that still plague many Latin American economies. And populism tapped into the undercurrent of anti-American sentiment arising from the long history of U.S. intervention in the region and the excesses of U.S. policy during the Cold War.[106] A combination of military rule and right-wing populism proved to be a compelling formula; at the end of the 1970s, fourteen of nineteen Latin American countries were still ruled by military regimes.[107]

## A Swing to the Left

In the 1980s, Latin America entered a period of democratization that relatively quickly brought military rule to an end. In most of the region, the transition to democracy and civilian rule was a largely ordered affair, with militaries willingly ceding control.[108] Military regimes chose to loosen their grip on power for a number of reasons. A combination of deteriorating economic conditions, discontent within the business community, and greater activism among civic groups eroded the military's confidence in its ability to sustain political stability. More moderate elements within the officer corps, particularly in Brazil, were concerned about the growing power of hardliners in the security apparatus. Moderates saw engagement with civil society as a way of strengthening their hand and preserving the professionalism of the officer corps. Finally, the international community—with the United States in the lead—was putting increasing pressure on Latin American regimes to end repression and authoritarian rule.[109]

Unlike in Europe, where an expanding middle class anchored the process of political liberalization, in Latin America democratization has proceeded while the working class and urban and rural poor still represent a substantial majority of the population. On average, Latin America's middle class represents roughly twenty percent of the population, meaning that democratization in the region has occurred absent the sizable bourgeoisie that shaped political liberalization in the West.[110] The result has been the political empowerment of an underclass long excluded from the economic bargains that authoritarian regimes struck with the business community and unionized workers. As a consequence, the political center of gravity in Latin America has swung decidedly to the left. The pro-market policies favored by the economic elite have not been abandoned, but they are now complemented by efforts to advance social welfare and address the needs of the poor.

The wave of democratization that has swept across Latin America since the 1980s has thus transformed its political landscape, causing a dramatic swing from right-wing to left-wing populism. Among the region's nineteen countries, fifteen were as of 2010 governed by center-left or left-wing governments; the only exceptions were Colombia, Honduras, Mexico, and Panama. This pull to the left resulting from the mobilization and growing electoral power of the poor has led to the proliferation of ambitious programs to alleviate poverty. A leader on this front was Brazil's president, Luiz Inácio Lula da Silva, a union organizer turned politician. Lula introduced *Bolsa Familia*, a program of direct cash payments to poor families, conditioned on their children's attendance at school and participation in vaccination programs. During Lula's first term in office, the poverty rate in Brazil fell by over twenty-five percent. Although its governments have been tilting to the right, Mexico administers a similar program, called *Oportunidades*, which reaches over one-quarter of the country's population.[111]

The expansion of social welfare from the organized working class to the poor has been accompanied by the continuation, if not the intensification, of populism. Even though Brazil and many other countries in the region have succeeded in reducing poverty, some forty percent of Latin America's population still lives below the poverty line, and the region's income inequality remains the world's highest. Widespread poverty and inequality profoundly affect public attitudes. More than two-thirds of Latin Americans believe that their countries are governed for the benefit of a powerful minority rather than the general good. Democratization has been accompanied by disillusion about the persistence of inequality and of a political system skewed to serve the interests of the wealthy few.[112] A recent Latino barometer poll revealed that roughly half of Latin Americans would accept a non-democratic government as long as it improved economic conditions.[113] Such discontent has encouraged leaders to embrace a left-wing populism that targets social injustice and economic and political inequities.

Adding to the populist flavor of politics is the fact that many Latin American countries have electoral systems that combine presidential and parliamentary rule—a recipe for gridlock. Most legislatures in the region are elected through proportional representation, meaning that presidents often lack ruling majorities. In Brazil's 2002 election, for example, nineteen parties won seats in the parliament and Lula's Worker's Party accounted for only eighteen percent of legislators. A 2005 study of recent elections in eighteen Latin American countries found that the president's party on average enjoyed lower-house majorities in only one in six elections. Political fragmentation, clashes between the executive and legislative branches, and prolonged bouts of stalemate encourage leaders to rely on populist appeal to circumvent gridlock.[114]

A further source of left-wing populism is the continuing political marginalization of minorities, for whom calls for income redistribution and social justice have particular electoral appeal. Although democratization and wealth redistribution have elevated the voice and living standards of blacks and indigenous groups, they remain underrepresented in governing institutions; the racial hierarchy of the colonial era has left a lasting imprint. In a recent session of Brazil's lower house of parliament, for example, only fifteen of 513 members were black even though black and *pardo* (brown) citizens represent about forty-four percent of the population. In a recent Guatemalan congress, Mayan Indians, who represent over sixty percent of the population, accounted for only fourteen of 133 legislators.[115]

The mobilization of underrepresented groups has, in some instances, led to a radical brand of left-wing populism, personified by Venezuelan president Hugo Chavez. After his election in 2002, Chavez, a Venezuelan of mixed European, African, and indigenous descent, became a champion of the country's underclass. He resorted to "resource nationalism" to take on Venezuela's own elite as well as foreign multinationals, asserting state control over the oil industry and other sectors. Chavez effectively toppled Venezuela's political class by garnering support among less advantaged sectors of the electorate through a mix of wealth redistribution, anti-American rhetoric, and suppression of dissent. Evo Morales in Bolivia, Rafael Correa in Ecuador, Daniel Ortega in Nicaragua, Ollanta Humala in Peru—although these leaders embraced milder versions of Chavez's populism, all followed in his footsteps and rode to power by appealing to the poor through promises of wealth redistribution and social justice.

Chavez's hard-edged brand of socialist-style populism is the exception, not the rule. It has generally prevailed in countries with fragmented and polarized party systems; stalemate among traditional political elites provides an opening for more radical populists.[116] It is also more likely in countries rich in natural resources—oil and minerals—in which nationalization promises to provide governments sizable revenues.[117] Filling state coffers through nationalized industries, according to the likes of Chavez and Morales, is needed to advance the cause of social justice.

Throughout most of Latin America, where more stable party systems have led to compromise between the middle-class establishment and political movements arising from the mobilization of the poor, left-wing populism has taken milder forms. Lula's electoral success depended in large part on his appeal to Brazil's underclass. But he defended private capital, macroeconomic stability, and open markets—key ingredients of the country's impressive economic growth. His successor, Dilma Rousseff, has relied on the same basic formula. On foreign policy, Lula avoided Chavez's taunting anti-American rants, but nonetheless kept his distance from the United States and generally aligned Brazil with the BRICs, not with the West. His friendliness toward Iran and his staunch support for Palestinian statehood were consistent irritants in his relationship with Washington.

There are exceptions to this swing to the left, Mexico among them. In 2000, the National Action Party (PAN) broke the seventy-year lock of the Institutional Revolutionary Party (PRI) on the Mexican presidency. PAN was able to do so in part by promising market-oriented reforms to the country's growing middle class, of particular appeal to the northern regions of the country that have benefited most from globalization and free trade. President Vincente Fox, a former executive of Coca-Cola, represented the new turn in Mexican politics.[118] PAN succeeded in retaining power in the 2006 elections, but the center-right's political margin was paper-thin; Felipe Calderón, Fox's successor, defeated López Obrador by less than 0.5 percent of the vote. Obrador drew much of his support from the rural poor and ethnic minorities in the south and center of the country. Had Obrador prevailed, he would have orchestrated a dramatic shift to the populist left to cater to his electoral base.

As Latin America continues to develop economically, its political mainstream is likely to remain under the sway of left-wing populism. Due to income inequality and the political marginalization of indigenous groups, the hard left will have a steady constituency. But Chavez's brand of socialist-style populism has its limits, as made clear by the plunging fortunes of the Venezuelan economy. The need for foreign capital and the allure of foreign markets is poised to make Lula's more moderate brand of left-wing populism the standard bearer. A Brasilia Consensus, not a Caracas Consensus, is likely to carry the day.

Over the coming decades, Latin America, more than any other region of the world, will likely follow a path not that divergent from the Western model of development. After all, the region is today populated primarily by countries that are, for the most part, democratic and capitalist. But due to a long history of autocracy, income inequality, racial hierarchy, and anti-Americanism, Latin America will be dominated by a unique brand of left-wing populism that represents a break with the Western model.

Democratization in Latin America has brought an impoverished underclass into the political arena well before the consolidation of a broad middle class. The wealth and power of the region's traditional political and economic elite as well as the market disciplines imposed by globalization will, with some exceptions, provide a check against ideological extremes of the sort embraced by Chavez. But an entrenched left-wing populism will captivate Latin America's politics as this century unfolds, setting the region apart from the West amid the emerging debate about the terms of the next world.

## Democracies with Attitude

Robert Kagan recently wrote that, "In today's world, a nation's form of government, not its 'civilization' or its geographical location, may be the best predictor of its geopolitical alignment."[119] Kagan is not alone in holding this view. In the run-up to the 2008 election in the United States, Democrats and Republicans alike touted the benefits of a League of Democracies—a global directorate of democratic states whose like-mindedness would supposedly enable them to forge a durable consensus on how best to address most international challenges.[120] This conviction that the world's democracies will naturally align with each other bolsters confidence that the Western approach to international order will endure even as the Euro-Atlantic zone loses its preponderance of wealth and military strength. It is widely presumed, for example, that India will ally with the United States as it climbs the ranks of the great powers. During his visit to the country in November 2010, President Obama lauded India as "the world's largest democracy," and declared that "the relationship between the United States and India—bound by our shared interests and our shared values—will be one of the defining partnerships of the twenty-first century."[121]

It is illusory, however, to presume that a country's form of government will be such an important determinant of its geopolitical alignment; democracies are simply not destined to ally with each other as a matter of course. On the contrary, democratic countries not infrequently go their separate ways on matters of statecraft. Consider India's relationship with the United States. India has been a democracy since it became independent in 1947, but it spent most of the Cold War aligned with the Soviet Union. To be sure, times have changed, and India and the United States have for the better part of a decade been building closer strategic and economic ties.

But the convergence is primarily a function of a shared interest in checking the power of China. Balancing against China's rise was the primary motive behind George W. Bush's readiness to sign a deal with India on nuclear cooperation—as well as Obama's subsequent endorsement of India's bid to join the UN Security Council as a permanent member.

Hedging against the rise of China is not the sole driving force behind a new strategic relationship between India and the United States; as Obama made clear during his visit in 2010, the United States sees India as an attractive suitor in part because it is a democracy. But a close look at the key foreign policy issues on the U.S.-India agenda suggests that their shared commitment to democratic governance is hardly a guarantor of common geopolitical interest.

Pakistan is India's archenemy; the two countries have fought three wars since they became independent states, and both keep their forces at the ready for another round. Nonetheless, the United States has been giving Pakistan billions of dollars in military and economic assistance in order to facilitate its help in fighting Islamic militants operating in the borderlands between Afghanistan and Pakistan. Moreover, in order to speed the eventual withdrawal of U.S. forces from Afghanistan, Washington has been working to cut a political deal with the Afghan Taliban (which is quietly in alliance with Pakistan), a move that enhances Islamabad's influence in Afghanistan—an outcome anathema to India. When it comes to Iran, America's archenemy, the tables are turned. In its effort to curb Iran's nuclear program, the United States has long sought to isolate Iran. But New Delhi has consistently balked at cutting off commercial and political links with Tehran. The United States and India have been similarly far apart on climate change and the global trade agenda. On all of these issues, differing national interests have overwhelmed whatever affinity arises from a shared commitment to democracy.

India's socioeconomic landscape and its place in the international pecking order also weigh at least as heavily as its democratic institutions in shaping the country's international alignments. A New Delhi consensus on matters of domestic and international governance, although still evolving, is closer to a Brazilian conception

than an American one. India's social stratification, ethnic and linguistic diversity, income inequities, and vast rural poor will ensure
a leftist brand of populism long into the future.

India has traditionally cast itself as a leader of the nonaligned
movement—a grouping of mostly developing countries that has
sought to resist the alliance networks shaped by the great powers.
New Delhi has also been reluctant to embrace the U.S.-led agenda
of democratization and the sanctioning of repressive regimes;
Indians tend to see such policies as unwelcome bouts of intervention by the leading powers. On trade, India often lines up with
other developing countries. In the UN General Assembly, India
over the past decade voted with the United States only about
twenty-five percent of the time—a good indicator of its mind-set
on many international issues, and another sign that its interests
and status as an emerging power are more important determi-
nants of its foreign policy than its democratic institutions.[122] As
a further indication of its alignment with rising powers, India's
prime minister, Manmohan Singh, recently called for "new global
'rules of the game'" and the "reform and revitalization" of international institutions.[123]

The same argument applies to many other emerging countries
that are democratic. Brazil has been a stable democracy since the
1980s, but it regularly differs with the United States on developments in Latin America (recently, over the U.S. military presence
in Colombia and the international response to the 2009 "coup" in
Honduras) and in the Middle East (Iran and the Palestine-Israel
conflict). Like many other leaders in the region, President Lula was
particularly sensitive to what he saw as the excesses of American
power. He practiced democracy at home and supported its spread
elsewhere. But as he stated in his inaugural address in 2003, equally
important was "the democratization of international relations,
without hegemony of any kind."[124] As discussed above, Brazil's
socioeconomic composition, like that of many democracies in Latin
America, puts it on a populist trajectory that militates against regularly following the West's lead.

Elsewhere, religion is combining with geopolitics to push emerging democracies toward foreign policies that diverge with Western

interests. Turkey has become more democratic as the ruling AKP Party has cut back the political sway of the military and the traditional economic elite. The result has been a clean break with Ankara's long tradition of orienting its foreign policy toward Europe and the United States. Turkey opposed the U.S. invasion of Iraq in 2003 and denied U.S. forces access to Iraq through Turkish territory. In 2010, Turkey canceled its regular military exercises with Israel, and instead carried out land and air maneuvers with China—the first time a NATO member had engaged in exercises with the Chinese military. The following year, Ankara expelled Israel's ambassador amid a dispute stemming from the fatal confrontation between Israeli forces and a naval flotilla that tried to breach the blockade of Gaza in May 2010. Indonesia now enjoys democratic rule after decades of repressive autocracy. But the role of Islam in its politics will induce Jakarta to keep Washington at arm's length, and geopolitical considerations will compel Indonesia to balance carefully between the United States and China.

Contrary to Kagan, a nation's geographical location and strategic interests, its socioeconomic makeup, its place in the international hierarchy, and, particularly in the Muslim world, its religious orientation, are at least as important in shaping its foreign policy as its form of government.

## A Global Dissensus

In a globalized economy, companies rise and fall on the basis of the quality and price of the products they offer. Firms at the top of the pecking order lose out when competitors find better technologies and business models. A Darwinian logic—the survival of the fittest—determines which companies rule the roost.

When it comes to geopolitics, the "business models" offered by major powers are only one factor shaping the pecking order. To be sure, certain political orders outperform others and spread through the appeal of success; a type of Darwinian logic does apply. Indeed, had socialist economies done better than capitalist ones during the twentieth century, socialism might well have emerged as the victor of the main ideological contest of the industrial era.

But just because capitalism has prevailed against socialism does not mean that the world is heading toward a homogeneous endpoint. For the foreseeable future, China's brand of authoritarian capitalism may well outperform—or at least hold its own against—the democratic alternative. Strongmen in Africa are hardly producing impressive results on the economic front—but they will decisively shape the politics of the continent for decades to come. The same goes for populists in Latin America and theocrats in the Middle East.

The bottom line is that states around the world are on very different political trajectories. The divergence is a function of profound variation on many dimensions, including political culture, path of socioeconomic development, and religion. Even among states that share a commitment to liberal democracy, competing interests and jockeying for position and status will stand in the way of international consensus. The next world will not march to the Washington Consensus, the Beijing Consensus, or the Brasilia Consensus. It will march to no consensus. Rather, the world is headed toward a global dissensus.

# 6 :: Reviving the West

The rise of the Western world—and its eventual domination of the international system—was a product of teamwork between North America and Europe. Western nations were at the leading edge of history, clearing the way for liberal democracy, industrial capitalism, and secular nationalism. Twice during the twentieth century, the Atlantic democracies allied with each other to defeat challenges to their security and values. And although the United States took the lead in shaping the international order that emerged after World War II, it would not have succeeded without the steady help of its European allies.

The globe's center of gravity may be shifting away from the Atlantic democracies, but they can nonetheless have considerable say as a post-Western order takes shape. If the West is to help guide the transition to multipolarity, however, it will have to rise to the occasion on two fronts. It will have to recover its political and economic vitality and retain its cohesion even as its era of primacy gradually comes to an end. And it must embrace a strategy and set of principles that succeed in forging a consensus between the West and the rising rest. Reviving the West is the subject of this chapter. Arriving at a consensual strategy for managing the transition to a post-Western world is the subject of the next.

## The Cohesion of the West

According to historical precedent, the end of the Cold War should have precipitated the dissolution of the Western alliance. After all, alliances tend to come apart when the threat that brought them into being disappears. But the Atlantic alliance proved to be an exception. Rather than closing shop, both NATO and the European Union took advantage of the collapse of the Soviet Union to expand eastward. Central Europe was successfully integrated into the West. As Yugoslavia came apart during the 1990s, NATO stepped in to stop the bloodshed and bring peace to the Balkans—albeit with a reluctant slowness that cost many lives. The United States and Europe also worked together on the economic front, enjoying a decade of robust growth and successfully containing the 1997–1998 financial crisis that hit emerging economies. The cohesion of the West during the 1990s suggested not a fraying alliance born of convenience, but a deeper community based on a common political logic and a shared sense of purpose.[1]

The first post–Cold War decade instilled optimism about the durability of the West, but the presidency of George W. Bush had the opposite effect. Bush backed away from the tradition of U.S. multilateralism to which Europe had grown accustomed. He withdrew from the Anti-Ballistic Missile Treaty and made clear his opposition to U.S. participation in the Kyoto Protocol on climate change, the International Criminal Court, and the Comprehensive Test Ban Treaty. After Bush had been in office only two months, a British journalist based in Washington expressed views that typified European attitudes toward his administration: "From here, the main voices in Washington seem to be working their way toward a host of fresh assessments: abrasive toward old enemies, mistrustful of internationalist compromise, America First when it comes to global threats, admonitory toward allies."[2]

The terrorist attacks of September 11, 2001, led to an initial outpouring of European solidarity with the United States and unanimous support within NATO for the U.S. invasion of Afghanistan and its offensive against the Taliban and Al-Qaeda. But Bush then decided to continue the "war on terror" by invading Iraq, a move that caused a deep rift among the Atlantic democracies. Britain, Spain, Italy, Poland, and a handful of other European countries supported the effort to topple Saddam Hussein and sent troops to help with the occupation of Iraq. France and Germany, however, led a coalition that opposed the war and mounted a successful effort to deny Washington UN approval of the invasion. This break over fundamental matters of war and peace called into question the integrity of the Atlantic partnership.[3]

Initially, many Europeans welcomed this crossroads; they longed to emerge from the shadow of U.S. power. And the Bush administration did not bemoan the rift, confident that the United States enjoyed the material superiority to act as it saw fit. Washington believed that allies should follow the leader—or get out of the way. On both sides of the Atlantic, however, minds readily changed; Europeans and Americans alike soon came to regret the consequences of a divided West. Europe found itself in disarray; the prospect of life without the American guardian was more unsettling than initially presumed. And the United States found itself in deep trouble in both Afghanistan and Iraq, making clear to Washington that it could not run the world on its own. The Bush administration was suddenly in search of help on all fronts—and Europe was the best place to turn for that help.

Soon after his second inauguration, Bush flew to Brussels to repair relations with Europe and to reaffirm America's commitment to NATO. His administration began consulting European allies far more regularly than during the first term. European governments welcomed the outreach and reciprocated with their own gestures of goodwill. Bush remained an unpopular figure in Europe, but transatlantic solidarity was on the mend. The repair of relations was a testament to the resilience of the bond. Even amid the rift over Iraq and discord over a host of other issues, the Atlantic democracies were drawn back to their partnership by the recognition that they remained each others' best partners.

The election of Barack Obama then consolidated the repair of Atlantic relations. Obama's charisma and multicultural background earned him extraordinary popularity in Europe. He restored to U.S. foreign policy the multilateral traditions favored by Europeans.

And his campaign pledges to fight global warming, abolish nuclear weapons, and close the controversial prison in Guantanamo were warmly greeted across Europe. To be sure, Obama proved unable to deliver on some of his promises, and Washington's preoccupation with the Middle East and East Asia engendered feelings of disappointment and neglect across Europe. But, on balance, Obama succeeded in restoring Europe's confidence in the appeal and reliability of its American partner.

The Obama administration's take on the transatlantic link, like the Bush administration's, went through ups and downs. Washington initially expected Europe to demonstrate its revived enthusiasm for partnership with America by shouldering additional burdens, particularly in Afghanistan. Obama was then frustrated by Europe's unwillingness to do more in Afghanistan, its embrace of economic austerity when Washington was calling for more fiscal stimulus, and an EU that seemed to be spending more time sorting out quarrels among its member states than addressing global challenges. Well aware of Washington's impatience, Europeans worried that Obama might forsake the Atlantic link in favor of a "G-2"—a global condominium between the United States and China.

Such anxieties, however, readily proved unfounded. From Washington's perspective, the prospect of a new Sino-American partnership was snuffed out by Beijing's stubborn protection of its undervalued currency, its embrace of a regional muscularity that rattled China's neighbors, and its unwillingness to confront North Korea's military provocations. Obama also faced domestic pressure—in no small part arising from job losses and slow growth at home—to get tough with China. Washington was simultaneously struggling to smooth out relations with other potential partners, Russia and Turkey among them. Facing an uphill battle on these fronts as well, Obama came to realize, just as George W. Bush did, that Europe remained America's best partner. As Obama explained in a *New York Times* op-ed in advance of the 2010 NATO Summit in Lisbon, "our relationship with our European allies and partners is the cornerstone of our engagement with the world, and a catalyst for global cooperation. With no other region does the United States have such a close alignment of values, interests, capabilities and goals."[4] In May 2011, Obama spent a full week in Europe, primarily to stress the enduring value of the transatlantic link. And he followed Europe's lead on the intervention in Libya, an operation that, despite its unexpected length, confirmed the solidity and efficacy of transatlantic partnership.

The revival of the transatlantic link is good news; the world needs a cohesive West as it navigates the global turn. If the Atlantic democracies hang together, they have a far better chance of anchoring the transition to multipolarity and ensuring that it occurs by design rather than default. Both sides of the Atlantic are certainly aware that a shift in the global balance of power is under way and understand the attendant geopolitical challenges. According to the U.S. National Security Strategy released in May 2010, the United States is "working to build deeper and more effective partnerships with other key centers of influence—including China, India, and Russia, as well as increasingly influential nations such as Brazil, South Africa, and Indonesia.... International institutions must more effectively represent the world of the 21st century, with a broader voice—and greater responsibilities—for emerging powers."[5]

Europe is on the same page. Soon after becoming Europe's foreign policy czar, Catherine Ashton laid out a similar perspective:

> I intend to invest a lot in strengthening partnerships across the world: China, India, South Africa, Brazil, Mexico, and Indonesia. For too long we have seen these countries mainly through an economic prism. But it is clear that they are major political and security players too, with increasing political clout. Our mental map has to adjust—and fast. My sense is that the European response should be more generous—in making space at the top tables of global politics. Early on, when strategies are formed, not just when resources are needed for implementation.[6]

The United States and the EU thus appreciate that the West must make room for rising powers—precisely why they teamed up to expand the G-8 into the G-20. Transatlantic differences will surely emerge over the details of how best to accommodate the newcomers; giving up primacy is never an easy task. But the West is headed in the right direction; it is well aware that the transition to multipolarity has commenced and it has begun to adjust its collective diplomacy accordingly.

## The (Un)Governability of the West

Although the Western democracies appreciate the need to anchor the coming transition in global power, it is very much open to question whether the United States and Europe, individually and collectively, will be up to the task. At the same time that rising powers like China, Turkey, and Brazil have a new spring in their step, the industrialized democracies have headed in the opposite direction. The West has entered a prolonged period of sluggish economic growth, political polarization, and self-doubt. Accordingly, even though they have the opportunity to anchor the global turn, it is unclear that the Atlantic democracies will have the wherewithal to do so.

In Europe, the crisis of governability is manifesting itself through the renationalization of politics. The project of European integration has begun to falter just at the moment that the collective will and capability of the European Union are needed to help guide global change. If this reversal continues and the EU's individual nations ultimately fail to aggregate their voices and resources, they risk becoming geopolitically irrelevant. In the United States, the crisis of governability is taking a different form: a partisan polarization so intense that it produces ineffectual policy and, not infrequently, political paralysis. The absence of consensus, coupled with partisan animosity, has prevented progress on important domestic priorities, such as controlling the deficit and reforming immigration policy. Bipartisanship on foreign policy has been equally hard to come by, hampering America's ability to provide steady leadership at a time of global uncertainty.

It is no accident that both sides of the Atlantic are simultaneously experiencing significant problems of governance. The same goes for Japan, which has of late been saddled with one ineffective and unpopular prime minister after another. Globalization is weakening state capacity at the same time that it confronts electorates with new challenges that they look to their governments to address.

The resulting gap between the demand for good governance and its short supply alienates voters and leaves governments only more ineffectual and vulnerable.

A vicious cycle of sorts has emerged. In a globalized world, open and liberal democracies do not have as much control over their destinies as they used to. Immigration, flows of capital, goods, and services, the information revolution, social movements and networks, international terrorism, global warming—states need to be fleet-footed and adaptive to manage effectively these and other transnational issues. But these transnational forces also challenge state capacity by penetrating borders and rooting around the normal levers of control that governments have at their disposal. Moreover, globalization in its various guises is also sapping the West of the political will needed to adjust policy; the economic dislocation it has spawned is fostering popular discontent across the industrialized democracies, in turn producing weak governments. Globalization is increasing disaffection by widening the gap between winners and losers. Outsourcing, immigration, and the threat of terrorism are causing further disquiet among democratic electorates. Global markets and global threats require policy adaptation, but at the same time they foster populist reactions that undermine the ability of governments to respond appropriately. Sluggish and ineffective responses only intensify popular discontent, fueling the vicious cycle that has been stoking the renationalization of politics across Europe and the polarization of politics across America.

## The Renationalization of Europe

In the bitter years after World War II, Europeans embarked on efforts to inoculate themselves against future war.[7] Political and economic integration was to stitch together Europe's nation-states in order to end rivalries between them and leave behind centuries of bloodshed. The project of integration was formally launched in 1951, when the European Coal and Steel Community brought under collective control the coal and steel production of Germany, France, Italy, Belgium, the Netherlands, and Luxembourg. In the decades that followed, Europe expanded its membership from six to over two dozen, and it progressively deepened its union. Plans for a single market went into effect in 1987, and a single currency—the euro— began circulating in 2002. Next, the EU embarked on efforts to adopt the Constitutional Treaty, which was to consolidate the union's legal and political character and provide for more centralized decision making on matters of foreign and security policy. Many European leaders portrayed the move as a turning point, comparing it to the U.S. Constitutional Convention, which took place in 1787 and fashioned the legal and political foundation of the federation that would come into being in 1789 upon the Constitution's ratification.

The attempt to adopt the European Constitutional Treaty was indeed a turning point—but not in the way that its supporters intended. When faced with the prospect of passing more power from national capitals to EU institutions in Brussels, Europe's citizens balked. Amid the process of ratification, French voters rejected the treaty in a referendum in May 2005. Dutch voters followed suit in June. The EU thereafter abandoned the effort to ratify its would-be constitution, instead drafting a dramatically scaled-down version known as the Lisbon Treaty. Because the streamlined version amended rather than replaced existing treaties, it required parliamentary ratification, not popular approval. The only exception was Ireland, whose laws required a public referendum. The Irish proceeded to reject the Lisbon Treaty in 2008. They changed their minds the following year, but only after ensuring that the treaty would not jeopardize national control of taxation and military neutrality.

After entering into force on December 1, 2009, the Lisbon Treaty endowed the EU with a new presidential post, a foreign policy czar, and its own diplomatic service. Nonetheless, the discomfort of member states with a more centralized union became readily apparent when they selected Herman Van Rompuy as the EU's president and Catherine Ashton as its foreign policy chief. Both were low-profile individuals who would not threaten the authority of national leaders. The ratification of the Lisbon Treaty was a long-awaited success for the EU. But it took place amid clear signs that the union's constituent nations were having second thoughts about further diluting their sovereignty in favor of collective governance.

The problem is that Europe's institutions and its politics are on divergent paths; its institutions are getting more European and its politics more national. As a consequence of the Lisbon Treaty, the member states are to give Brussels more say over foreign policy. In response to the euro-zone crisis, the EU has deepened fiscal and financial integration. All the while, however, politics in the European street is heading in the opposite direction—away from Brussels and back to the nation-state—risking that Europe's more powerful institutions prove hollow and lack popular legitimacy.

Popular pushback against the EU has been taking many forms. Right-wing populism is on the upswing across Europe. It is the product primarily of a backlash against immigration (particularly of Muslims), not against European integration. Nevertheless, this hard-edged nationalism targets not only minorities but also the compromise of sovereignty that comes with political union. 2010 was a banner year for the far right. Hungary's Jobbik Party, which borders on xenophobic, won forty-seven seats—up from zero in 2006. In elections in Sweden, the anti-immigrant Swedish Democrats won twenty seats in the parliament—the party's first entry into the legislature since its founding in 1988. Even in the historically tolerant Netherlands, the far-right Party of Freedom recently won over fifteen percent of the vote, giving it only seven fewer seats than the leading party. Finland joined the club in the spring of 2011, when the populist True Finns won almost twenty percent of the vote.

In countries in which the far right has fared less well, political trends have nonetheless not augured well for the EU. British voters in 2010 brought to power a coalition dominated by the Conservative Party, which is well known for its antipathy toward the EU. And in Belgium, which held the EU's rotating presidency during the second half of 2010, elections failed to produce a new government; the country was effectively paralyzed by the divide between Dutch-speaking Flemish citizens and French-speaking Walloons. It speaks volumes that the country tasked with guiding the European project during such a critical period in the union's evolution suffered exactly the kind of nationalist antagonism that the EU was created to eradicate.

Germany has long been the engine behind European integration, driven by its obsession with banishing the national rivalries in which it was a prominent participant. But even Germany's enthusiasm for the EU has been fast dissipating. A poll conducted in the spring of 2009 found that seventy-four percent of Germans think that the EU "takes too many powers from Germany."[8] The same year the German Constitutional Court issued a ruling strengthening the sway of the national parliament over EU legislation. As the influential weekly *Der Spiegel* commented, the ruling "threatens future steps toward European integration."[9]

Germany's shifting attitudes toward the EU have been amply manifested in its policies. Berlin no longer sees the need to stay in lockstep with Paris, weakening Europe's Franco-German anchor. German Chancellor Angela Merkel and French President Nicolas Sarkozy have not mixed well on a personal level, and have parted company on many issues, including how to deal with the economic crisis within the euro-zone.[10] When Greece in 2010 was on the verge of a financial meltdown, Berlin was initially reluctant to come to the rescue, irking Paris as well as Athens. Merkel procrastinated for months, constituting a breach of the spirit of common welfare that is the hallmark of a collective Europe. Only after the Greek crisis threatened to engulf the euro-zone did Merkel override strong popular opposition and approve a bailout. Voters in local elections in North Rhine-Westphalia promptly punished her decision; the Christian Democrats suffered their most severe defeat in the postwar era. Merkel then spent much of 2011 caught between domestic opposition to further bailouts and the urgent need for Germany to devote resources and leadership to shoring up the euro-zone.

Germany's readiness to break with Britain and France on the 2011 military intervention in Libya was particularly striking. Berlin abstained on the authorizing vote in the UN Security Council, aligning with the BRICs rather than its EU partners. Merkel's decision to do so was no doubt motivated primarily by domestic considerations. Her governing coalition had been losing electoral support of late, and Merkel calculated—incorrectly, it turned out—that she could reverse her slide by embracing an anti-war stance. It is revealing that Merkel's preferred domestic strategy entailed setting Berlin against the European mainstream.

Katinka Bayrsch, an astute observer of Germany, sums up these changes as follows:

> In the aftermath of the [financial] crisis, a new EU reality has emerged; the dynamics that pushed the European project forward over the past sixty years can no longer be relied on to drive future integration. The crisis has brought to light, and accelerated, a number of trends already visible in recent years: decision-making power is shifting from Brussels to the national capitals of EU member countries...and the alliance between France and Germany—long the motor of European integration—is weakening. Underlying and exaggerating these changes is Germany's growing euro-skepticism....It is difficult to see how the EU could make progress on anything...with a reluctant, grumpy and inward-looking Germany at its heart.[11]

## The Causes and Consequences of Europe's Renationalization

A confluence of different developments—a perfect storm of sorts— has been driving this striking renationalization of European politics. Global competition, the financial downturn, and the euro-zone crisis have intensified economic insecurity and fostered political divisions within the EU. The EU's larger and more prosperous members resent having to bail out their weaker neighbors. In return, the recipients of the largess resent the austerity that has accompanied financial assistance. Meanwhile, globalization is threatening Europe's comfortable welfare state. To contain debt and become more competitive, member states are increasing retirement ages and cutting benefits. Although European integration in many respects enhances economic performance, the EU often gets blamed for economic hardship. In France, for example, anti-Europe campaigns have targeted the EU's "Anglo-Saxon" assault on social welfare and the "Polish plumber" who takes jobs from Frenchmen due to the EU's open labor market.

The lack of progress in integrating Muslim immigrants into the social mainstream has intensified discomfort over labor mobility and open borders. Social tension between majority populations and Muslim minorities has fueled far-right parties that, as mentioned, target not only immigration but also the EU. With many EU member states facing demographic decline and insolvent pension systems in the years ahead, they can ill afford to shun immigrants from North Africa, Turkey, and the Middle East, where youthful populations will provide generous labor pools. Nonetheless, the transition toward more social diversity is proving uniquely controversial across Europe, stoking nationalist sentiment that then undercuts support for the EU.

Generational change is similarly eroding popular enthusiasm for European integration. Europeans who came of age during World War II or the Cold War assign the EU sacred status; it is the vehicle through which Europe has escaped its bloody past. But younger Europeans have no past from which they seek escape. According to a recent poll, French citizens over fifty-five are twice as likely to see the EU as a guarantor of peace as those under thirty-six.[12] And Germany, as Bayrsch notes, "is now run by a group of leaders with no living memory of the horrors of World War II.... Today, many Germans think they have paid their historical dues."[13] Whereas their predecessors viewed the European project as an article of faith, current European leaders tend to assess the value of the EU through a cold calculation of costs and benefits. European integration simply does not animate national politics as it used to.

The EU's rapid enlargement to the east and south is also taking a toll on its political vitality. Absent the familiarity of the smaller union that existed before the Berlin Wall fell, the EU's original members in Western Europe have turned inward. And the new members from Central Europe, who have enjoyed meaningful sovereignty only since the collapse of the Soviet bloc, are reluctant to give it away again—even to consensual institutions in Brussels rather than autocratic ones in Moscow. As Poland's late president Lech Kaczynski stated soon after taking office in 2005, "What interests the Poles is the future of Poland and not that of the EU."[14]

Apathy toward the EU also stems from a lack of popular enthusiasm for a more onerous European role in global affairs. Many European nations sat out the war in Iraq, and most of those that participated withdrew their troops by 2009. The war in Afghanistan initially enjoyed more public support, but the enthusiasm was short-lived. A poll conducted in the spring of 2010 indicated that almost two-thirds of the German public opposed the presence of German troops in Afghanistan.[15] Although the German government bucked public opinion, the Dutch did not; the Netherlands was the first NATO member to quit Afghanistan, withdrawing its troops during the summer of 2010. Against this backdrop, most EU nations chose to sit out NATO's intervention in Libya in 2011.

Such widespread aversion to a more ambitious and expansive foreign policy rests uneasily with the Lisbon Treaty, which is intended in part to raise the EU's geopolitical profile. But this objective, at least for now, enjoys scant popular support; wars in remote lands, coupled with plunging defense expenditures due to fiscal austerity, are curbing Europe's enthusiasm for greater geopolitical responsibility. After all, member states have never shown much appetite for a union-wide security policy, instead jealously protecting their sovereignty on matters of defense.

The likely consequences of Europe's renationalization are far from calamitous. With its nations having left behind geopolitical rivalry, Europe is hardly headed back to armed conflict. Nonetheless, absent a dramatic turnaround, European politics is poised to become less European and more national, undercutting the EU's ability to help manage the global turn. The more time and energy EU member states spend haggling with each other, the less time and energy they will devote to tasks farther afield. Moreover, Europe's individual states are not sizable enough to make their presence felt on the global stage. The EU's largest member—Germany—has a population of roughly eighty million, compared with 1.4 billion in China. Only if EU members aggregate their wealth and military capability will they be able to help anchor the coming transition in global power. In a world that sorely needs the EU's collective will, a divided and introverted Europe would constitute a historical setback.

So too would the United States be bereft of the partner that it needs and wants. The vitality of the transatlantic link depends upon Europe's ability to recover its equanimity, deepen its collective character, and shoulder greater international burdens. Former Secretary of Defense Robert Gates bluntly stated as much in February 2010: "The demilitarization of Europe—where large swaths of the general public and political class are averse to military force and the risks that go with it—has gone from a blessing in the 20th century to an impediment to achieving real security and lasting peace in the 21st."[16] During NATO's Libya campaign, Gates was even more forthright, suggesting that the alliance's future could be "dim, if not dismal" and venturing that "future U.S. political leaders . . . may not consider the return on America's investment in NATO worth the cost."[17]

As they seek to adjust the international system to the rise of emerging powers, Americans will look to Europe for help and support. If Europe continues to fall well short of these expectations, the transatlantic link will pay a considerable price. Indeed, Europe could slip off America's geopolitical radar screen. As the United States tries to reduce its debt and the burden on its armed forces, it will weigh the value of its allies by their concrete contributions to collective efforts. In the case of Europe, the offering could be increasingly paltry—unless the EU recovers its political momentum.

## The Polarization of the United States

Bipartisanship in the United States has fallen off a cliff.[18] Not only has partisan confrontation been rising, but it has also been spreading from domestic issues to foreign policy. During the Cold War, elected officials regularly cordoned off national security from partisan gamesmanship. As Republican Senator Arthur Vandenberg famously put it in 1950, "'bipartisan foreign policy' means a mutual effort, under our indispensable two-party system, to unite our official voice at water's edge."[19] Such political discipline has come to a definitive end. Bipartisan cooperation on foreign policy dropped sharply during the 1990s as a consequence of both the end of the Cold War and the confrontation between President Bill Clinton and a Congress that was controlled by the Republicans after the midterm elections in 1994. A brief hiatus followed the terrorist attacks of September 11, 2001, but partisan conflict then proceeded to intensify during the balance of the Bush presidency. By the end of Bush's second term, bipartisan voting on foreign policy had plunged to levels not experienced since internationalists and isolationists faced off during the 1930s.[20]

Senator Barack Obama's appeal as a presidential candidate stemmed in part from his pledge to restore bipartisan civility to U.S. politics. As Obama insisted in his victory speech in November 2008, "we have never been just a collection of individuals or a collection of red states and blue states; we are and always will be the United States of America."[21] Even before taking office, he courted congressional Republicans as well as George Will, David Brooks, and other conservative commentators. Obama believed that if he reached across the aisle in a spirit of respect and compromise, Republicans would reciprocate.

Obama soon found otherwise. As he stated toward the end of his first year in office, "What I haven't been able to do...is bring the country together....That's what's been lost this year...the whole sense of changing how Washington works."[22] Try as he might, Obama could not bridge the partisan divide through gestures of goodwill because the problem was principally one of substance, not style. Simply put, Democrats and Republicans have been miles apart on most policy issues. Moreover, the partisan gap has of late been widening, not closing. Consider the results of the 2010 midterm elections. The Democrats lost a good number of their moderate members, moving the party's center of gravity substantially to the left. Meanwhile, although the Republicans picked up a few moderates, their ranks swelled with many Tea Party members, pushing the party further to the right. All along, the ideological center in Congress has been fast thinning out.[23]

On Capitol Hill, Democrats and Republicans have crossed swords on just about every issue—from taxation and the budget, to social issues, to virtually all aspects of foreign policy. Democrats generally opposed Obama's decision in December 2009 to send additional troops to Afghanistan, while Republicans thought the size of the surge was insufficient and criticized his pledge to begin withdrawing troops in the summer of 2011. On Cuba, congressional Democrats complained that Obama was not moving fast enough to scale back sanctions, whereas Republicans accused him of coddling a dictatorship. On trade, Democrats have been skittish about new deals to liberalize commerce, while Republicans want to forge ahead. The American public has been similarly divided. Democratic and Republican voters sharply disagree about most foreign policy issues, including defense spending, how best to fight terrorism, the role of the United Nations, and Obama's overall handling of U.S. statecraft.[24] Jim Leach, a moderate Republican from Iowa who lost his House seat in the 2006 midterm election, aptly summed up the state of affairs as follows: "[The United States'] middle has virtually collapsed. And how to reconstruct a principled center, a center of gravity in American politics, may be the hardest single thing at this particular time."[25]

## The Causes and Consequences of a Polarized America

America's political fragmentation is a product of some of the same underlying conditions that have been plaguing Europe. The housing bust and financial crisis came on the heels of a long stretch of stagnant wages for America's middle class. During the first decade of the twenty-first century, median income declined by roughly five percent. In counties dependent upon manufacturing, the decline was nine percent.[26] Globalization and outsourcing hit particularly hard America's manufacturing sector, which has not been able to maintain the same qualitative edge as Germany's. At the same time, America's social safety net is considerably less generous than Europe's, meaning that unemployment in the United States comes with greater hardship.

The hard times have fueled polarization and populism. Exacerbating the discontent is the reality that income inequality has been on a steady rise over the past two decades, making the United States the most unequal country in the industrialized world.[27] The boom that followed World War II led to broad gains for American workers, easing ideological clashes over socioeconomic issues and helping establish a bipartisan center. In contrast, the economic uncertainties and inequities of globalization are bringing those clashes back to life and strengthening the ideological extremes.[28]

Generational change is taking an additional toll on political comity. The World War II generation is fast retiring from political life, denying Congress the bipartisan relationships built up over decades. And older legislators are not being replaced by individuals who have also forged civic bonds through military service. In the Congress that took office in January 2011, twenty percent of members had served in the military—compared with more than seventy-five percent in the 1970s.[29] Moreover, most members were elected to Congress after 1989; these representatives will not have experienced first-hand the political discipline and bipartisan compromise that accompanied the Cold War. Compressed schedules do not help matters; lawmakers tend to begin work in Washington on Tuesday and return to their districts on Thursday, providing few opportunities for interaction across partisan lines.

As in Europe, immigration is roiling America's political waters. Although the United States has been much more successful than European countries in integrating immigrants into the social mainstream, the continuing inflow of Hispanic migrants has provoked a sharp political divide. Republicans have generally focused on border control and the use of law enforcement to locate and deport illegal immigrants. Democrats favor an approach that combines better border control with reforms that would enable illegal workers to earn the right to stay in the United States. The result has been political stalemate and a polarized debate that risks intensifying ethnic divisions within American society.

Polarization in the United States is also being driven by several developments not present in Europe. The United States has been experiencing the return of important regional cleavages, making it more difficult to bridge partisan divides.[30] The Republicans dominate in the geographic zone called the "Big L"—the states stretching from Montana south to Arizona and east to Georgia. Moderate "Rockefeller" Republicans have all but disappeared from the party; its ideological center has accordingly moved considerably to the right. Meanwhile, Democrats in Congress increasingly come from the liberal states in the Northeast and along the Pacific coast. Conservative Democrats in the south have tended to lose their seats to Republicans, pushing the Democratic caucus decidedly to the left.

During the decades after World War II, the delegations that states sent to Congress had a healthy partisan mix. So did the regional coalitions that formed on Capitol Hill. Centrism and bipartisanship were the beneficiaries; aspirants to public office had to cater to a diverse electorate, and party delegations in Congress were consequently ideologically heterogeneous. In the last twenty years, congressional delegations have become more politically homogeneous. During the 111th Congress (2009–2011), for example, the House delegation from New England did not contain a single Republican. That ideology and party affiliation are increasingly running along regional lines makes bipartisan compromise all the more elusive.

As if these factors are not enough, the campaign finance system, congressional redistricting, and broadcast media that provoke more than inform are adding to the combative nature of U.S. politics. Lawmakers and candidates for office need to raise money constantly, rendering them beholden to special-interest groups and giving them strong incentives to cater to narrow constituencies.[31] Efforts to reform the campaign finance system have been repeatedly blocked by the courts. Congressional redistricting has made matters worse by becoming a regular mechanism for protecting incumbents. Politicians in homogeneous districts have little reason to tack to the center to capture swing voters and independents, discouraging ideological moderation and encouraging a narrow conformity.[32]

The media also appear to be contributing to polarization—particularly among the public—through a sharp increase in partisan and confrontational broadcasts. As cable stations and radio talk shows vie for market share, they opt for verbal fisticuffs or political programs that cater to audiences of a particular political persuasion. Fox News has become the channel of the right, and MSNBC the favorite of the left. CNN has struggled to maintain a more evenhanded approach—only to see its prime-time ratings plunge. On a sample day in October 2010, CNN at 8:00 p.m. had an audience of 311,000, compared with three million for Fox and one million for MSNBC.[33]

The political polarization that is infecting American politics risks tying the country in knots at the very moment that the United States needs a singular sense of purpose to address pressing challenges at home and abroad. President Obama's signature domestic policies— health care reform and fiscal stimulus—proved uniquely divisive. His health care bill did not win a single Republican supporter in the House or Senate, and House Republicans passed legislation seeking to repeal it days after the opening of the 112th Congress. The fiscal stimulus received no Republican support in the House and only three Republican votes in the Senate. Democrats and Republicans did reach a deal on tax cuts late in 2010, but the bill represented a lowest common denominator that succeeded only in adding some $860 billion to the federal budget deficit. In similar fashion, the deal on deficit reduction struck in August 2011 averted national default, but did little to rein in the nation's indebtedness. More responsible plans for restoring the fiscal health of the U.S. economy—such as that put forward by the National Commission on Fiscal Responsibility and Reform—were dead on arrival. No progress has been made on other pressing issues, such as reforming immigration policy and reducing greenhouse gas emissions; Democrats and Republicans have been at loggerheads. When it comes to fixing problems at home, polarization is poised to produce inadequate policies—or no policies at all.

On foreign policy, the main consequence of continued polarization is likely to be inconstancy. As Walter Lippmann presciently warned in the 1940s, partisan division has the potential to prevent the United States from finding "a settled and generally accepted foreign policy." "This is a danger to the Republic," Lippmann continued. "For when a people is divided within itself about the conduct of its foreign relations, it is unable to agree on the determination of its true interest. It is unable to prepare adequately for war or to safeguard successfully its peace.... The spectacle of this great nation which does not know its own mind is as humiliating as it is dangerous."[34]

As Lippmann would have predicted, today's partisan divide has denied the United States "a settled and generally accepted foreign policy." With Democrats and Republicans disagreeing on most matters of statecraft, policy is poised to swing widely as power changes hands in Washington. Indeed, that is precisely what happened when Obama succeeded Bush in 2009. The Bush administration had emphasized the assertive use of U.S. power and shied away from cooperative multilateralism. In contrast, a signature aspect of Obama's foreign policy has been his emphasis on multilateral cooperation. Bush's ambassador to the United Nations, John Bolton, was openly hostile to the body, whereas Obama pledged to the United Nations General Assembly that "The United States stands ready to begin a new chapter of international cooperation."[35] While Bush shunned engagement with America's adversaries, arguing that the likes of Iran and North Korea constituted an "axis of evil," Obama has made a point of reaching out to belligerent regimes.[36] In tone and substance, U.S. foreign policy went through a sea change after Obama came into office—and could swing again when power next changes hands.[37]

Polarization has the potential to produce not just not unsteadiness, but also a retreat toward isolationism. During the interwar period, partisan rancor and political stalemate encouraged Americans to opt for the illusory safety of isolation.[38] The United States might again be headed in the same direction, encouraged not just by partisan paralysis, but also the weariness born of the wars in Iraq and Afghanistan and the country's economic woes.

A poll at the end of 2009 revealed that forty-nine percent of the public believed that the United States "should mind its own business"—the highest response to that question ever recorded, far surpassing the thirty-two percent expressing that attitude in 1972, during the height of opposition to the Vietnam War. The poll also found that seventy-six percent of the public thought the United States should focus less on international problems and "concentrate more on our own national problems and building up our strength and prosperity here at home."[39] The advent of the Tea Party movement may well strengthen such neo-isolationist inclinations. Its backers, after all, hail from a libertarian tradition holding that American ambition abroad comes at the expense of liberty and prosperity at home. It does not help matters that public approval of Congress stood at thirteen percent at the end of 2010, the lowest level recorded since Gallup began tracking assessments of congressional performance over three decades ago.[40] According to a *New York Times/ CBS News* poll, public disapproval of Congress hit another new low in the summer of 2011 following the partisan confrontation over raising the debt ceiling.[41] Such discontent with the country's legislature makes only more likely popular disaffection with the country's politics at home and its policies abroad.

To be sure, the United States has hardly been shunning international commitments in recent years. The wars in Iraq and Afghanistan suggest the opposite, as does the intervention in Libya. But the problem is not that the United States has done too little, but that it has done too much, risking a backlash amid economic hardship and polarization on the home front. If a sharp turning inward is forthcoming, it would not augur well for the readiness of the United States to guide the coming transition in global power. Indeed, in combination with the EU's travails, America's polarization suggests that the West is anything but ready to anchor the global turn.

## Restoring Western Solvency

These are unquestionably tough times for the Western democracies. Their economies have been stumbling. Their electorates are dyspeptic and divided, making effective governance hard to come by. In the United States, Europe, and Japan as well, elites and publics alike are aware that Western primacy is waning, fueling a sense of apprehension about the future.[42]

That the world is in the midst of tectonic change is, however, cause not for the West's retreat, but for its renewal. It is precisely because a global turn is under way that the West must seek to emerge from its doldrums and help manage that turn. The West's track record provides reason for hope; one of the great assets of liberal democracy is its capacity for self-correction. Political accountability and the marketplace of ideas have regularly helped democracies change course. To be sure, such responsiveness is currently threatened by populism and polarization. But the energy that is today expended in the service of partisan warfare can and should be put to much more productive use.

The guiding concept for reviving the West should be *restoring solvency*—recovering a balance between resources and commitments both economically and politically.[43] The West is suffering from an acute disequilibrium between means and ends. Economically, the Atlantic democracies have been spending more than they have been producing, leading to asset bubbles and budget and trade deficits. Politically, governments enjoy scant public support, leaving them enfeebled and timid. On matters of foreign policy, Europe aspires to have more clout, but for now, it lacks the requisite collective strength and is instead falling prey to renationalization. Meanwhile, the United States has overreached, assuming an onerous range of commitments that has been provoking popular discontent. By the end of 2010, for example, sixty percent of the American public deemed the war in Afghanistan not worth fighting.[44] The strategic weariness of the U.S. electorate helped convince President Obama that the United States should take a back seat during NATO's intervention in Libya. Continued overextension risks chipping away at the public's appetite for internationalism, thereby increasing the chances of an isolationist backlash.

The starting point for bringing means and ends back into balance is having realistic expectations about the West's ability to restore stable and steady leadership both at home and abroad. Structural changes, not just temporary conditions, are hampering the practice of liberal democracy and weakening the West's influence over international politics. Globalization is making democratic governance more difficult by at once weakening state capacity and inducing electorates to expect more of their states. Polarization in the United States has deep roots in the regionalization of party politics, the power granted to special interests by the campaign finance system, and generational change. The quality of leadership matters, but it can go only so far in restoring centrism and pragmatism. The same goes for Europe. With the causes of renationalization running deep, there is no easy fix for the EU's loss of momentum. An economic recovery would certainly restore a measure of political vitality to both sides of the Atlantic. But the West should also face the reality that it may well have to live with political lethargy for some time to come.

In similar fashion, the West's diminishing sway over global affairs is a function of the secular diffusion of power and is therefore inevitable. Even as Western economies recover from the Great Recession, they will together represent a declining share of global output; the West should recognize that its economic footprint and geopolitical leverage have peaked. No country or region stays number one in perpetuity. Expectations and ambitions need to be brought into line with these global realities.

## Learning from the Rest: Social Cohesion and Strategic Planning

In no one's world, different kinds of political systems will have their strengths and weaknesses. Capitalist autocracies like China certainly have much to learn from the West. The Chinese economy has been performing admirably, but its reliance on low-wage manufacturing and exports has its own vulnerabilities, which will become increasingly apparent as more firms leave China to take advantage of even lower wages in other developing countries. China needs to import from the West the capacity for economic innovation and adaptation rather than relying so heavily on basic manufacturing. Doing so will require a more open society that nurtures technological, scientific, and entrepreneurial advance.

At the same time, the West has much to learn from China and other countries that have state-managed markets. If China is still far too communitarian, the West, and the United States in particular, may have become too individualistic and socially balkanized. All too often, American politics is about catering to narrow segments of the electorate in order to stay in office, not about pursuing policies that are in the interests of the nation as a whole. Such segmentation is also occurring among the public. As Robert Putnam documents in *Bowling Alone*, civic engagement in the United States has experienced a secular decline.[45] Meanwhile, the EU is pulling apart as individual member states pursue their own interests rather than those of the collective union.

Programs of national service can be effective antidotes to social segmentation, but they are in short and decreasing supply in the West. Germany recently ended military conscription, abandoning its aversion, grounded in the experience of World War I and World War II, to a professional military capable of flouting civilian control. Germany certainly needs a more capable military, but

REVIVING THE WEST    169

the Western democracies must also consider how to compensate for the social effects of abandoning conscription. Alternative programs of national service are one option. In the United States, Teach for America, which channels talented college students into the public school system, provides a successful model. So do Americorps and the Peace Corps, programs that provide community service at home and abroad. Local programs through schools, religious institutions, and civic associations, as well as more civics education and volunteer opportunities in schools, provide alternative vehicles for promoting social engagement and cohesion.[46] Other promising programs offer forgiveness of student loans in return for public service.[47]

The West can also learn from China and other state-led economies the benefits of strategic economic planning. When it comes to foreign policy, the Western democracies do their best to think strategically. In the United States, the National Security Council, the State Department, and the Pentagon all have offices charged with long-range planning. But when it comes to economic matters, the market is generally left to its own devices. To be sure, laissez-faire competition produces innovation and entrepreneurship, both of which are in much shorter supply in state-led economies. But while China builds its infrastructure to fulfill its long-range plans, the United States watches its sewers, bridges, highways, and mass transit systems erode from neglect. The U.S. government has no high-level official or agency charged with long-range economic planning. Moreover, most of the new jobs created in the United States over the past two decades were in sectors not engaged in international trade, such as government and health care, boding ill for employment and wages in the absence of credible plans for domestic economic renewal.[48] Europe faces similar challenges. While the EU has made admirable attempts to engage in strategic planning in order to promote jobs and growth, Brussels has had little success herding together its individual member states for that purpose.[49]

The United States should establish in both the executive and legislative branches offices tasked with providing long-range economic planning. Negotiations between the two branches could produce an annual plan of targeted investments in sectors such as infrastructure, education and training, and business development,

providing coherence to a budgetary process that is currently politi-
cized, uncoordinated, and divided among dozens of congressional committees and executive agencies. A National Infrastructure
Bank could make available initial funding and serve to attract private investment.⁵⁰ Although some EU members, due to their larger
state sectors, already do better than the United States on matters of
infrastructure, Europe would also benefit from more effective long-
range planning.

Of particular importance is investment in higher education and
human capital, which will shore up the "knowledge and technology
underpinnings of the economy." Washington should also provide
targeted support for research and technology, and offer incentives
for similar investment from the private sector.⁵¹ While such initiatives would certainly provoke controversy on Capitol Hill, political
support for these and other proposals to boost competitive strength
may be more solid than commonly presumed. In March 2011, for
example, a broad-based group representing business, education,
science, and engineering urged President Obama and the congressional leadership to develop a strategic plan for economic growth.
"Economic growth and job creation," the group affirmed, "require
federal investment to prepare our children with world-class edu-
cations and to support the scientific and technology research and
innovation infrastructure that enable the private sector to create
jobs and compete in the global economy."⁵²

Efforts should also be made to boost the competitiveness of
U.S. companies doing business abroad. American diplomacy can
more effectively augment existing government programs to provide
financing and loan guarantees to such companies. Diplomats in
foreign embassies already provide useful business contacts as well
as knowledge of local conditions. Diplomatic negotiations should
more regularly include a healthy dose of economic as well as political deal making. Foreign visits and access to high-ranking officials,
for example, could be tied to closing lucrative business deals.⁵³ EU
diplomats could play a similar role for European companies.

The need for strategic planning also applies to regulation of international markets. Without greater oversight of the international
financial system, the global economy will be permanently vulnerable

to crises of the sort that unfolded in 2008. Speculative excesses and trade and financial imbalances are inevitable in a world of inter-dependent but diverse economies—especially as the West loses its capacity to mind the store. A more hands-on Western approach to managing trade and investment is by no means inconsistent with a rules-based commercial and financial system. Instead, the rules of the system need to be updated to moderate volatility and reflect the growing diversity of the world's major economies. Reforms aimed at taming volatility include the following: higher capital require-ments for financial institutions; global accounting standards; more transparency of complex financial instruments; and the establish-ment of oversight bodies to monitor adherence to such standards and to sanction noncompliance.

Such efforts to give more purpose to the West's economic policies are just that—modest steps to make the United States and Europe more strategic and competitive. As Michael Spence and Sandile Hlatshwayo argue, economic strategies that represent a "benign form of competition among nation-states" are far preferable to protectionist alternatives.[54] And when up against countries wield-ing autocratic brands of capitalism, the West has little choice but to fight back. As Steven Pearlstein argues, "With its state-controlled economy, China can force its companies to act collaboratively to achieve the country's strategic economic objectives. And that gives it a tremendous advantage in negotiating the terms of trade with a country like [the United States]. . . . We have no choice but to respond in kind—if for no other reason than as a way to negotiate a more level playing field for American firms and American workers."[55] Long-term economic planning is not to abandon Western princi-ples. Rather, it is to accentuate the advantages of a liberal economic order by combining strategic guidance with the dynamism that comes with market competition.

*Riding the Tiger: Progressive Populism*

Electorates in the industrialized democracies are understandably angry and frustrated. Many Americans have watched their real wages decline as the country's income inequality widens. Germans

are tired of footing the bill for shoring up Europe's weaker economies, while electorates in the EU's smaller members resent Berlin's
haughtiness. Japan's voters have been saddled with an economy
that has been stagnant for well over a decade and shows few signs
of coming back to life; the earthquake and tsunami of March
2011 and the nuclear crisis that followed hardly helped matters. A
turnaround in economic conditions would certainly improve the
mood in the United States, Europe, and Japan. But the problems
confronting the practice of liberal democracy run much deeper.
Even as healthier growth rates return, globalization will continue
to confront the Western democracies with economic and social
dislocation. Immigration will polarize electorates in the United
States and Europe. Japan has thus far resisted opening its doors to
immigrants, but the costs of its insularity will only increase as its
population ages.

It is also the case that democratic institutions in the West, often
for very sound reasons, enjoy scant public confidence. Since 2006,
one Japanese prime minister after another has seen his tenure truncated by scandal, incompetence, or both. Europe's main center-left
and center-right parties, which have dominated politics for decades,
have been steadily losing ground to more strident parties on the left
and right. Fragile governments result, weakening both national and
EU institutions.

The problem is perhaps most acute in the United States, where
an electorate confronted with economic distress and inequality
correctly senses that special interests have captured a political system beholden to campaign finance. "To a striking degree," Paul
Pierson writes, "the construction of policies that might address
long-term national challenges has become subject to an effective
veto by powerful, concentrated interests."[56] Even when Congress
succeeds in passing important legislation, the effectiveness of the
resulting policies is regularly limited by corporate lobbying. As the
recent economic crisis unfolded, Washington did an impressive job
of bailing out Wall Street and averting a financial meltdown. But
the corporations saved from collapse did an equally impressive job
of blocking the types of reforms needed to prevent a repeat performance. The health care bill passed in 2010 marked a historic

achievement: extending coverage to the uninsured. But it did little to contain costs—a sacrifice necessary to win over insurers, drug companies, and medical associations. This capture of American politics by special interests is rooted in a campaign finance system that, for both political and legal reasons, appears set in stone.

If Americans cannot address the root cause of the problem, then they must seek to transcend it. The best antidote is a progressive populism that taps into public discontent and channels it toward productive ends. Populist anger has thus far decidedly advantaged groups like the Tea Party in the United States, the Jobbik Party in Hungary, and the Northern League in Italy—movements that gravitate toward a nationalist, anti-government, and anti-immigrant discourse. Particularly in the United States, as Leslie Gelb has noted, "moderates generally don't fare well in the political trenches; their distinctions and subtleties fade in the fray."[57]

Rather than continuing to cede ground to extremist voices, centrists must encourage a brand of populism that supports a pragmatic and progressive agenda. After all, a substantial majority of the U.S. electorate consists of moderate and centrist voters who want results, not the party faithful or special interests committed to narrow ideological platforms.[58] The No Label movement, launched late in 2010 to provide a centrist brand of activism, is a welcome, if small, step in the right direction. With American voters more moderate and pragmatic than their elected representatives, greater public engagement and pressure offers at least one pathway to better policy. Through exercising its voice, the broader electorate can help ensure that its objectives take precedence over those of the mobilized interest groups that too often carry the day.

Making the case for a progressive populism is straightforward: In an interdependent world, multilateral cooperation, state-led growth, and immigration are all vital to economic success. Multilateral cooperation—not going it alone—offers the most effective means of combating nuclear proliferation, terrorism, cyber-attack, and other threats. Improvements in schools, worker retraining, and state-led investment in infrastructure, innovation, and job creation—not protectionism—are the right instruments for remaining competitive. Managed immigration and naturalization—not closed borders—are the best means of sustaining the population growth vital to economic advance. Even though the party establishments would lock horns over these assertions, they should appeal to centrist voters who are more interested in results than ideology. The challenge for leaders is to deploy a progressive brand of populism that mobilizes the pragmatic center and enables it to fend off the ideological extremes. The same goes for Europe. Progressives should rally publics behind a stronger and more unified EU instead of letting right-wing populists chip away at the union, potentially producing a Europe that is fragmented, introverted, and geopolitically sidelined.

In the United States, electoral reform can help broaden the political influence of the moderate center. Facilitating voter registration—allowing it on election day or making it automatic upon application for a driver's license—would increase electoral turnout among less politically active citizens, many of whom are centrists. Assigning responsibility for redistricting to nonpartisan commissions rather than state legislatures would mute the polarizing effects of gerrymandering.[59] A change in the congressional schedule might also help. Rather than operating on a three-day workweek, Congress could move to a five-day workweek, punctuated by a weeklong visit to the home district each month. This schedule would provide more time for deliberation and legislation and for professional and social contact across party lines.

The internet and community organizing also hold promise for helping revitalize democracy. The internet is usually seen as an effective vehicle for disseminating information from governments, organizations, and media outlets to consumers. But just as the internet has been used to organize mass political movements in the Middle East, perhaps it could play a role in making established democratic governments more responsive and responsible. The main political parties could hold "internet referenda," the results of which might give them the popular mandate needed to resist corporate pressure. Rather than casting ballots once every few years, voters might feel that they have continuing input into policy deliberations and outcomes. Such attempts to augment representative government with an element of direct democracy might help cultivate greater public engagement and confidence in Western institutions.[60] In addition, local governments and community organizations could more regularly hold town halls or small-group meetings intended to bring politics closer to the voter.[61]

A complementary approach to improving democratic governance entails establishing technocratic panels of experts and politicians tasked with generating pragmatic, results-oriented proposals. Such panels could address a range of issues, including deficit reduction, health care, reform of entitlement programs, investment in infrastructure, immigration, trade, and foreign policy. The National Commission on Fiscal Responsibility and Reform, headed by Alan Simpson and Erskine Bowles, was a case in point; it provided a realistic set of proposals for bringing down the U.S. deficit and sustaining economic growth over the long term. The commission was forthright in acknowledging that a combination of spending cuts and revenue increases, not either alone, is essential to tackling the deficit—an obvious reality, but one many politicians were unwilling to accept. It is hardly surprising that the commission's sensible recommendations failed to advance once exposed to partisan confrontation on Capitol Hill. Under such circumstances, civic activism or internet referenda could be useful in pressuring Congress to act on the recommendations of nonpartisan expert panels.

Discrete logrolls that cut across partisan divides offer another means of circumventing gridlock and advancing a pragmatic policy agenda.[62] Evangelicals on the right and social progressives on the left can close ranks on climate change, human rights, and international development. Corporations that rely on low-wage labor may be able to team up with pro-immigration constituencies on the left. Democrats who support multilateralism on principle can form coalitions with Republicans who support international cooperation as a vehicle for reducing costs. These and other political bargains are only temporary palliatives, but they may lead to reasoned and reasonable policy outcomes, which over time can help repair partisan cleavages by producing results. Although good politics is often a precondition for good policies, good policies can help restore good politics.[63]

## Foreign Policy: Aligning Means and Ends

On matters of foreign policy, means and ends must also be brought back into balance. On this front, the two sides of the Atlantic face opposite challenges. Europe needs to increase its means if it is to make credible its ambition to become a more capable actor on the global stage. Meanwhile, the United States has to rein in its ends if it is to pursue a solvent grand strategy—one that is in equilibrium with available resources and public support.

Europe's current approach to foreign and security policy is schizophrenic. On the one hand, the Lisbon Treaty provides Europe with institutions meant to enhance its ability to take on a new level of international leadership and responsibility. The EU's new diplomatic corps—the External Action Service—came into being on January 1, 2011, and is busily developing its portfolio. On the other hand, the renationalization of Europe is undercutting the EU's aspirations to fashion a more collective and robust foreign policy. The problem is not just the continuing reluctance of member states to pool their sovereignty on matters of defense. The readiness of EU members to contemplate new burdens has been significantly tempered by the unpopularity of the mission in Afghanistan. Meanwhile, the NATO mission in Libya, although successful in toppling the Qaddafi regime, proved uniquely divisive. Not only did most EU members refuse to contribute aircraft to the combat mission, but Germany could not even muster the will to support the mission at the UN Security Council, instead choosing to abstain. To their credit, France and Britain did take the lead in the air campaign in Libya, but the mission underscored just how divided Europe is on matters of security.

In addition, the resources Europe has available to assume a greater geopolitical profile are shrinking. The defense budgets of most member states are small and getting smaller. Even Britain, despite its long tradition of projecting power on a global basis, has been slashing its spending on defense. In 2010, the British government announced cuts in defense expenditure of some eight percent, prompting it to turn to France to share aircraft carriers, develop a joint forces brigade, and collaborate on research facilities to test the reliability of nuclear warheads. Proposals also circulated to combine the French and British nuclear arsenals as a cost-saving measure.

If deep cuts in European defense spending have a silver lining, it is that they have the potential to push EU members toward greater defense cooperation. The sharing of assets and coordination of policy recently exhibited by Britain and France—although the product of cost-cutting necessity rather than a new appetite for a more collective EU—is Europe's only hope for increasing the means needed to shoulder more international responsibilities. If the forces of renationalization continue to prevail, the EU's individual member states will gradually slip into geopolitical oblivion. Taken individually, they do not have the raw capability needed to make their presence felt on the global stage. For example, Germany, the EU's most populous and wealthiest member, in 2010 spent $40 billion on defense and decided to downsize its armed forces from 240,000 to 185,000 personnel. By means of comparison, the United States in 2010 spent some $700 billion on defense and maintained roughly 1.6 million personnel under arms.[64]

Europe needs not only to aggregate its military strength, but also to allocate its defense resources more wisely. Collectively, EU members spend about $400 billion on defense and maintain approximately three million personnel under arms.[65] However, many of these troops are not combat-ready and European countries lack the lift needed to deploy their forces in a timely fashion. The EU thus needs to rationalize defense spending by formulating a sensible division of labor among member states and producing more capable forces able to operate under a unified command. The resources are available; missing is the political will to embrace a union-wide approach to defense planning and policy.

Accordingly, the central challenge for Europe is to reverse the trend of renationalization and instead recover enthusiasm for deeper integration of the union. Restoring economic stability and growth will certainly help. But the most important ingredient is leadership. The EU desperately needs new leaders committed to the European project and willing to expend political capital to further integration—particularly on matters of foreign policy. Especially as the World War II generation passes from the scene, the goal of projecting Europe's voice on the global stage will help provide a new narrative justifying the European project. The Lisbon Treaty gives the EU the institutions needed to assert itself diplomatically and geopolitically. It is now up to Europe's leaders to generate the political will needed to bring those institutions to life. Rather than following public opinion, they need to rally it behind the cause of European integration—just as Europe's founding fathers did during the years after World War II.

Populism in Europe therefore must be channeled in a direction that strengthens rather than weakens the union. Leaders can do so by stressing how much stronger each nation would be if part of a broader Europe, and how much stronger Europe would be in the world if it cohered as a more collective actor. When it comes to the EU, the whole would be much more than the sum of its parts.

While Europe needs to aggregate its resources to bring its means into line with its aspirations, the United States needs to moderate its ends to bring them into line with diminishing economic and political means. In the aftermath of the events of September 11, 2001, the United States pursued a foreign policy relatively unfettered by constraints on either military spending or political will. The Defense Department's annual base budget alone grew from roughly $300 billion in 2001 to $550 billion in 2010. Meanwhile, since 2006, yearly supplemental appropriations for the wars in Iraq and Afghanistan have ranged between $100 billion and $190 billion. By the end of the Bush administration, fighting two wars simultaneously—without raising taxes or reducing other government spending—had already added over one trillion dollars to the national debt.[66]

The political largess that sustained such expenditures is, however, drying up. The inconclusive wars in Iraq and Afghanistan, coupled with the economic downturn and mounting debt, are producing a stingier brand of American internationalism. Indeed, it speaks volumes that during NATO's 2011 intervention in Libya, the Obama administration left it to the Europeans to lead the military operation. Pressure for a judicious retrenchment has emerged from the need to downsize the defense budget as well as a growing conviction that the country should spend more time and money on its own problems and less on the problems of others.

Restoring the political solvency of U.S. foreign policy will require a more discriminating and selective strategy based on the following principles.[67] Rather than seeking to uphold an expansive range of global commitments in the absence of sufficient domestic support, Washington should devolve more geopolitical responsibility to its partners. This approach means persistent pressure on the European Union to shoulder greater defense burdens. It entails updating the U.S.-Japan alliance in order to shift more responsibility to Tokyo, a move that may require revision of Japan's constitutional clause maintaining that "the Japanese people forever renounce war as a sovereign right of the nation." South Korea has recently purchased advanced fighter aircraft, upgraded its ground forces, and expanded its navy; Seoul is capable of shouldering additional burdens. India, Indonesia, Turkey, Saudi Arabia—cooperation with these and other countries offers the United States opportunities to lighten its load in important strategic theaters.

In addition to relying more heavily on individual allies, the United States can pursue retrenchment by building up regional organizations, such as the Association of Southeast Asian Nations, the Gulf Cooperation Council, and the African Union, so that they can help fill the gap as the United States reduces its geopolitical footprint. The Pentagon can also husband its resources by shuttering some of its 750 overseas bases. This consolidation need not come at the expense of America's ability to project power on a global basis. Rather, U.S. forces stationed at home and at select forward bases would be deployed as needed to deal with emerging crises.

The United States would by no means withdraw from its presence in the strategically important regions of Northeast Asia and the Middle East. But it would shrink the size of its deployments and, especially in the Middle East, gradually move to an offshore posture. The wars in Iraq and Afghanistan have made clear that attempts to pursue regime change and nation-building are bottomless pits. If liberal democracy is to emerge in countries whose politics have long turned on tribal, sectarian, and ethnic politics, it can only come from within. As the West's own experience reveals, political pluralism must rest on underlying socioeconomic conditions. It cannot be engineered or imposed by an outside power.

Looking ahead, the military component of the fight against terrorism should focus narrowly on destroying terrorist cells and networks. After all, the most significant accomplishment to date on that front—the killing of Osama Bin Laden in May 2011—was the product not of full-scale war but of painstaking intelligence gathering and a surgical military operation. Meanwhile, civilian agencies should use primarily economic tools to address the long-term sources of instability in the Middle East. The popular uprisings that began in 2010 represent an auspicious opening—but only that; it will take generations for prosperous and more liberal societies to emerge in the Middle East. Recognizing that reform in the region will be slow in coming, Washington should pursue policies that patiently support economic development, respect for human rights, and religious tolerance. Gradual liberalization from the top down rather than radical change from below offers the best prospects for a durable and benign evolution of the region's politics.

American leaders should also view international partnerships in a more pragmatic light. In an era of partisan polarization, it is difficult to win congressional approval of international pacts and institutions—as Woodrow Wilson's defeat over the League of Nations made clear. Today, proposals for building grand alliances of democracies and new mechanisms of global governance are likely to find scant domestic support. If the United States is to remain a team player in world politics and prevent a break with the many nations still supporting institutionalized multilateralism, presidents will have to rely more on pragmatic partnerships, flexible concerts, and task-specific coalitions. The "contact group" for the Balkans, the quartet in the Middle East, the EU-3/U.S. coalition dealing with Iran, the six-party talks for negotiating with North Korea—these and other informal groupings are fast becoming some of the most promising vehicles for effective diplomacy.

This recipe for a modest retrenchment in U.S. strategy would help bring the country's foreign policy back into line with its political will. In a polarized America looking to lighten its load, selective engagement may well attract bipartisan support. The lack of consensus at home has been in part a product of overreaching abroad. Accordingly, strategic retrenchment holds promise of freeing up both the financial resources and the political capital needed to advance the country's renewal. Moreover, retrenchment would effectively preempt the more strident isolationism embraced by at least some members of the Tea Party movement. It is far preferable for the United States to pursue a more modest foreign policy that enjoys domestic support than to pursue an overly ambitious statecraft that further polarizes the nation and leaves a world in the midst of change without the benefit of measured and steady U.S. engagement. Strategic restraint is also essential to make room for the rising rest as they seek to emerge from the shadow of Western power, the subject of the next chapter.

# 7 :: Managing No One's World

Postwar settlements are usually ordering moments. At these historical turning points, diplomats seek not only to forge the terms of peace, but also to establish new rules and mechanisms aimed at taming the causes of war. The Thirty Years' War ended with the Peace of Westphalia, which sought to eliminate wars of religion and codified conceptions of sovereignty and diplomacy that would come to anchor the Western world. The Napoleonic Wars concluded with the Congress of Vienna, which founded the Concert of Europe and put in place a cooperative order that preserved great-power peace for decades. The Versailles Treaty not only marked the end of World War I, but also launched the League of Nations—a bold attempt to prevent war through collective security rather than the balance of power. The close of World War II was accompanied by similar intellectual and institutional ferment. At a series of seminal gatherings, including those at Dumbarton Oaks and Bretton Woods, diplomats hashed out plans for the United Nations and a new international financial architecture.

In contrast with these previous post-war junctures, the close of the Cold War was followed by continuity rather than change. Decades of East-West rivalry ended quietly and bloodlessly, encouraging the West to conclude that its winning ways would do just fine to anchor the post–Cold War world. The word in Washington was that the new order would be defined by the "status quo plus."

Admittedly, this complacency gave way to an acute sense of vulnerability following the terrorist attacks of September 11, 2001. But the United States was thereafter preoccupied with the threat of terrorism and the wars in Afghanistan and Iraq, pressing matters that distracted attention from most other foreign policy issues. Against this backdrop, it is not surprising that Washington has been flat-footed when it comes to debating the shape of the next world.

A second obstacle to forward thinking about the coming global turn is intellectual disarray among those states that are fast headed toward the top ranks. If the world's emerging powers enjoyed a consensus among themselves about the nature of the post-Western world, they could drive debate about the nature of that world. But rising powers are far from arriving at a shared view of the rules of the next order. They know what they do *not* want—a world under the continued hegemony of the West. But they do not have a coherent vision of what should replace the Western order. Indeed, with the exception of China, which has well-funded ministries and think tanks tasked with mapping out the country's grand strategy, other rising powers are just getting in the game. India's diplomatic service is only 600 strong; by way of comparison, the United States employs roughly 12,000 diplomats.[1] Brazil is fast seeking to expand its diplomatic representation abroad; it has recently opened some sixteen embassies in Africa alone. Turkey's more assertive foreign policy and its deepening engagement in the Middle East are brand new; its changing orientation will take years to mature. Rising nations need additional time and resources to develop the ambitions and institutions that will mark their arrival as major powers.

It is precisely because the interests and strategic visions of emerging powers will vary widely that the next world will be no one's world. The global turn will bring to an end the era of Western dominance. But what comes next will not be the Chinese century, the Asian century, or anyone else's century. Rather, no one's world will exhibit striking diversity; alternative conceptions of domestic and international order will compete and coexist on the global stage.

The next world will hardly be the first one in which different great powers operate according to different conceptions of order. But, due to the onset of global interdependence, it will be the first time that such a diverse set of orders intensely and continuously interact with each other. During the seventeenth century, the Holy Roman Empire, Ottoman Empire, Mughal Empire, and Qing Dynasty each governed according to its own rules and culture. But these imperial actors were largely self-contained; there was little interaction among them and thus little need to agree upon a set of common norms to preserve order.

Not so today. In a world in which both markets and security are global in nature, the Washington Consensus (to the degree it still exists), Brussels Consensus, Beijing Consensus, New Delhi Consensus, Brasilia Consensus—and other developing conceptions of order—will regularly interact with each other. Globalization is of course not a twenty-first–century development. But a globalized world that is no longer guided by the hand of Western hegemony—these waters are uncharted.

The weight of history should be sufficient to ward off complacency about the challenges that will accompany the coming shift to multi-polarity and global dissensus. The past makes amply clear that transitions in the balance of power are dangerous historical moments; most of them have been accompanied by considerable bloodshed. It is true that at the opening of the twentieth century Great Britain peacefully ceded hegemony of the Western Hemisphere to the United States. But that transition occurred within the Western family; hegemony did change hands, but the baton was passed between two countries steeped in the traditions and practices of Anglo-Saxon culture and politics—and was facilitated by the emergence of common enemies. It is also true that the bipolar world of the Cold War turned into America's unipolar moment without a major war. But the Soviet Union effectively imploded; it was largely incapable of putting up a fight. Apart from these anomalies, previous changes in the international pecking order have left behind the deep scars of hegemonic war.

The presence of nuclear weapons may well make the coming shift in the global balance of power more peaceful than previous hegemonic transitions. Great powers with nuclear arsenals will exercise caution and restraint toward each other—as the United States and the Soviet Union did during the Cold War. But the strategic landscape will be far more complicated and fluid than it was during the era of East-West rivalry. Bipolarity entailed two nuclear-armed blocs carefully balancing against each other. The next world will host at least nine nuclear powers operating in a much less predictable strategic environment. Emerging powers that do not have nuclear arsenals—such as Turkey and Brazil—may feel the need to acquire them. And even though nuclear weapons engender restraint, they also dramatically increase the costs if such restraint fails. It is simply too dangerous to count on nuclear deterrence to tame the geopolitical rivalries that will inevitably be stoked by the onset of multipolarity.

The spread of democracy and commercial interdependence, some analysts contend, also have the potential to pacify the coming transition in global order.[2] But such arguments do not hold up under scrutiny. The next world will be populated by powers of many different regime types, not just by democracies. Moreover, emerging powers that are democracies may well align themselves with their rising compatriots rather than with the West. And even if all the world's countries were democratic, it cannot be taken for granted that the relationships among them would be reliably cooperative. Unable to direct their competitive energies against nondemocracies, democratic great powers may engage in geopolitical rivalry with each other. After all, great-power rivalry is often the product of competition for prestige and status—a yearning from which democracies are hardly immune.[3]

The peace-causing effects of commercial interdependence are similarly illusory. Economic interdependence among Europe's great powers did little to avert the hegemonic war that broke out in 1914. Geopolitical competition made short shrift of economic ties. And when lasting peace does break out, deepening economic ties are usually a consequence rather than a cause of political reconciliation.[4] It is also the case that interdependence can actually fuel conflict by serving as a source of vulnerability. During the 1930s, for example, Japan viewed its reliance on imports of oil and steel from the United States as a major economic threat. This perception of economic vulnerability ultimately convinced Tokyo to embark on a southward advance to access the oil and minerals of Southeast

Asia, a move that precipitated U.S. sanctions and Japan's consequent attack on Pearl Harbor.

In similar fashion, China's vast holdings of U.S. debt may for now give both countries a vested interest in preserving a political environment conducive to stable economic ties. But should unforeseen developments foster geopolitical competition between the two countries, an economic link that today appears as benign interdependence would quickly become just the opposite—a powerful source of Chinese leverage and a major American vulnerability. In the midst of strategic rivalry, commercial interdependence can do more harm than good. It is worth keeping in mind that China in 2010 suspended the sale of rare earth metals to Japan during a row over the status of a Chinese fishing boat captain, whom Japan had arrested after he rammed a Japanese coast guard vessel in waters near the disputed Senkaku/Diaoyu islands. Beijing is more than ready to exploit economic interdependence for geopolitical purpose. So too is Moscow, which has on several occasions curtailed the flow of natural gas to its neighbors in order to enhance its political leverage.

Simply put, the coming global turn has considerable potential to bring with it geopolitical peril. It is for this reason that the West and the rising rest must address with urgency how to peacefully manage the transition.

## Principles for the Next World

Although Western hegemony is in its waning days, it still provides a significant level of global stability. Teamwork between the United States and the EU continues to represent the world's most important partnership. The EU's aggregate wealth rivals America's, and the U.S. economy will remain number one into the next decade. The American military will maintain its primacy well beyond the next decade, and Washington's diplomatic clout will be second to none for the foreseeable future.

Nonetheless, the stability afforded by Western predominance will slip away in step with its material and ideological primacy. Accordingly, the West must work with emerging powers to take

advantage of the current window of opportunity to map out th
rules that will govern the next world. Otherwise, <u>multipolarity cou-</u>
<u>pled with ideological dissensus will ensure balance-of-power com-</u>
<u>petition and unfettered jockeying for power, position, and prestige.</u>
It is far preferable to arrive at a new rules-based order by design
rather than head toward a new anarchy by default.

The goal should be to forge a consensus among major states about
the foundational principles of the next world. The West will have to
be ready for compromise; the rules must be acceptable to powers
that adhere to very different conceptions of what constitutes a just
and acceptable order. The political diversity that will characterize
the next world suggests that aiming low and crafting a rules-based
order that endures is wiser than aiming high and coming away
empty-handed. What follows is a sketch of what the rules of the next
order might look like—a set of principles on which the West and the
rising rest may well be able to find common ground.

## Defining Legitimacy

Under American leadership, the West has propagated a conception
of order that equates political legitimacy with liberal democracy. If
a new rules-based order is to emerge, the West will have to embrace
political diversity rather than insist that liberal democracy is the
only legitimate form of government. To be sure, nondemocracies
currently have their say in global institutions, such as the United
Nations, the World Bank, and the G-20. But even as the West does
business with autocracies in these and other settings, it also dele-
gitimates them in word and action.

The United States leads the charge on this front. In his second
inaugural address, George W. Bush stated that, "America's vital
interests and our deepest beliefs are now one....So it is the policy
of the United States to seek and support the growth of democratic
movements and institutions in every nation and culture."[5] Although
of different political stripes, Barack Obama told the UN General
Assembly in 2010 that "experience shows us that history is on the
side of liberty; that the strongest foundation for human progress
lies in open economies, open societies, and open governments. To

put it simply, democracy, more than any other form of government, delivers for our citizens."[6] Obama also made clear his commitment to democracy promotion in outlining the U.S. response to the Arab Spring:

> The United States supports a set of universal rights. And these rights include free speech, the freedom of peaceful assembly, the freedom of religion, equality for men and women under the rule of law, and the right to choose your own leaders....Our support for these principles is not a secondary interest...it is a top priority that must be translated into concrete actions, and supported by all of the diplomatic, economic and strategic tools at our disposal.[7]

Europe generally shares this outlook. Catherine Ashton, the EU's foreign policy chief, declared in 2010 that, "democracy, human rights, security, governance and sustainable development are intrinsically linked. Democratic principles have their roots in universal norms and values."[8] Such statements affirm Robert Kagan's observation that elites in the West "have operated on the ideological conviction that liberal democracy is the only legitimate form of government and that other forms of government are not only illegitimate but transitory."[9]

This stance is morally compelling and consistent with values deeply held among the Atlantic democracies. But the equation of legitimacy with democracy undermines the West's influence among emerging powers. Even countries like Brazil and India, both of which are stable democracies, tend to view the West's obsession with democracy promotion as little more than uninvited meddling in the affairs of others. The backlash is of course considerably harsher in autocracies such as China and Russia, which regularly warn the United States and the EU to stay out of the domestic affairs of other countries. In Putin's words, "We are all perfectly aware of the realities of domestic political life. I do not think it is really necessary to explain anything to anybody. We are not going to interfere in domestic politics, just as we do not think that they should prevent practical relations...from developing. Domestic politics are domestic politics."[10]

For the West to speak out against political repression and overt violations of the rule of law is not only warranted but obligatory. But to predicate constructive relations with rising powers on their readiness to embrace a Western notion of legitimacy is another matter altogether. Senator John McCain is off course in insisting that "It is the democracies of the world that will provide the pillars upon which we can and must build an enduring peace."[11] On the contrary, only if the West works cooperatively with all regimes willing to reciprocate—democracies and nondemocracies alike—will it be able to build an enduring peace. Terrorism, nuclear proliferation, climate change, energy security, water and food security, financial crisis—these challenges are global in nature and can be effectively addressed only in partnership with a wide array of countries.

It makes little sense for the West to denigrate and ostracize regimes whose cooperation it needs to fashion a secure new order; the stakes are too high. Western countries only harm their own interests when they label as illegitimate governments that are not liberal democracies. Recognizing the next world's inevitable political diversity and thereby consolidating cooperation with rising powers of diverse regime type is far more sensible than insisting on the universality of Western conceptions of legitimacy—and alienating potential partners. The West and rising rest must arrive at a new, more inclusive, notion of legitimacy if they are to agree on an ideological foundation for the next world.

As a starting point, responsible governance, rather than liberal democracy, should be adopted as the standard for determining which states are legitimate and in good standing—and thus stakeholders in the next order.[12] Put simply, a state would be in good international standing if it is dedicated to improving the lives of its citizens and enables them to pursue their aspirations in a manner broadly consistent with their preferences. States that fall short of this standard would be those that aim primarily to extract resources from their citizens, wantonly expose them to widespread privation and disease, or carry out or enable the systematic persecution or physical abuse of minorities. Beyond these strict prohibitions, however, societies should have considerable latitude in how they organize their institutions of government and go about meeting the needs of their citizens. As long as they are committed to improving the welfare and dignity of their people, states should enjoy the rights of good standing.

It is true that equating good standing with responsible governance would be to acknowledge the legitimacy of states that do not adhere to Western conceptions of rights and liberties. But the globe's inescapable political diversity necessitates this relaxation in standards; different kinds of polities take different approaches to furthering the material and emotional needs of their peoples. In liberal states, citizens pursue their aspirations individually and privately. Other types of polities—China, Russia, the United Arab Emirates, and Singapore, for example—put less emphasis on individual liberties in favor of a more collective approach to promoting the welfare of their citizens. Peoples with communitarian political cultures or a long history of deprivation may prefer a state-led brand of governance to a laissez-faire one that risks exposing them to political strife and poverty. Muslim societies may view a separated mosque and state as alien, and deem a fusion of the sacred and secular as not only acceptable, but obligatory. In patrimonial cultures, loyalty to tribe, clan, and family regularly take precedence over individual rights. To acknowledge that different kinds of polities can practice different forms of responsible governance is to respect diversity. In contrast, to compel other societies to embrace a certain form of government would be to impose a type of un-freedom.

Clearing the way for a more inclusive global order entails recognizing that there is no single form of responsible government; the West does not have a monopoly on the political institutions and practices that enable countries to promote the welfare of their citizens. As long as other countries adhere to reasonable standards of responsible governance, the West should respect their political choices as a matter of national discretion and as a reflection of the intrinsic diversity of political life.

These same standards should also apply to the conduct of foreign policy. States in good standing must safeguard not only the welfare of their own citizens, but also those of other countries. They must respect the sovereignty and political preferences of other states in good standing, and they must refrain from actions that compromise the security and well-being of other states and their citizens. Countries that commit aggression or engage in prohibited actions, such as systematically sponsoring terrorism or exporting weapons of mass destruction, should not be considered in good standing and should be denied the rights enjoyed by responsible states.

Consistently abiding by these standards for inclusion—in rhetoric as well as in policy—would increase the number of stakeholders in the international system. It would also allow for the clear demarcation of those states that do not deserve such rights, and therefore facilitate the delegitimation and isolation of the world's most dangerous actors. The West would enjoy the backing of democracies and nondemocracies alike in taking a principled stand against regimes that prey on their own citizens—such as Sudan, North Korea, and Zimbabwe. So too would a broad coalition likely form to confront any state or non-state actor that consistently breaches international norms and commits acts of aggression against other states. With membership in the community of nations inclusively defined, a consensus might well emerge on how to deal with states that are predatory at home and abroad, providing legitimacy and widespread support for humanitarian and preventive intervention.

Marshaling coalitions that span regime type and region is particularly important when it comes to one of the most pressing challenges of this era: confronting and containing rogue states with nuclear weapons programs. Countries such as Iran and North Korea represent threats in their own right. They also have the potential to transfer weapons of mass destruction to non-state terrorist groups. A major obstacle to reining in their behavior has been the reluctance of rising powers such as China, India, Turkey, and Brazil to join the West's efforts to apply intense political pressure and impose economic sanctions. The West's willingness to embrace a more inclusive conception of legitimacy—one based on responsible governance rather than democracy—would certainly help widen the circle of nations ready to stand against countries that are predatory toward their own citizens and threatening toward the international community.

So too would this recasting of the notion of legitimacy encourage the United States to moderate its over-zealous promotion of democracy. Rushing to the ballot box in places like Bosnia, Iraq, and Afghanistan has done more harm than good. In societies that lack experience with constitutional rule, expedited transitions to democracy often produce civil war. In immature democracies, winners usually take all, leading to the majority's exploitation and persecution of the minority. It is worth keeping in mind that the West's own transition to democracy was long and bloody. Promoting responsible and responsive governance promises to yield better results than insisting on a hurried transition to democracy.

To be sure, some will legitimately question whether the moral authority of liberal democracies would be tarnished by this more pragmatic approach. But the costs of moral compromise would be more than offset by the likely gains in international security. Moreover, the West need not abandon efforts to promote democracy as it embraces a broader definition of legitimacy. On the contrary, it should continue to speak out against repression and use political and economic incentives to encourage democratization. Citizens in democratic societies have every reason to be confident that liberal democracy, from both a moral and material perspective, is superior to the alternatives. Nonetheless, the spread of democracy should be one component of a long-term vision rather than serve as a defining objective. If the West is right about the strengths of liberal democracy, it will spread of its own accord as a consequence of its appeal and effectiveness. In the meantime, promoting responsible governance and respect for alternative approaches to providing it offers the most promise of advancing the international stability needed for democracy to demonstrate its virtues.

This redefinition of international legitimacy does not violate Western values, but instead draws heavily on the West's own experience. Compromise, tolerance, and pluralism were all vital to the West's rise. Along the way, regimes of differing types lived side-by-side, more often than not respecting each other's political, religious, and ideological choices. The West has long celebrated and benefited from pluralism at home, and should do the same in approaching the rest of the world. As Steven Weber and Bruce Jentleson recognize, acknowledging the heterogeneity of political life "takes hold of the great diversity of human experience to turn it into a virtue not a vice, a source of new and recombinant ideas, not fear and hatred."[13]

It is also the case that focusing more on eradicating tyranny than spreading democracy is entirely consistent with the Western experience. As John Gaddis notes, "the objective of ending tyranny...is as deeply rooted in American history as it is possible to imagine....Spreading democracy suggests knowing the answer to how people should live their lives. Ending tyranny suggests freeing them to find their own answers."[14] In short, the West's own liberal tradition recognizes the diverse pathways available for promoting human dignity and well-being.

As the world's dominant power, the United States should take the lead in constructing this more pluralist approach to legitimacy. The United States will be better off if it gets ahead of the curve and helps craft a new order that enjoys support in most quarters of the globe than if it clings to an outmoded vision backed primarily by its traditional Western allies. Working with states that govern responsibly rather than haranguing those who fail to govern democratically would ultimately elevate America's moral authority and enhance its credibility abroad, important assets as it works with rising powers to manage the global turn.

## Defining Sovereignty

Globalization, the growing influence of non-state actors, rising concern about failing and failed states—these and other developments are stimulating debate within the international community, and particularly among the Western democracies, about the need for a formal attenuation of national sovereignty.[15] Kofi Annan, UN secretary general from 1997 through 2006, strongly supported the notion of a collective "responsibility to protect," a new norm maintaining that responsible states have both a right and an obligation to intervene to alleviate widespread human suffering. The UN-backed intervention in Libya in 2011 in many respects marked the implementation of this doctrine. Different proposals envisage a broader range of circumstances justifying the abrogation of sovereignty. For example, the international community might intervene militarily to disarm states producing weapons of mass destruction or to remove regimes that flagrantly abuse and exploit their citizens. Others contend that the spread of globalization and the proliferation of non-state actors are leading to the withering away of the nation-state; borders have become so porous that states no longer wield the traditional prerogatives of sovereignty.[16] Global rules, the argument runs, need to be updated accordingly.

Holding all countries to the standard of responsible governance would subject states that fall below that standard to isolation and sanction. In this sense, equating good standing with responsible governance is entirely consistent with enforcing the "responsibility to protect." However, a broader dilution of sovereignty would be impractical and counter-productive. Many emerging powers argue that formal attempts to abrogate or attenuate the traditional practice of sovereignty set a dangerous precedent. They see such attempts as veiled efforts to give the Western democracies the leeway to act as they see fit. As President Lula warned President George W. Bush in São Paolo in 2007, Brazil's relationship with the United States depends upon Washington's readiness to respect "the sovereign political decision of each state."[17] Russia and China, in particular, treat with suspicion Western efforts to fashion new rules of the road that would justify infringements on the sovereignty of other states. Such discomfort prompted both Moscow and Beijing to oppose the West's decision to guide Kosovo to independence from Serbia in 2008 and to object to NATO's effort to topple the Qaddafi regime after ostensibly intervening to protect Libyan civilians.

As to claims that the nation-state is withering away, the opposite is true. It is certainly the case that a series of developments— globalization, migration, the proliferation of non-governmental organizations, the information revolution—are making borders more porous and eroding state capacity. But far from sitting back and ceding sovereignty, states are resisting and fighting back. The threat of terrorism and illegal immigration have prompted the United States to tighten its northern and southern borders, increase security at all ports of entry, and ramp up domestic surveillance. The economic dislocation caused by globalization is sapping support for free trade, while the Great Recession has led to a new level of government oversight of financial markets.

The same is happening across Europe, which is seeing its national borders come back to life. In the spring of 2011, for example, France reintroduced patrols on its frontier with Italy to stem the flow of migrants escaping instability in North Africa. Meanwhile, Denmark decided to reinstate some of its border controls. As discussed above, such creeping renationalization raises troubling questions about the future of Europe's project of integration. These efforts to reclaim the traditional prerogatives of sovereignty are daily fare in the West. In much of the rest of the world, no such reassertion is taking place—because it is not needed; throughout most of the developing world states have maintained a relatively tight grip on sovereignty. Far from withering away, the nation-state is bulking up.

The West and rising rest should seek agreement on the need to invoke the "responsibility to protect" with regard to states that do not meet minimal standards of responsible governance. But reaching a consensus on the terms of the next order will otherwise require dialing back more ambitious proposals to attenuate sovereignty.[18] Most of the rising rest have little interest in compromising their own or anyone else's sovereignty. The sovereign nation-state is here to stay.

## Balancing Representation and Efficacy

If the main multilateral institutions charged with global governance are to maintain their legitimacy, their decision-making structures must be adapted to reflect the growing influence of emerging powers. Some institutions are off to a good start. In 2010, the World Bank and International Monetary Fund agreed to increase the voting weight of developing countries in Asia, Africa, and South America, a change that came at the expense of the influence of the developed West. China's voting share was increased from 2.78 percent to 4.42 percent, which puts it in third place behind the United States and Japan. China now has more weight in these financial institutions than the United Kingdom, France, and Germany.[19] The G-8 decided at its 2009 summit in Pittsburgh that the more inclusive G-20 should henceforth serve as the main global forum for coordinating economic policies. Whereas the G-8 is primarily a Western club, the G-20 offers seats at the table to South Africa, Mexico, Argentina, Brazil, China, South Korea, India, Indonesia, Saudi Arabia, Turkey, and Australia. In 2009 as well, the BRIC grouping held its first summit meeting in Russia, followed by a second in 2010 in Brazil and a third in 2011 in China. At the China summit, South Africa joined the grouping.

Expanding the UN Security Council, despite widespread appreciation of the need to do so, is proving far more difficult. Sensible proposals have been circulating, but regional rivalries stand in the way of a plan able to pass muster in the General Assembly any time soon. Nonetheless, ongoing discussion makes clear that the West and emerging powers alike understand that the legitimacy of the UN requires the eventual expansion of the Security Council. The most realistic plans on the table foresee new seats for Brazil, Germany, India, and Japan, as well as places for countries from the Islamic world and Africa (such as Indonesia, Egypt, Nigeria, and South Africa).

The ongoing effort to bring more players into the tent is essential—but also problematic. The more seats at the table, the more difficult it will be to arrive at effective decisions. The G-20 may be representative, but its size and diversity stand in the way of efficacy. The obstacles may only grow more formidable as power continues to shift from the established to the emerging powers, magnifying the potentially adverse consequences of their differences in perspective and interest.

To offset the tension between legitimacy and efficacy, the move to make global councils more inclusive may need to be combined with efforts to fashion smaller and more informal groupings, such as great-power directorates or concerts, as well as task-specific coalitions. Accordingly, efforts to update the institutions and modes of global governance may require not just a broadening of the circle, but also a simultaneous move toward exclusivity. The most sensible and least controversial approach to forming global and regional coalitions is to convene them on an ad hoc basis. Depending upon the issue area being addressed, nations with the most capability to act and the most interest in doing so would participate. Also worth consideration is the establishment of a more regularized

great-power concert—perhaps consisting only of the United Sta[
the EU, Japan, Brazil, China, India, and Russia—which might n[
on the margins of G-20 meetings and as needed to address crises.

## Facilitating Regional Devolution

Enhancing the efficacy of international institutions will also require
the devolution of greater responsibility and capability to regional
actors.[20] Deliberations at the global level are certainly required
to set broad policies as well as coordinate responses to crises. But
global governance has its limits; as the UN and G-20 have made
clear, reaching consensus and taking effective action do not come
easily.

The diffusion of global power ultimately means the diffusion
of international responsibility—from the Atlantic community of
democracies to a broad array of states in good standing in all quarters of the globe. A new distribution of power necessitates a new distribution of responsibility, and effectively tackling many of today's
challenges requires broad cooperation across region and regime
type. Proposals that envisage the world-wide extension of Western
institutions—such as a global NATO or a League of Democracies—
are destined to fall woefully short.[21] Important rising powers would
be excluded and Western democracies have little appetite for such
an expansion of commitments.

Instead, Western institutions should serve as a model, not a
substitute, for regional governance elsewhere. In the same way that
NATO and the European Union helped bring security and prosperity to the Atlantic community, similar institutions can do the
same in other areas. Regional devolution makes sense for a number of reasons. Countries closest to a crisis are those most likely to
take effective action, if only for reasons of proximity. And with the
West likely to be more focused on its own problems in the coming
years, tapping the potential of other states increases the likelihood
of timely diplomatic and military initiatives. Finally, the West's
intervention beyond the Atlantic zone always invites resistance and
resentment. In contrast, action by local states is more likely to enjoy
support and legitimacy within the region in question.

The devolution of authority to regional bodies has already been occurring, aided by the evolving capacities for governance and engagement at the regional level. The Association of Southeast Asian States (ASEAN), the Gulf Cooperation Council (GCC), the African Union (AU), the Economic Community of West African States (ECOWAS), the defense union taking shape in South America (UNASUR)—as these and other regional organizations mature, they have considerable potential to assume greater responsibility for their respective regions.

## Taming Globalization

The liberalization of markets, the construction of a globalized economy, and the spread of prosperity are defining legacies of the era of Western primacy.[22] The fundamentals of this order are firmly in place, anchored by institutions like the World Bank and World Trade Organization. But the maintenance of this order faces significant challenges. Due to the West's political and economic troubles, the Atlantic democracies may no longer be up to minding the store. The United States already seems to have lost its traditional enthusiasm for being the engine behind the global liberalization of trade. In addition, emerging powers with alternative views of how to manage their own economies and global commerce may want to change the rules in ways that advantage their interests and values. These new conditions are likely to necessitate scaled-back goals for the liberalization of the international economy, more state intervention in markets, and efforts to make globalization more equitable.

Even as the West and the rest address ways to advance the liberalization of markets, they should pay at least as much attention to warding off protectionism. The global downturn and volatility in currency markets tempt states to erect barriers against the intrusions of the international market. Despite a 2008 pledge by G-20 members that they would resist protectionism, the World Bank reported the following year that seventeen of the group's twenty countries had already violated this commitment and restricted trade at the expense of other countries.[23] A world without a dominant economic power able and willing to manage the global system could also clear the way for the emergence of regional blocs and new impediments to commerce. Global liberalization is at risk not only of slowing, but actually slipping into reverse. Preventing this backsliding toward protectionism requires reciprocal restraint at the national level as well as multilateral compacts.

Financial markets also require greater regulation—as made clear by the banking and debt crises that have afflicted both sides of the Atlantic. Globalization was expected to most advantage laissez-faire economies, but less oversight has proved to have significant liabilities as well as assets. New global rules of the road make more sense than a go-it-alone approach that risks stoking economic nationalism. In the same vein, rectifying structural imbalances in the global economy would help address some of the root causes of financial instability. The United States needs to consume less, save more, and increase its exports. In return, top exporters like China and Germany need to step up domestic demand and take in more imports from the rest of the world. The G-20 offers the appropriate venue for negotiating when and how the necessary adjustments might take place.

Finally, the next order should promote a brand of globalization in which prosperity is shared more equally. A globalized economy has widened wealth inequalities inside countries as well as between them. A global rebalancing will help matters, but a more equitable distribution of the benefits of global flows will also require additional steps. Bringing down agricultural subsidies and textile tariffs in the West would deliver major benefits to struggling economies in the developed world. Within the West, worker retraining, strategic investment, and programs aimed at job creation can help reduce inequality.

Guarding against protectionism, fashioning new financial rules of the road, mitigating wealth inequality—fulfilling these objectives would admittedly require significant adjustments to the liberal economic order erected by the West. But such adjustments offer the best hope of preserving its foundational principles and guiding the West and rising rest toward a new rules-based system for promoting global growth.

## Managing the Rise of China

Adjusting to the rise of the rest and the accompanying reconfiguration of the global order is partly about forging an international consensus on new standards of legitimacy and norms of behavior. But it is also about managing the geopolitical contests over position, status, and influence that will be awakened by a shift in the pecking order. When past transitions in the balance of power have led to war, the clash has usually occurred between the reigning hegemon and the rising challenger. The global turn thus has considerable potential to trigger a dangerous confrontation between number one and the emerging contender for primacy—that is, between the United States and China.

The potential for a Sino-American struggle for hegemony is not immediate; it is likely to begin during the next decade, not the current one. Over the course of this decade, China's military might— its navy in particular—will not be sufficiently strong to challenge America's dominating presence in East Asia. By the next decade, however, China will likely have the capability to pose a more direct strategic challenge to the United States. The contest is poised to focus primarily on the western Pacific, not a global theater of operations. A conflict over Taiwan is certainly possible—but is a relatively remote prospect. Beijing is likely to continue pursuing a foreign policy sufficiently shrewd and agile to avoid an overt confrontation over Taiwan. Moreover, relations between Beijing and Taipei have been on an upward trajectory, as demonstrated in the growing air links between the two countries. After starting direct flights between China and Taiwan in 2008, the two governments in 2010 raised the number of allowed flights per week from 270 to 370.[24] Peaceful reunification, perhaps with considerable autonomy for Taiwan, is increasingly in the realm of the thinkable.

Even if the Taiwan issue is effectively contained or resolved, the ongoing modernization of China's surface and submarine fleets and the development of anti-ship weapons, including ballistic missiles, will eventually compromise the ability of the U.S. fleet to control the waters inside the first island chain.[25] As it reaches this strategic threshold, China is likely to adjust its declaratory policy to match its

capability. Just as the United States unfurled the Monroe Doctrine
to ward off European powers that challenged U.S. hegemony in the
Western Hemisphere, China is set to lay claim to a sphere of influence in Northeast Asia and guardianship of the region's vital sea
lanes. Indeed, Beijing has already called the South China Sea an
area of "core interest."

As China's naval strength grows, the United States will face a
strategic dilemma in the western Pacific similar to the one that Great
Britain faced in the western Atlantic roughly a century earlier. When
confronted with the rapid growth of the U.S. Navy during the 1890s,
Britain chose to accept the arrival of U.S. hegemony in the Western
Hemisphere, effectively recognized the Monroe Doctrine, and
granted U.S. warships primacy in the western Atlantic. A peaceful
power transition followed, facilitated by a shared sense of common
values and heritage, and by Britain's keen interest in withdrawing
from the western Atlantic to focus its battle fleet on other, more
pressing threats.[26]

Sino-American rapprochement is likely to be more elusive; the
two countries do not share political values or a common culture,
and U.S. defense commitments to South Korea, Japan, and Taiwan
would make U.S. accommodation of China's regional ambition both
unwise and improbable. The upshot is that both the United States
and China have strong incentives to turn to diplomacy to tame their
relationship over the course of this decade. If they succeed in doing
so—and enter the next decade having escaped a zero-sum view of
the naval balance in the western Pacific—then a peaceful power
transition is likely. If not—and China is intent on pushing out of
regional waters a U.S. Navy determined to stay put—a historic confrontation may well loom.

Pursuing rapprochement with China does not mean adopting
a policy of blanket accommodation. On the contrary, the United
States must pursue a nuanced mix of engagement and containment.
Giving too much ground could invite too much Chinese ambition;
Beijing needs to know its limits. On the other hand, it would be
dangerously premature to conclude that China, unless coerced to
do otherwise, will inevitably pursue policies of predatory expansion
in step with its rising power. To confront Beijing with the prospect

of encirclement would risk fueling a vicious cycle of mounting rivalry. The onset of World War I provides sobering lessons about the potential for naval rivalry between the hegemon (Great Britain) and the rising challenger (Germany) to produce a catastrophic war that neither power intended.

Japan has an important role to play in shaping the strategic environment in the region. Just as Franco-German rapprochement anchored the evolution of a Europe at peace with itself, so too is reconciliation between China and Japan central to building stable peace in East Asia. If the Sino-Japanese relationship remains adversarial, Japan will maintain its reliance on the United States for its security, and the region will continue to play host to geopolitical tension and balance-of-power dynamics. In contrast, if Japan and China are able to put their troubled past behind them, they should be able to provide a foundation for a cooperative security order for the region as a whole. Rapprochement between France and Germany cleared the way for peace in Europe, ultimately reducing its dependence on U.S. power. Rapprochement between China and Japan can do the same for East Asia, reducing its dependence on U.S. power and diminishing the likelihood of a Sino-American contest for naval hegemony in the region.

Getting the Sino-American relationship right will require good politics, not just good policy. Leaders in Beijing face consistent pressure from domestic constituencies to stand up to the United States, and the same goes for leaders in Washington when it comes to China policy. A rising tide of Chinese nationalism makes it difficult for Chinese leaders to appear pliant in the face of U.S. pressure. Similarly, China's reluctance to significantly appreciate the value of its currency, the U.S. trade deficit with China, China's record on human rights, and its growing foreign ambition limit Washington's room for maneuver. Managing the domestic politics of Sino-American rapprochement will require as much tact as managing the diplomacy.

## Restoring U.S. Leadership

The United States will have more to say about the shape of the global turn than any other nation; America will remain the world's most powerful and influential country even as a multipolar landscape gradually emerges over this decade and the next. The United States must get its own house in order if it is to be able, along with its European allies, to anchor the coming transition in global order. Restoring the country's economic and political solvency will require greater focus on the home front and a more selective grand strategy that brings global commitments back into line with available resources.

Fortuitously, what the United States needs to do to restore solvency and domestic consensus—retrench—is also what it needs to do to make more room for rising powers. Efforts to maintain hegemony in most quarters of the globe would further erode domestic support for the nation's foreign policy, exacerbating polarization and inconstancy. A strategy of dominion would also alienate rising powers whose cooperation is essential to managing the global turn. In contrast, a judicious and selective retrenchment would rebuild the bipartisan foundations of a steady and sustainable brand of U.S. leadership. It would also devolve rights and responsibilities to emerging powers looking to wield influence commensurate with their growing capabilities.

Getting right the management of the global turn will also require the United States to put great-power politics back at the top of its list of priorities. Since the attacks of September 11, 2001, the United States has been preoccupied with the threat of terrorism and the consequent wars in Iraq and Afghanistan. The result has been a dramatic over-militarization of the fight against terrorism, leading to an excessive drain on resources and political capital. Instead, the United States should use force in a surgical fashion to combat terrorists, but stay far away from efforts to occupy and rebuild failing states. As it has found out in Iraq and Afghanistan, nation-building often knows no end.

The United States has not only been preoccupied by developments in the Middle East, but also lulled into complacency about the prospects for great-power competition. Since the end of the Cold War, great-power rivalries have admittedly been absent from the scene. But such quiescence is only temporary. Great-power contests over primacy and prestige have been in abeyance—put into suspension by the scope of U.S. power and the dominance of the

Western-led order. However, they will likely return with a vengeance as the West's preponderance subsides.

The United States is already waking up to the reality that it can no longer afford either its preoccupations in the Middle East or its complacency about great-power rivalry. Harsh realities are compelling Washington to reconfigure national priorities. In this respect, fiscal and political constraints on U.S. strategy may be a blessing in disguise. Voices from both the left and right have been insisting—correctly—that the billions of dollars spent in Iraq and Afghanistan would be better spent creating jobs at home. More generally, unemployment, mounting deficits, poisonous stalemate in Washington, the advent of the Tea Party's neo-isolationist voice within the Republican Party—these are all contributing to political pressure for a focus on the home front. Meanwhile, the intensifying activism of China, Russia, India, Brazil, Turkey, and other nations makes quite clear that rising powers have begun to stir.

Policy and rhetoric must now catch up with these emerging political and strategic realities. The United States still aspires to a level of global dominion for which it has insufficient resources and political will. American elites continue to embrace a national narrative consistent with this policy—"indispensable nation," "the American century," "America's moment"—these and other catchphrases like them still infuse political debate about U.S. strategy. They crowd out considered debate about the more diverse global order that inevitably lies ahead.

American elites would be wise to begin laying the domestic groundwork for a more modest conception of America's role in the world. To their surprise, they would likely find a public more than ready to shoulder fewer burdens and share more equitably with emerging powers the responsibilities of preparing for the next world. An opinion survey from the fall of 2010 revealed that roughly two-thirds of Americans view positively the rise of other nations because they will become less dependent on U.S. power and play a greater role in addressing global challenges.[27] At least for now, the U.S. public knows better than its leaders.

• • • •

The challenges associated with peacefully arriving at the next world should not be underestimated; power transitions are extremely dangerous moments in global affairs. It is an auspicious sign that the West and the rising rest alike recognize that the global turn has begun and have initiated a conversation on how to manage it. It is now up to the West to revive its internal strength and self-confidence, thereby endowing itself with the political wherewithal to guide the coming transition. The West must also generate the foresight to realize that the world is fast headed toward multiple versions of modernity, not toward the spread of a homogeneous brand of Western modernity. Accordingly, it must prepare for—and ultimately welcome—the political diversity and pluralism that inevitably lie ahead. For their part, the rising rest must arrive at their own conceptions of the next world, and work constructively with the West to get there peacefully.

The rise of the West was in many respects the product of the readiness of Europeans to countenance change and welcome a religious and political diversity that overturned the economic, political, and ideological status quo. The Reformation, the rise of the middle class, and the challenges these developments posed to monarchy, aristocracy, and church—these were the defining developments that propelled the West toward a remarkable era of progress and prosperity.

Today, such profound change is happening again, except it is occurring on a global scale. New players and diverging ideologies are challenging the Western order and the traditional institutions of authority on which it rests. If the West can help deliver to the rest of the world what it brought to itself several centuries ago—political and ideological tolerance coupled with economic dynamism—then the global turn will mark not a dark era of ideological contention and geopolitical rivalry, but one in which diversity and pluralism lay the foundation for an era of global comity.

# NOTES

ACKNOWLEDGMENTS

1   Charles Kupchan and Adam Mount, "The Autonomy Rule," *Democracy: A Journal of Ideas*, no. 12 (Spring 2009); Charles Kupchan and Peter Trubowitz, "Grand Strategy for a Divided America," *Foreign Affairs*, Vol. 86, no. 4 (July/August 2007); Charles Kupchan and Peter Trubowitz, "Dead Center: The Demise of Liberal Internationalism in the United States," *International Security*, Vol. 32, no. 2 (Fall 2007); and Charles Kupchan and Peter Trubowitz, "The Illusion of Liberal Internationalism's Revival," *International Security*, Vol. 35, no. 1 (Summer 2010).

CHAPTER ONE

1   Francis Fukuyama, *The End of History and the Last Man* (New York: Free Press, 1992).
2   "Obama the Party Crasher," *Washington Times*, December 23, 2009.
3   On the concept of multiple versions of modernity, see Shmuel Eisenstadt, ed., *Multiple Modernities* (Piscataway: Transaction Publishers, 2002).
4   G. John Ikenberry, "The Rise of China and the Future of the West," *Foreign Affairs*, Vol. 87, no. 1 (January/February 2008), pp. 25, 37.
5   Fareed Zakaria, *The Post-American World* (New York: Norton, 2008), p. 218.
6   See, for example, Charles Kupchan, *The End of the American Era: U.S. Foreign Policy and the Geopolitics of the Twenty-first Century* (New York: Knopf, 2002); Parag Khana, *Second World: How Emerging Powers Are Redefining Global Competition in the Twenty-first Century* (New York: Random House, 2008); Kishore Mahbubani, *The New Asian Hemisphere: The Irresistible Shift of Global Power to the East* (New York: Public Affairs, 2008); Zakaria, *The Post-American World*; Martin Jacques, *When China Rules the World: The End of the Western World and the Birth of a New Global Order* (New York: Penguin, 2009); Stefan Halper, *The Beijing Consensus: How China's Authoritarian Model Will Dominate the Twenty-First Century* (New York:

Basic Books, 2010); and Ian Morris, *Why the West Rules—For Now: The Patterns of History, and What They Reveal about the Future* (New York: Farrar, Straus and Giroux, 2010).

7   The emerging literature on this subject includes, Andrew Hurrell, *On Global Order: Power, Values, and the Constitution of International Society* (Oxford: Oxford University Press, 2007); Steven Weber and Bruce Jentleson, *The End of Arrogance: America in the Global Competition of Ideas* (Cambridge: Harvard University Press, 2010); and G. John Ikenberry, *Liberal Leviathan: The Origins, Crisis, and Transformation of the American World Order* (Princeton: Princeton University Press, 2011).

8   See Daniel Deudney and G. John Ikenberry, "The Logic of the West," *World Policy Journal*, Vol. 10, no. 4 (Winter 1993/94).

9   For a summary of the debate on the causes of Europe's rise, see Jack Goldstone, *Why Europe? The Rise of the West in World History 1500–1850* (New York: McGraw-Hill, 2008).

10  According to the rankings of Freedom House in 2010, forty-seven countries were "not free" and fifty-eight were "partly free."

11  Azar Gat, *Victorious and Vulnerable: Why Democracy Won in the 20th Century and How It Is Still Imperiled* (Lanham: Rowman & Littlefield, 2010), p. 79.

12  Henry Kissinger, "An End of Hubris," *The Economist*, November 19, 2008.

## CHAPTER TWO

1   Diarmaid MacCulloch, *The Reformation: A History* (New York: Penguin, 2003), p. 485.

2   Charles Tilly, "War-Making as State-Making," in Peter Evans, Dietrich Rueschemeyer, and Theda Skocpol, eds., *Bringing the State Back In* (Cambridge: Cambridge University Press, 1985).

3   See Daniel Nexon, *The Struggle for Power in Early Modern Europe: Religious Conflict, Dynastic Empires, and International Change* (Princeton: Princeton University Press, 2009), p. 6.

4   See Hendrik Spruyt, *The Sovereign State and Its Competitors* (Princeton: Princeton University Press, 1994), pp. 37–40.

5   L. Carl Brown, *Religion and the State: The Muslim Approach to Politics* (New York: Columbia University Press, 2000), p. 65.

6   William H. McNeill, *History of Western Civilization: A Handbook* (Chicago: University of Chicago Press, 1969), pp. 284–85. See also Marvin Perry, Myrna Chase, Margaret Jacob, James Jacob, and Theordore Van Laue, *Western Civilization: Ideas, Politics, and Society*, 9th ed. and (Boston: Houghton Mifflin Harcourt, 2008), p. 394; and John R. McNeill and William H. McNeill, *The Human Web: A Bird's-Eye View of World History* (New York: Norton, 2003), p. 142.

7   See MacCulloch, *The Reformation*, pp. 35–40.

8    Perry, et al., *Western Civilization*, p. 336; and McNeill, *History of Western Civilization*, p. 337

9    Craig A. Lockard, *Societies, Networks, and Transitions: A Global History*, Vol. 2 (Boston: Wadsworth, 2011), p. 434. See also Morris Rossabi, "The 'Decline' of the Central Asian Caravan Trade," in James D. Tracy, ed., *The Rise of Merchant Empires: Long Distance Trade in the Early Modern World, 1350–1750* (New York: Cambridge University Press, 1993); and William H. McNeill, *The Rise of the West: A History of Human Community* (Chicago: University of Chicago Press, 1963), p. 565.

10    McNeill, *History of Western Civilization*, pp. 268–69.

11    J. R. Hale, *Renaissance Europe, 1480–1520* (London: Wiley-Blackwell, 1992), p. 206; and Spruyt, *The Sovereign State*, pp. 65–66.

12    Spruyt, *The Sovereign State*, p. 26.

13    See S. R. Epstein, ed., *Town and Country in Europe 1300–1800* (Cambridge: Cambridge University Press, 2001); and Norman Pounds, *The Medieval City* (Westport: Greenwood Press, 2005).

14    See Eric Carlson, *Religion and the English People, 1500–1640: New Voices New Perspectives* (Kirksville: Thomas Jefferson University Press, 1998), pp. 77–79.

15    Spruyt, *The Sovereign State*, pp. 136–37.

16    McNeill, *History of Western Civilization*, p. 271.

17    McNeill, *History of Western Civilization*, pp. 273–74.

18    Hale, *Renaissance Europe*, p. 175. See also Richard Britnell, "Town Life," in Rosemary Horrox and W. Mark Ormrod, eds., *A Social History of England 1200–1500* (Cambridge: Cambridge University Press, 2006).

19    McNeill, *History of Western Civilization*, pp. 273–74.

20    Raymond de Roover, "The Account Books of Collard de Marke," *Bulletin of the Business Historical Society*, Vol. 12, no. 3 (June 1938), pp. 44–47.

21    Hale, *Renaissance Europe*, p. 48.

22    Hale, *Renaissance Europe*, pp. 11–12; and Spruyt, *The Sovereign State*, pp. 74–75.

23    MacCulloch, *The Reformation*, pp. 76–79.

24    Hale, *Renaissance Europe*, p. 189.

25    Hale, *Renaissance Europe*, pp. 283–84.

26    Hale, *Renaissance Europe*, p. 149.

27    Spruyt, *The Sovereign State*, pp. 116–125.

28    For comparative discussion of the different trajectories of Germany, England, France, and Italy, see Spruyt, *The Sovereign State*.

29    Mark Kishlansky, *A Monarchy Transformed: Britain 1603–1714* (New York: Penguin, 1997), pp. 8–20.

30    Spruyt, *The Sovereign State*, pp. 6, 64–66, 77, 89, 100–105.

31    Spruyt, *The Sovereign State*, pp. 66, 76, 132–85.

32  Nexon, *The Struggle for Power*, pp. 3–4.

33  On the role of necessity in encouraging religious tolerance, see John Owen, *The Clash of Ideas in World Politics: Transnational Networks, States, and Regime Change, 1510–2010* (Princeton: Princeton University Press, 2010), pp. 79–121.

34  Diarmaid MacCulloch, *The Later Reformation in England, 1547-1603* (New York: Palgrave, 2001), pp. 2–7.

35  See MacCulloch, *The Reformation*, pp. 11–12; and Patrick Collinson, *The Reformation: A History* (New York: Modern Library, 2004), pp. 128–29.

36  MacCulloch, *The Reformation*, p. 130.

37  MacCulloch, *The Reformation*, pp. 118–30; Perry, et al., *Western Civilization*, pp. 320–22; and Euan Cameron, *The European Reformation* (New York: Oxford University Press, 1991), pp. 172–74.

38  Cameron, *The European Reformation*, pp. 210–13; and Perry, et al., *Western Civilization*, p. 323.

39  MacCulloch, *The Reformation*, p. 171.

40  MacCulloch, *The Reformation*, p. 669; Collinson, *The Reformation*, p. 21.

41  MacCulloch, *The Reformation*, pp. 684–87.

42  Cameron, *The European Reformation*, pp. 210–13.

43  MacCulloch, *The Reformation*, p. 400.

44  MacCulloch, *The Reformation*, p. 191; and Cameron, *The European Reformation*, pp. 329–31.

45  MacCulloch, pp. 136, 202–203; and Collinson, *The Reformation*, p. 155.

46  Cameron, *The European Reformation*, pp. 301–302; and Perry, et al., *Western Civilization*, pp. 332–34.

47  MacCulloch, *The Reformation*, pp. 162–64; and Nexon, *The Struggle for Power*, pp. 132, 161.

48  Collinson, *The Reformation*, p. 10; Nexon, *The Struggle for Power*, pp. 196–201.

49  Massimo Firpo and John Tedeschi, "The Italian Reformation and Juan de Valdes," *The Sixteenth Century Journal*, Vol. 27, no. 2 (Summer 1996), p. 355. See also Frederic C. Church, *The Italian Reformers, 1534-1564* (New York: Columbia University Press, 1932); and Silvana Seidel Menchi, "Italy," in Robert Scribner, Roy Porter, and Mikuláš Teich, eds., *The Reformation in National Context* (Cambridge: Cambridge University Press, 1994).

50  Pierre Chaunu, *The Reformation* (New York: St. Martin's Press, 1990), pp. 158–59; Perry, et al., *Western Civilization*, p. 332; and Menchi, "Italy," pp. 181–201.

51  Perry, et al., *Western Civilization*, p. 332.

52  McNeill, *The Rise of the West*, p. 579. See also Spruyt, *The Sovereign State*, p. 136; and Nexon, *The Struggle for Power*, pp. 88–89.

53  Whereas Germany had only a handful of towns with a population over 25,000, Italy had thirty such towns. See Spruyt, *The Sovereign State*, pp. 112–13.

54  Spruyt, *The Sovereign State*, p. 97.

55  Mark Greengrass, *The French Reformation* (New York: Basil Blackwell, 1987), pp. 1–3.

56  Cameron, *The European Reformation*, pp. 286–89. See also Mack Holt, *The French Wars of Religion, 1562-1629* (Cambridge: Cambridge University Press, 1995), p. 14.

57  Spruyt, *The Sovereign State*, pp. 100–101.

58  Greengrass, *The French Reformation*, p. 57.

59  J.H.M. Salmon, *Society in Crisis: France in the Sixteenth Century* (New York: St. Martin's Press, 1975), pp. 102–104; and Roger Price, *A Concise History of France*, 2nd ed. (Cambridge: Cambridge University Press, 2005), pp. 63–65.

60  Spruyt, *The Sovereign State*, p. 6. See also Fernand Braudel, *The Wheels of Commerce: Civilization and Capitalism, 15th–18th Century* (New York: Harper & Row, 1982), pp. 474, 477, 479, 487.

61  MacCulloch, *The Reformation*, pp. 58–61; and Collinson, *The Reformation*, p. 107.

62  Chaunu, *The Reformation*, pp. 160–63.

63  MacCulloch, *The Reformation*, pp. 394–96; and Collinson, *The Reformation*, pp. 138–39.

64  Collinson, *The Reformation*, pp. 155–58; and Nexon, *The Struggle for Power*, p. 170.

65  Nexon, *The Struggle for Power*, p. 100. See also Owen, *Clash of Ideas*, pp. 79-121.

66  See Cameron, *The European Reformation*, pp. 294–97, 358–60; and Gat, *Victorious and Vulnerable*, pp. 26–27, 32.

67  MacCulloch, *The Reformation*, pp. 158–59.

68  Collinson, *The Reformation*, pp. 155–56; and Nexon, *The Struggle for Power*, pp. 164–65, 168–69.

69  McNeill, *History of Western Civilization*, p. 386; and Collinson, *The Reformation*, pp. 156–58.

70  Nexon, *The Struggle for Power*, p. 178.

71  One such conflict occurred in Cologne. The Peace of Augsburg excluded ecclesiastical territories from the provision that princes would be able to determine the religion of their territories. The Cologne War broke out when the prince-elector of Cologne converted to Protestantism. Rather than stepping aside as the city's ruler, as stipulated in the Peace of Augsburg, he sought to retain power and withdraw Cologne from the Catholic fold. Complicating matters, he converted to Calvinism rather than Lutheranism. Fighting soon broke out, with Dutch, Scottish, and English mercenaries

joining the Protestant side, and Bavarian and papal forces fighting on behalf of the Catholics. On these isolated conflicts, see Owen, *Clash of Ideas*, pp. 110–11.

72   France fought on the side of the Protestants despite its adherence to Catholicism. Geopolitical considerations—its rivalry with the Habsburg Empire—trumped support for co-religionists.

73   On the war, see Peter Wilson, *The Thirty Years War: Europe's Tragedy* (Cambridge: Harvard University Press, 2009).

74   As McNeill writes, as a consequence of wars, "administrative consolidation inched ahead in nearly all the states of Europe.... As European armaments became more elaborate and expensive, monarchs could more easily monopolize organized violence within their states, thus strengthening domestic sovereignty." McNeill, *The Rise of the West*, p. 582. See also McNeill, *History of Western Civilization*, p. 402.

75   Charles A. Kupchan, *How Enemies Become Friends: The Sources of Stable Peace* (Princeton: Princeton University Press, 2010), pp. 295–303.

76   MacCulloch, *The Reformation*, p. 307.  See also Greengrass, *The French Reformation*, pp. 42–43.

77   Menna Prestwich, "Calvinism in France, 1559–1629," in Menna Prestwich, ed., *International Calvinism, 1541–1715* (Oxford: Clarendon Press, 1985), pp. 71–108. See also Holt, *The French Wars of Religion*, p. 38; and Collinson, *The Reformation*, p. 98.

78   Greengrass, *The French Reformation*, p. 48.

79   Greengrass, *The French Reformation*, pp. 53–54

80   Greengrass, *The French Reformation*, pp. 68–69.

81   Nexon, *The Struggle for Power*, pp. 188–225.

82   The word "Anglican" is derived from *ecclesia anglicana*, Latin for "the English church." Although the term did not come into common use until the nineteenth century, it began to be used to refer to the Church of England during the 1500s. I will use the two terms interchangeably.

83   McNeill, *History of Western Civilization*, pp. 403–404; and Robert Ashton, *The English Civil War: Conservatism and Revolution, 1603–1649* (New York: W.W. Norton, 1979), p. 9.

84   MacCulloch, *The Reformation*, pp. 198–201; and Kishlansky, *A Monarchy Transformed*, p. 63.

85   Kishlansky, *A Monarchy Transformed*, pp. 76–77.

86   Kishlansky, *A Monarchy Transformed*, pp. 111–12; and Ashton, *The English Civil War*, pp. 15, 18.

87   Collinson, *The Reformation*, p. 149.

88   Kishlansky, *A Monarchy Transformed*, pp. 127–29.

89   Kishlansky, *A Monarchy Transformed*, pp. 145–49; and Ashton, *The English Civil War*, pp. 143–48.

90   Kishlansky, *A Monarchy Transformed*, pp. 152–57.

91  Anglicans preferred a uniform national church overseen by bishops, Presbyterians wanted a national church without bishops, and Puritans and other "independent" denominations argued that each congregation should govern itself. See Kishlansky, *A Monarchy Transformed*, pp. 168–69; and McNeill, *History of Western Civilization*, p. 407.

92  Kishlansky, *A Monarchy Transformed*, p. 159.

93  Gary de Krey, *Restoration and Revolution in Britain: Political Culture in the Era of Charles II and the Glorious Revolution* (New York: Palgrave Macmillian, 2007), pp. 21–24.

94  Kishlansky, *A Monarchy Transformed*, p. 225; and de Krey, *Restoration and Revolution in Britain*, pp. 29–31.

95  Kishlansky, *A Monarchy Transformed*, p. 226.

96  Kishlansky, *A Monarchy Transformed*, pp. 229–34; and de Krey, *Restoration and Revolution in Britain*, pp. 34–35.

97  Kishlansky, *A Monarchy Transformed*, pp. 263–89; and Steven Pincus, *1688: The First Modern Revolution* (New Haven: Yale University Press, 2009), pp. 432–33.

98  Pincus, *1688: The First Modern Revolution*, pp. 349–50.

99  Kishlansky, *A Monarchy Transformed*, p. 23.

100 Kishlansky, *A Monarchy Transformed*, p. 16.

101 Gerald Newman, ed., *Britain in the Hanoverian Age, 1714–1837: An Encyclopedia* (London: Routledge, 1997), p. 453.

102 Goldstone, *Why Europe?*, pp. 93–94.

103 Morris, *Why the West Rules*, p. 491.

104 Paul Kennedy, *The Rise and Fall of British Naval Mastery* (London: Macmillan, 1983), p. 70.

105 MacCulloch, *The Reformation*, pp. 676, 703.

106 Michael Mann, *The Sources of Social Power: The Rise of Classes and Nation-States, 1760–1914* (Cambridge: Cambridge University Press, 1993).

## CHAPTER THREE

1  *Karen Barkey, Empire of Difference: The Ottomans in Comparative Perspective* (Cambridge: Cambridge University Press, 2008), pp. 9, 17–18.

2  Barkey, *Empire of Difference*, pp. 77–79, 86–87, 93–94.

3  Barkey, *Empire of Difference*, pp. 93–95.

4  Barkey, *Empire of Difference*, pp. 85–88.

5  Barkey, *Empire of Difference*, p. 131.

6  Daniel Goffman, *The Ottoman Empire and Early Modern Europe* (Cambridge: Cambridge University Press, 2002), p. 73.

7  Spruyt, *The Sovereign State*, p. 16; and Suraiya Faroqhi, *The Ottoman Empire and the World Around It* (New York: I.B. Tauris, 2007), pp. 16–17, 94, 156.

8   For a comprehensive study of Ottoman commercial and financial practices, see Timur Kuran, *The Long Divergence: How Islamic Law Held Back the Middle East* (Princeton: Princeton University Press, 2011). Kuran's main argument is that "The Middle East fell behind the West because it was last in adopting key institutions of the modern economy." Quotation from p. 5.

9   Cities in the Middle East substantially expanded in size and number during the Abbasid dynasty (750–1258). Merchants grew in wealth and status as urban areas expanded, becoming an early Muslim bourgeoisie. This merchant class would enjoy considerably less autonomy and influence during the Ottoman era. See Bernard Lewis, *Islam in History: Ideas, People, and Events in the Middle East* (Chicago: Open Court, 1993), pp. 307–308.

10   Brown, *Religion and State*, p. 65.

11   Halil Inalcik, *The Ottoman Empire: The Classical Age 1300–1600* (New York: Praeger, 1976), pp. 165–78.

12   Donald Quataert, *The Ottoman Empire, 1700–1922* (New York: Cambridge University Press, 2005), pp. 169–70.

13   Bernard Lewis, *Islam and the West* (New York: Oxford University Press, 1993), pp. 156–65; and Vali Nasr, *The Shia Revival: How Conflicts within Islam Will Shape the Future* (New York: W.W. Norton, 2006), pp. 38–39, 49–52, 57.

14   Nasr, *The Shia Revival*, p. 34, 35–52.

15   Lewis, *Islam in History*, pp. 279–80, 303–308; and McNeill, *The Rise of the West*, pp. 632–33.

16   Lewis, *Islam in History*, p. 293. See also Lewis, *Islam and the West*, pp. 4, 35–136, 181.

17   See Brown, *Religion and State*, pp. 1–80.

18   Barkey, *Empire of Difference*, p. 55.

19   Barkey, *Empire of Difference*, p. 81.

20   McNeill, *The Rise of the West*, p. 626.

21   Barkey, *Empire of Difference*, p. 201.

22   Barkey, *Empire of Difference*, pp. 251–56.

23   Barkey, *Empire of Difference*, pp. 257–62.

24   Barkey, *Empire of Difference*, p. 295.

25   Kenneth Pomeranz, *The Great Divergence: China, Europe, and the Making of the Modern World Economy* (Princeton: Princeton University Press, 2000), pp. 31–106; and R. Bin Wong, *China Transformed: Historical Change and the Limits of European Experience* (Ithaca: Cornell University Press, 2000), pp. 13–38.

26   Braudel, *The Wheels of Commerce*, pp. 586–88, 595.

27   Ross Terrill, *The New Chinese Empire* (New South Wales: University of New South Wales Press, 2003), pp. 58–59.

28   Wong, *China Transformed*, pp. 43–44, 96–112.

29   McNeill, *The Rise of the West*, p. 644. See also Willard J. Peterson, *The Ch'ing Empire to 1800*, Vol. 1 (Cambridge: Cambridge University Press, 2002), p. 8.

30    David Scott, *China and the International System, 1840–1949: Power, Presence, and Perceptions in a Century of Humiliation* (Albany: State University of New York, 2008), pp. 11, 13.

31    The urban communities that emerged along the Indus River were by the third millennium BC some of the most advanced cities of their time. Beginning around 1750 BC, Indus civilization entered a long period of decline, due primarily to successive waves of invasion and foreign rule. The empires established by these invaders generally relied on centralized and vertical institutions of control, which stymied the area's previous economic dynamism. After the collapse of the Mauryan dynasty around 150 BC, India passed through an extended period of weak rule, which helped foster an economic renaissance.

32    Stanley Wolpert, *A New History of India* (New York: Oxford University Press, 2009), p. 70.

33    Wolpert, *A New History of India*, pp. 113–15.

34    John F. Richards, *The Mughal Empire* (Cambridge: Cambridge University Press, 1996), pp. 165–85. See also Barbara N. Ramusack, *The Indian Princes and Their States* (Cambridge: Cambridge University Press, 2004); and Stephen Dale, "India Under Mughal Rule," in David Morgan and Anthony Reid, eds., *The Eastern Islamic World Eleventh to Eighteenth Centuries*, Vol. 3 (Cambridge: Cambridge University Press, 2010), pp. 266–314.

35    Conrad Totman, *Early Modern Japan* (Los Angeles: University of California Press, 1995), pp. 12–13.

36    Braudel, *The Wheels of Commerce*, pp. 589, 591.

37    Totman, *Early Modern Japan*, p. 19.

38    Scott MacDonald and Albert Gastmann, *A History of Credit and Power in the Western World* (New Brunswick: Transaction Publishers, 2001), p. 259.

39    McNeill, *The Rise of the West*, p. 646.

40    On the interplay between modernization and traditional Japanese values and social structures, see Josefa M. Saniel, "The Mobilization of Traditional Values in the Modernization of Japan," in Robert Bellah, ed., *Religion and Progress in Modern Asia* (New York: The Free Press, 1965), pp. 124–49; Ming-Cheng Lo and Christopher Bettinger, "The Historical Emergence of a 'Familial Society' in Japan," *Theory and Society*, Vol. 30, no. 2 (April 2001), pp. 237–79; and Kashiwagi Hiroshi, "On Rationalization and the National Lifestyle," in Elise Tipton and John Clark, eds., *Being Modern in Japan: Culture and Society from the 1910s to the 1930s* (Honolulu: University of Hawaii Press, 2000).

41    Hedley Bull and Adam Watson, eds., *The Expansion of International Society* (Oxford: Clarendon Press, 1984), pp. 3, 6. See also Adam Watson, *The Evolution of International Society: A Comparative Historical Analysis* (London: Routledge, 1992).

42    Daniel Philpott, *Revolutions in Sovereignty: How Ideas Shaped Modern International Relations* (Princeton: Princeton University Press, 2001), p. 33;

and Bernard Porter, *The Lion's Share: A Short History of British Imperialism 1850–2004*, 4th ed. (Harlow: Longman, 2004), p. 21.

43  C. A. Bayly, *The Birth of the Modern World: 1780–1914* (Oxford: Blackwell, 2004), p. 476. See also Ian Brownlie, "The Expansion of International Society: The Consequences for the Law of Nations," in Bull and Watson, eds., *The Expansion of International Society*, p. 358.

44  For elaboration of these principles, see Adam Watson, "European International Society and Its Expansion," in Bull and Watson, eds., *The Expansion of International Society*, pp. 23–24; and Adda Bozeman, *Politics and Culture in International History* (Princeton: Princeton University Press, 1960), pp. 438-522.

45  Watson, "European International Society and Its Expansion," p. 18.

46  Martin Lynn, *Commerce and Economic Change in West Africa: The Palm Oil Trade in the Nineteenth Century* (Cambridge: Cambridge University Press, 1997), p. 60.

47  Watson, "European International Society and Its Expansion," pp. 21–22.

48  Watson, "European International Society and Its Expansion," p. 22. See also Jürgen Osterhammel and Niels Petersson, *Globalization: A Short History*, Dona Geyer, trans. (Princeton: Princeton University Press, 2005), pp. 59–60.

49  On the role of technology in facilitating imperial expansion, see Daniel R. Hedrick, *The Tools of Empire: Technology and European Imperialism in the Nineteenth Century* (New York: Oxford University Press, 1981).

50  See Paul Kennedy, *The Rise and Fall of British Naval Mastery* (London: Macmillan, 1983); and C. A. Bayly, *Imperial Meridian: The British Empire and the World 1780–1830* (Harlow: Longman, 1989).

51  Watson, "European International Society and Its Expansion," p. 27.

52  Watson, "European International Society and Its Expansion," p. 27.

53  Edward Keene, *Beyond the Anarchical Society: Grotius, Colonialism, and Order in World Politics* (Cambridge: Cambridge University Press, 2002), p. xi.

54  See Benedict Anderson, *Imagined Communities: Reflections on the Origin and Spread of Nationalism* (New York: Verso, 1991), pp. 163–85.

55  Percival Spear, *The Oxford History of Modern India, 1740–1975*, 2nd ed. (New Delhi: Oxford University Press, 1978), p. 7. See also Stanley Wolpert, *India*, 3rd ed. (Berkeley: University of California Press, 2005), pp. 44–55.

56  Thomas Naff, "The Ottoman Empire and the European States System," in Bull and Watson, eds., *The Expansion of International Society*, p. 158. See also Edhem Eldem, "Capitulations and Western Trade," in Suriaya Faroqhi, ed., *The Cambridge History of Turkey, Vol. 3: The Later Ottoman Empire, 1603–1839* (Cambridge: Cambridge University Press, 2006), p. 284; Faroqhi, *The Ottoman Empire and the World Around It*, p. 17; and Lockard, *Societies, Networks, and Transitions*, pp. 434, 588–90.

57  Porter, *The Lion's Share*, pp. 21, 158; Gerrit W. Gong, "China's Entry into International Society," in Bull and Watson, eds., *The Expansion of International Society*, p 178; and Morris, *Why the West Rules*, pp. 6–11.

58   Gat, *Victorious and Vulnerable*, p. 43.

59   Hedley Bull, "The Emergence of a Universal International Society," in Bull and Watson, eds., *The Expansion of International Society*, p. 123.

60   Hedley Bull, "The Revolt Against the West," in Bull and Watson, eds., *The Expansion of International Society*, pp. 217–18.

61   On the evolution of the U.S.-led order after World War II, see G. John Ikenberry, *After Victory: Institutions, Strategic Restraint, and the Rebuilding of Order after Major Wars* (Princeton: Princeton University Press, 2000), pp. 163-256; G. John Ikenberry, "Liberal Internationalism 3.0: America and the Dilemmas of Liberal World Order," *Perspectives on Politics*, Vol. 7, no. 1 (March 2009); Michael Mandelbaum, *The Ideas That Conquered the World: Peace, Democracy, and Free Markets in the Twenty-first Century* (New York: Public Affairs, 2002); and Stewart Patrick, *The Best Laid Plans: The Origins of American Multilateralism and the Dawn of the Cold War* (Lanham: Rowman and Littlefield, 2009).

62   Stephen Ambrose and Douglas Brinkley, *Rise to Globalism: American Foreign Policy Since 1938*, 8th ed. (New York: Penguin Books, 1997), p. 61.

63   See John Montgomery, *Forced To Be Free: The Artificial Revolution in Germany and Japan* (Chicago: University of Chicago Press, 1957); and Ambrose and Brinkley, *Rise to Globalism*, pp. 49–50.

64   Alan Milward, *The Reconstruction of Western Europe, 1945–51* (Berkeley: University of California press, 1984), p. 56. See also Tony Judt, *PostWar: A History of Europe Since 1945* (New York: Penguin Books, 2005), pp. 63–99.

CHAPTER FOUR

1   See Zakaria, *The Post-American World;* and Mahbubani, *The New Asian Hemisphere.*

2   I include Japan as part of the West since it has been an industrialized democracy and aligned itself with the West since the end of World War II.

3   Goldman Sachs estimates from: Jim O'Neill and Anna Stupnytska, "The Long-Term Outlook for the BRICs and N-11 Post Crisis," Goldman Sachs Global Economics Paper no. 192, December 4, 2009, http://www2.goldmansachs.com/our-thinking/brics/brics-reports-pdfs/long-term-outlook.pdf, p. 23. In April 2011, the IMF estimated that the Chinese economy will overtake that of the United States in 2016. This calculation is based on purchasing power parity, a measure of the amount of goods a currency can buy rather than GDP at market exchange rates. See Brett Arends, "IMF Bombshell: Age of America Nears End," *MarketWatch*, http://www.marketwatch.com/story/imf-bombshell-age-of-america-about-to-end-2011-04-25.

4   At its third summit meeting in 2011, South Africa formally joined the BRIC grouping, thereafter known as the BRICS grouping. See Jack A. Smith, "BRIC becomes BRICS: Changes on the Geopolitical Chessboard," *Foreign Policy*

*Journal*, January 21, 2011, http://www.foreignpolicyjournal.com/2011/01/21/bric-becomes-brics-changes-on-the-geopolitical-chessboard/.

5  Goldman Sachs estimates from: O'Neill and Stupnystka, "The Long-Term Outlook for the BRICs and N-11 Post Crisis," p. 4.

6  James Politi, "World Bank Sees End to Dollar's Hegemony," *Financial Times*, May 18, 2011.

7  Uri Dadush and Bennett Stancil, "The World Order in 2050," Carnegie Endowment for International Peace, *Policy Outlook*, April 2010, http://www.carnegieendowment.org/files/World_Order_in_2050.pdf, p. 8.

8  Central Intelligence Agency, "World Factbook 2010: Current Account Balance," https://www.cia.gov/library/publications/the-world-factbook/rankorder/2187rank.html.

9  Bureau of Economic Analysis, "National Income and Product Accounts Tables," Table 1.1.5 Gross Domestic Product, and Table 2.1 Personal Income and Its Disposition, http://www.bea.gov/iTable/iTable.cfm?ReqID=9&step=1.

10  Eswar Prasad, Kai Liu, and Marcos Chamon, "The Puzzle of China's Rising Household Savings Rate," Brookings Institution, January 18, 2011, http://www.brookings.edu/articles/2011/0118_china_savings_prasad.aspx; Christopher Power, ed., "How Household Savings Stack Up in Asia, the West, and Latin America," *BusinessWeek*, June 10, 2010; and Martin Wolf, "East and West Are in Together," *Financial Times*, January 18, 2011.

11  Robin Wigglesworth, Andrew England, and Simeon Kerr, "Sovereign Wealth Funds Open Up Books," *Financial Times*, March 17, 2010.

12  David Herszenhorn, "G.O.P Bloc Presses Leaders to Slash Even More," *New York Times*, January 21, 2011; IMF World Economic Outlook Database, "General Government Gross Debt, percent of GDP," August, 2011, http://www.imf.org/external/pubs/ft/weo/2011/02/weodata/weorept.aspx?sy=2010&ey=2011&scsm=1&ssd=1&sort=country&ds=.&br=1&pr1.x=58&pr1.y=14&c=111&s=GGXWDG%2CGGXWDG_NGDP&grp=0&a=.

13  Federal Reserve Board, "Major Foreign Holders of Treasury Securities," Department of the Treasury, September 16, 2011, http://www.treasury.gov/resource-center/data-chart-center/tic/Documents/mfh.txt; Francis E. Warnock, "How Dangerous Is U.S. Government Debt?" Council on Foreign Relations, June 2010, http://www.cfr.org/financial-crises/dangerous-us-government-debt/p22408.

14  The United States and the EU both admit between one and 1.5 million legal immigrants per year. The U.S. population stands at roughly 300 million as compared with 500 million for the EU, giving the U.S. a considerably higher rate of immigration as a percent of total population. Fertility rates in the United States stand at roughly 2 children per woman as compared with about 1.4 in Europe, contributing to the differential rates of population growth on the two sides of the Atlantic. See "Demography and the West:

Half a Billion Americans?" *The Economist*, August 22, 2002, http://www. economist.com/node/1291056.

15   The data in this paragraph can be found at: Commission on Professionals in Science and Technology, "Temporary Residents Earn Majority of Doctorates in Engineering," May 29, 2010, http://www.cpst.org/hrdata/documents/ pwm13s/C473A063.pdf; and National Science Foundation, "Doctorate Recipients from U.S. Universities: Summary Report 2007–08," December 2009, http://www.nsf.gov/statistics/nsf10309/start.cfm.

16   Mabubhani, *The New Asian Hemisphere*, p. 59.

17   Richard Levin, "Top of the Class: The Rise of Asia's Universities," *Foreign Affairs*, Vol. 89, no. 3 (May/June 2010), p. 65.

18   National Science Foundation, "Science and Engineering Indicators, 2010," January, 2010, http://www.nsf.gov/statistics/seind10/figures.htm, Graph 0.30.

19   Todd Woody, "On Land, Air and Sea, a Retrofit Mission" *New York Times*, August 17, 2010, http://green.blogs.nytimes.com/2010/08/17/on-land-air-and-sea-a-retrofit-mission/; Joseph S. Nye, "Understanding 21st Century Power Shifts," The European Financial Review, June 19, 2011, http://www. europeanfinancialreview.com/?p=3287; "Hulls Listed by Name," United States Navy, http://www.nvr.navy.mil/quick/INDEX.HTM. In terms of the tonnage of its battle fleet, the U.S. Navy is larger than the next thirteen navies combined. See Robert M. Gates, "A Balanced Strategy: Reprogramming the Pentagon for a New Age," *Foreign Affairs*, Vol. 88, no. 1 (January/February 2009), p. 32.

20   It is worth noting that U.S. shipyards that produce warships have been steadily decreasing in number. In the 1950s and 1960s, three shipyards were constructing aircraft carriers, twelve yards were building surface warships, and seven yards were building submarines. Today, only one shipyard builds aircraft carriers, two construct other surface warships (such as destroyers and cruisers), and two build submarines. See "Shipbuilding History," http:// shipbuildinghistory.com/index.html; Newport News Shipbuilding, "Fact Sheet," August 24, 2011, http://www.huntingtoningalls.com/nns/assets/ NN_Fact_Sheet.pdf; Congressional Budget Office, "The Cost-Effectiveness of Nuclear Power for Navy Surface Ships," May 2011, http://www.cbo.gov/ ftpdocs/121xx/doc12169/05-12-NuclearPropulsion.pdf; and Ronald O'Rourke, "Navy Nuclear-Powered Surface Ships: Background, Issues and Options for Congress," Congressional Research Service, September 29, 2010, http://www. fas.org/sgp/crs/weapons/RL33946.pdf.

21   See United States Navy, "U.S. 7th Fleet Forces," http://www.c7f.navy.mil/ about.htm.

22   See Ronald O'Rourke, "China Naval Modernization: Implications for U.S. Navy Capabilities," Congressional Research Service, April 9, 2010, pp. 9–15, http://www.fas.org/sgp/crs/row/RL33153.pdf; and Office of Naval Intelligence, "The People's Liberation Army Navy: A Modern Navy with

Chinese Characteristics," August 2009, http://www.fas.org/irp/agency/oni/pla-navy.pdf, p. 17.

23 Office of Naval Intelligence, "The People's Liberation Army Navy," August 2009, p. 5; Nan Li and Christopher Weuve, "China's Aircraft Carrier Ambitions: An Update," *Naval War College Review* (Winter 2010), p. 17.

24 David Scott, "India's Drive for a 'Blue Water' Navy," *Journal of Military and Strategic Studies*, Vol. 10, no. 2 (Winter 2007–2008), p. 4.

25 Scott, "India's Drive for a 'Blue Water' Navy," p. 13. India already has one operational carrier. See Donald Berlin, "India in the Indian Ocean," *Naval War College Review*, Vol. 59, no. 2 (Spring 2006), p. 89.

26 "Indian Navy to Take Part in Multi-nation Exercises," BBC Worldwide Monitoring, May 31, 2009.

## CHAPTER FIVE

1 McNeill, *The Rise of the West*, pp. 806–807.

2 Robert Kagan, "End of Dreams, Return of History," *Policy Review*, no. 144 (August/September 2007), pp. 18–19.

3 Robert Kagan, *The Return of History and the End of Dreams* (New York: Knopf, 2008), p. 57.

4 See, for example, Edward S. Steinfeld, *Playing Our Game: Why China's Economic Rise Doesn't Threaten the West* (Oxford: Oxford University Press, 2010).

5 Minxin Pei, *China's Trapped Transition: The Limits of Developmental Autocracy* (Cambridge: Harvard University Press, 2006), pp. 2–3.

6 Kellee S. Tsai, *Capitalism without Democracy: The Private Sector in Contemporary China* (Ithaca: Cornell University Press, 2007), p. 3.

7 Karl Wittfogel, *Oriental Despotism: A Comparative Study of Total Power* (New Haven: Yale University Press, 1957).

8 See John Makeham, "Introduction," in John Makeham, ed., *New Confucianism: A Critical Examination* (London: Palgrave, 2003), pp. 1–23.

9 Tsai, *Capitalism without Democracy*, p. 169.

10 Pei, *China's Trapped Transition*, pp. 26–27.

11 Pew Global Attitudes Project, "Obama More Popular Abroad Than at Home, Global Image of U.S. Continues to Benefit," Pew Research Center, June 17, 2010, http://pewglobal.org/files/pdf/Pew-Global-Attitudes-Spring-2010-Report.pdf, p. 6.

12 Pei, *China's Trapped Transition*, p. 207.

13 Bruce Dickson, *Red Capitalists in China: The Party, Private Entrepreneurs, and the Prospects for Political Change* (Cambridge: Cambridge University Press, 2003), p. 159.

14 David Shambaugh, *China's Communist Party: Atrophy and Adaptation* (Washington, DC: Woodrow Wilson Center Press, 2008), p. 175.

15    See Tsai, *Capitalism without Democracy.*

16    Dickson, *Red Capitalists in China*, pp. 57, 83.

17    Pei, *China's Trapped Transition*, pp. 31, 93.

18    Michael Wines, "China Fortifies States Businesses to Fuel Growth," *New York Times*, August 30, 2010.

19    Tsai, *Capitalism without Democracy*, pp. 65–66.

20    On party recruitment during the reform era, see Dickson, *Red Capitalists in China*, pp. 29-55.

21    Dickson, *Red Capitalists in China*, p. 104.

22    Tsai, *Capitalism without Democracy*, p. 123.

23    Dickson, *Red Capitalists in China*, pp. 35–36.

24    Dickson, *Red Capitalists in China*, p. 85.

25    Tsai, *Capitalism without Democracy*, pp. 4, 201.

26    Dickson, *Red Capitalists in China*, p. 84; and Tsai, *Capitalism without Democracy*, p. 16.

27    Pei, *China's Trapped Transition*, p. 55.

28    Nick Mackie, "China's highway to economic growth," *BBC News*, July 19, 2005, http://news.bbc.co.uk/2/hi/business/4633241.stm.

29    "China Is Pulling Ahead in Worldwide Race for High-Speed Rail Transportation," *Washington Post*, May 12, 2010.

30    Shai Oster, "World's Top Polluter Emerges as Green-Technology Leader," *Wall Street Journal*, December 15, 2009.

31    Keith Bradsher, "China Leading Global Race to Make Clean Energy," *New York Times*, January 30, 2010.

32    Mahbubani, *The New Asian Hemisphere*, p. 64.

33    Zakaria, *The Post-American World*, p. 96; and Chen Jia, "Government to Increase Spending on Education," *China Daily*, March 1, 2010, http://www.chinadaily.com.cn/china/2010-03/01/content_9515384.htm.

34    Mahbubani, *The New Asian Hemisphere*, pp. 64–66.

35    Joseph Kahn and Daniel Wakin, "Western Classical Music: Made and Loved in China," *New York Times*, April 2, 2007.

36    Mahbubani, *The New Asian Hemisphere*, pp. 147–48.

37    Nga Pham, "Vietnam orders submarines and warplanes from Russia," *BBC News*, December 16, 2009, http://news.bbc.co.uk/2/hi/8415380.stm; "Australia spending $10B on navy; neighbors fear arms race," *CBC News*, June 20, 2007, http://www.cbc.ca/world/story/2007/06/20/australia-navy.html; Yuka Hayashi and Jeremy Page, "Japan Refocuses Its Defense With an Eye Toward China," *Wall Street Journal*, December 16, 2010; and Martin Fackler, "Japan Plans to Propose Closer Military Ties with South Korea," *New York Times*, January 5, 2010.

38    Mark Landler, "Offering to Aid Talks, U.S. Challenges China on Disputed Islands," *New York Times*, July 23, 2010.

39  John Pomfret, "China Makes Money Talk in Pursuit of Worldwide Influence," *Washington Post*, July 26, 2010.

40  See Edward Luce, *In Spite of the Gods: The Strange Rise of Modern India* (New York: Random House, 2007).

41  Meghnad Desai, "India and China: An Essay in Comparative Political Economy," in Wanda Tseng and David Cowen, eds., *India's and China's Recent Experience with Reform and Growth* (Basingstoke: Palgrave Macmillan, 2005), p. 18.

42  See Carl Walter and Fraser Howie, *Red Capitalism: The Fragile Financial Foundation of China's Extraordinary Rise* (Singapore: John Wiley & Sons, 2011), pp. 21, 43.

43  See Elizabeth Economy, *The River Runs Black: The Environmental Challenge to China's Future* (Ithaca: Cornell University Press, 2004).

44  Steinfeld, *Playing Our Game*.

45  See Gordon Chang, *The Coming Collapse of China* (New York: Random House, 2001); Bruce Gilley, *China's Democratic Future: How It Will Happen and Where It Will Lead* (New York: Columbia University Press, 2004); and Susan Shirk, *China: Fragile Superpower* (Oxford: Oxford University Press, 2007).

46  Pei, *China's Trapped Transition*, pp. 166, 207-208.

47  China's 2010 census suggests that its urban and rural populations are evening out. A significant number of urban workers are, however, temporary laborers from the countryside. Michael Wines and Sharon LaFraniere, "New Census Finds China's Population Growth Has Slowed," *New York Times*, April 28, 2011.

48  World Bank Group, "Doing Business: Measuring Business Regulations, 2010, http://www.doingbusiness.org/economyrankings/.

49  CIA, "The World Factbook 2010: Stock of Direct Foreign Investment at Home," https://www.cia.gov/library/publications/the-world-factbook/rankorder/2198rank.html?countryName=China&countryCode=ch&regionCode=eas&rank=10#ch.

50  Anders Aslund and Andrew Kuchins, *The Russia Balance Sheet* (Washington, DC: Peterson Institute for International Economics/Center for International and Strategic Studies, 2009), p. 51.

51  Aslund and Kuchins, *The Russia Balance Sheet*, pp. 40-42; Masha Lippman, "Russia's Apolitical Middle," *Washington Post*, June 4, 2007.

52  The polling data is from December 2009. See The Levada Center, "Russia Votes," http://www.russiavotes.org/national_issues/national_issues_politics.php?S776173303132=d23e94164c884dea6cdb6776ed33fcf8.

53  Fred Hiatt, "Around the World, Freedom Is in Peril," *Washington Post*, July 5, 2010.

54  Vladimir Putin, "Prepared Remarks at 43rd Munich Conference on Security Policy," February 10, 2007, http://www.washingtonpost.com/wp-dyn/content/article/2007/02/12/AR2007021200555.html.

55  See Charles A. Kupchan, "NATO's Final Frontier: Why Russia Should Join the Atlantic Alliance," *Foreign Affairs*, Vol. 89, no. 3 (May/June 2010).

56  Scattered protests also occurred in Oman, although on a smaller scale than in Bahrain. Ibadi Muslims make up over fifty percent of Oman's population, and most of the rest are Sunni.

57  Ali Mohammed Khalifa, *The United Arab Emirates: Unity in Fragmentation* (Boulder: Westview Press, 1979), p. 60.

58  Christopher M. Davidson, "After Shaikh Zayed: The Politics of Succession in Abu Dhabi and the UAE," *Middle East Policy*, Vol. 13, no. 1 (Spring 2006), p. 55.

59  Christopher M. Davidson, *The United Arab Emirates: A Study in Survival* (Boulder: Lynne Rienner, 2005), p. 90.

60  Library of Congress, "Country Profile: Saudi Arabia," September 2006, http://memory.loc.gov/frd/cs/profiles/Saudi_Arabia.pdf, p. 7.

61  Jad Mouawad, "The Construction Site Called Saudi Arabia," *New York Times*, January 20, 2008.

62  Yaroslav Trofimov, "Kuwait's Democracy Faces Turbulence," *Wall Street Journal*, April 9, 2009; Robert Worth, "In Democracy Kuwait Trusts, But Not Much," *New York Times*, May 6, 2008; and Andrew Hammond, "Kuwait's Democracy Troubles Gulf Arab Rulers," Reuters, June 24, 2009, http://www.reuters.com/article/idUSLH677342.

63  R.K. Ramazani, *The Gulf Cooperation Council: Record and Analysis* (Charlottesville: University of Virginia Press, 1988), p. 15.

64  See Pew Research Center, "Muslim Publics Divided on Hamas and Hezbollah," http://pewglobal.org/files/2010/12/Pew-Global-Attitudes-Muslim-Report-FINAL-December-2-2010.pdf, p. 3; and David Kirkpatrick and Mona El-Naggar, "Poll Finds Egyptians Full of Hope about Future," *New York Times*, April 26, 2011.

65  Lewis, *Islam in History*, pp. 284–85.

66  Oliver Roy, *Secularism Confronts Islam*, George Holoch, trans. (New York: Columbia University Press, 2007), p. 49.

67  Bernard Lewis, *Islam and the West* (New York: Oxford University Press, 1993), pp. 166–70.

68  Roy, *Secularism Confronts Islam*, p. 64.

69  Olivier Roy, *Globalized Islam: The Search for a New Ummah* (New York: Columbia University Press, 2006), p. 91.

70  Roy, *Globalized Islam*, pp. 97–98.

71  Tariq Ramadan, *Islam, the West and the Challenges of Modernity* (Leicester: The Islamic Foundation, 2009). See also Charles Kupchan, "The Controversy over Tariq Ramadan," *The Huffington Post*, November 28, 2007, http://www.huffingtonpost.com/charles-kupchan/the-controversy-over-tari_b_74552.html.

72  Kirkpatrick and El-Naggar, "Poll Finds Egyptians Full of Hope about Future."

73  In accordance with general practice, I use the term "Africa" to refer only to sub-Saharan Africa.

74  Martin Meredith, *The Fate of Africa: From the Hopes of Freedom to the Heart of Despair* (New York: Public Affairs, 2005), p. 154.

75  Meredith, *The Fate of Africa*, p. 154.

76  Michael Bratton and Nicholas van de Walle, *Democratic Experiments in Africa: Regime Transitions in Comparative Perspective* (Cambridge: Cambridge University Press, 1997), p. 69.

77  Meredith, *The Fate of Africa*, p. 165.

78  Samuel Decalo, "The Process, Prospects and Constraints of Democratization in Africa," *African Affairs*, Vol. 91, no. 362 (January 1992), pp. 13–18.

79  Daniel Posner and Daniel Young, "The Institutionalization of Political Power in Africa," in Larry Diamond and Marc Plattner, eds., *Democratization in Africa: Progress and Retreat* (Baltimore: The Johns Hopkins University Press, 2010), pp. 60–62.

80  Nicolas van de Walle, "Presidentialism and Clientelism in Africa's Emerging Party Systems," *The Journal of Modern African Studies*, Vol. 41, no. 2 (June 2003), p. 307.

81  H. Kwasi Prempeh, "Presidents Untamed," in *Democratization in Africa*, p. 19. See also Richard Joseph, "Challenges of a 'Frontier' Region," in *Democratization in Africa*, pp. 10–11; and Larry Diamond, "The Rule of Law versus the Big Man," in *Democratization in Africa*, p. 48.

82  Hermann Giliomee, James Myburgh, and Lawrence Schlemmer, "Dominant Party Rule, Opposition Parties and Minorities in South Africa," *Democratization*, Vol. 8, no. 1 (Spring 2001); Steven Friedman, "An Accidental Advance? South Africa's 2009 Elections," in *Democratization in Africa*, pp. 265–79; and Neil Southern, "Political Opposition and the Challenges of a Dominant Party System: The Democratic Alliance in South Africa," *Journal of Contemporary African Studies*, Vol. 29, no. 3 (July 2011).

83  Bratton and van de Walle, *Democratic Experiments in Africa*, pp. 61–96.

84  Posner and Young, "The Institutionalization of Political Power in Africa," p. 64.

85  Rotimi Suberu, "Nigeria's Muddled Elections," in *Democratization in Africa*, pp. 127, 132.

86  Penda Mbow, "Senegal: The Return of Personalism," in *Democratization in Africa*, pp. 152–53.

87  Barak Hoffman and Lindsay Robinson, "Tanzania's Missing Opposition," in *Democratization in Africa*, pp. 219–32.

88  E. Gyimah-Boadi, "Another Step Forward for Ghana," in *Democratization in Africa*, pp. 145–46.

89   See William Easterly and Ross Levine, "Africa's Growth Tragedy: Policies and Ethnic Divisions," *Quarterly Journal of Economics*, Vol. 112, no. 4 (November 1997).

90   Meredith, *The Fate of Africa*, p. 156.

91   See, for example, Gyimah-Boadi, "Another Step Forward for Ghana," p. 148.

92   Maina Kiai, "The Crisis in Kenya," in *Democratization in Africa*, pp. 213–14.

93   Prempeh, "Presidents Untamed," p. 19.

94   Prempeh, "Presidents Untamed," pp. 20–23.

95   For further discussion of the political evolution of African states, see Jeffrey I. Herbst, *States and Power in Africa: Comparative Lesson in Authority and Control* (Princeton: Princeton University Press, 2000); and Robert Bates, *When Things Fell Apart: State Failure in Late-Century Africa* (Cambridge: Cambridge University Press, 2008).

96   Meredith, *The Fate of Africa*, p. 380.

97   Kiai, "The Crisis in Kenya," p. 214.

98   Prempeh, "Presidents Untamed," p. 25.

99   Suberu, "Nigeria's Muddled Elections," p. 132.

100  Andrew Mwenda, "Personalizing Power in Uganda," in *Democratization in Africa*, pp. 245–46.

101  Bratton and van de Walle, *Democratic Experiments in Africa*, p. 89.

102  See J. Samuel Fitch, *The Armed Forces and Democracy in Latin America* (Baltimore: Johns Hopkins University Press, 1998), pp. 1–36.

103  Michael Reid, *Forgotten Continent: The Battle for Latin America's Soul* (New Haven: Yale University Press, 2007), p. 68.

104  Reid, *Forgotten Continent*, p. 217.

105  Reid, *Forgotten Continent*, p. 226.

106  Jorge Castaneda, "Latin America's Left Turn," *Foreign Affairs*, Vol. 85, no. 3 (May/June 2006), pp. 28–43; Reid, *Forgotten Continent*, pp. 78–79; and Julia Sweig, *Friendly Fire: Losing Friends and Making Enemies in the Anti-American Century* (New York: Public Affairs, 2006).

107  Robert H. Dix, "Military Coups and Military Rule in Latin America," *Armed Forces and Society*, Vol. 20, no. 3 (Spring 1994), p. 442.

108  See Samuel Huntington, "How Countries Democratize," *Political Science Quarterly*, Vol. 106, no. 4 (Winter 1991/92), pp. 579–616; and David Pion-Berlin, "Military Autonomy and Emerging Democracies in South America," *Comparative Politics*, Vol. 25, no. 1 (October 1992), pp. 83–102.

109  Dix, "Military Coups and Military Rule in Latin America," pp. 445–50.

110  Reid, *Forgotten Continent*, p. 219.

111  Reid, *Forgotten Continent*, pp. 233–34.

112   Cynthia Arnson, ed., *The New Left and Democratic Governance* (Washington, DC: Woodrow Wilson Center for International Scholars, 2007), p. 6.

113   Sebastian Chaskal, "Great Expectations," *Foreign Policy*, July 10, 2009, http://www.foreignpolicy.com/articles/2009/07/10/great_expectations.

114   Reid, *Forgotten Continent*, pp. 282–87.

115   Reid, *Forgotten Continent*, p. 280.

116   Robert Kaufman, "Conceptual and Historical Perspectives," in Arnson, ed., *The New Left and Democratic Governance*, p. 25.

117   Kenneth Roberts, "Political Economy and the 'New Left,'" in Arnson, ed., *The New Left and Democratic Governance*, p. 29.

118   See Luis Rubio and Jeffrey Davidow, "Mexico's Disputed Election," *Foreign Affairs*, Vol. 85, no. 5 (September/October 2006).

119   Kagan, "The Return of History," p. 73.

120   Ivo Daalder and James Lindsay, "Democracies of the World, Unite," *American Interest*, Vol. 2, no. 3 (January/February 2007); G. John Ikenberry and Anne-Marie Slaughter, "Forging a World of Liberty Under Law: U.S. National Security in the 21st Century," The Princeton Project on National Security, September 27, 2006, http://www.princeton.edu/~ppns/report/FinalReport.pdf; Senator McCain Addresses The Hoover Institution on U.S. Foreign Policy, May 1, 2007, http://media.hoover.org/sites/default/files/documents/McCain_05-01-07.pdf; and Robert Kagan, "The Case for the League of Democracies," *Financial Times*, March 13, 2008.

121   The White House, "Remarks by the President to the Joint Session of the Indian Parliament in New Delhi, India," November 8, 2010, http://www.whitehouse.gov/the-press-office/2010/11/08/remarks-president-joint-session-indian-parliament-new-delhi-india.

122   U.S. Department of State, "Voting Practices in the United Nations, 2000–2010," http://www.state.gov/p/io/rls/rpt/.

123   Mahbubani, *The New Asian Hemisphere*, p. 235.

124   Luiz Inácio Lula da Silva, "Pronunciamento do Presidente da República," January 1, 2003, http://www.info.planalto.gov.br/.

## CHAPTER SIX

1   See Deudney and Ikenberry, "The Logic of the West." For a thorough overview of U.S. strategy during the 1990s, see Derek Chollet and James Goldgeier, *America Between the Wars: From 11/9 to 9/11* (New York: Public Affairs, 2008).

2   Hugo Young, "We've Lost That Allied Feeling," *Washington Post*, April 1, 2001.

3   See Charles Kupchan, "The End of the West," *The Atlantic Monthly*, Vol. 290, no. 4 (November 2002); and Ivo Daalder, "The End of Atlanticism," *Survival*, Vol. 45, no. 2 (Summer 2003), pp. 147–66.

4   Barack Obama, "Europe and America, Aligned for the Future," *New York Times*, November 18, 2010.

5   National Security Council, *National Security Strategy of the United States*, May 2010, http://www.whitehouse.gov/sites/default/files/rss_viewer/national_security_strategy.pdf, p. 3.

6   Catherine Ashton, Remarks at the Munich Security Conference, February 6, 2010, http://www.consilium.europa.eu/uedocs/cms_data/docs/pressdata/EN/foraff/112774.pdf.

7   This analysis of the European Union draws on Charles A. Kupchan, "As Nationalism Rises, Will the European Union Fall?" *Washington Post*, August 29, 2010; and Charles A. Kupchan, "The Potential Twilight of the European Union," Council on Foreign Relations, http://www.cfr.org/eu/potential-twilight-european-union/p22934.

8   "Shrinking Germany," *The Brussels Journal*, May 9, 2009, http://www.brusselsjournal.com/node/3906.

9   "Brussels Put Firmly in the Back Seat," *Der Spiegel*, July 6, 2009, http://www.spiegel.de/international/germany/0,1518,634506,00.html.

10   Steven Erlanger, "Europe's Odd Couple," *New York Times*, January 16, 2011.

11   Katinka Bayrsch, "A New Reality for the European Union," Council on Foreign Relations, http://www.cfr.org/publication/22936/new_reality_for_the_european_union.html.

12   "NotreFamille Publie les Résultats du Sondage Les Français et l'Europe," June 4, 2009, http://www.big-presse.com/big-article-Famille-9787.php.

13   Bayrsch, "A New Reality for the European Union."

14   Andrew Borowiec, "Europe Struggles to Become Superpower: National Ambitions, Foreign-policy Issues Continue to Divide the Continent," *Washington Times*, March 12, 2006.

15   "Suicide blasts kill 3 foreigners, 3 Afghans," Associated Press, April 15, 2010, http://www.msnbc.msn.com/id/36565230/ns/world_news-south_and_central_asia/.

16   "Gates: European Demilitarization a Hindrance," *CBSNews.com*, http://www.cbsnews.com/stories/2010/02/23/politics/main6235395.shtml.

17   Andre de Nesnera, "Gates Delivers Blunt Message to NATO Partners," *VOA*, June 10, 2011, http://www.voanews.com/english/news/europe/Gates-Delivers-Blunt-Message-to-NATO-Partners-123654909.html.

18   This section draws on three essays co-authored by Charles Kupchan and Peter Trubowitz: "Grand Strategy for a Divided America," *Foreign Affairs*, Vol. 86, no. 4 (July/August 2007); "Dead Center: The Demise of Liberal Internationalism in the United States," *International Security*, Vol. 32,

no. 2 (Fall 2007); and "The Illusion of Liberal Internationalism's Revival," *International Security*, Vol. 35, no. 1 (Summer 2010).

19  Richard Heindel, "Review of *The Private Papers of Senator Vandenberg*," *American Historical Review*, Vol. 58, no. 2 (January 1953), p. 402.

20  Kupchan and Trubowitz, "The Illusion of Liberal Internationalism's Revival," p. 105.

21  Barack Obama, "Victory Speech," November 5, 2008, http://elections. nytimes.com/2008/results/president/speeches/obama-victory-speech.html.

22  Larry Hackett, "An Exclusive Interview with the Obamas: Our First Year," *People*, January 25, 2010, pp. 60–65.

23  See Kupchan and Trubowitz, "Dead Center," p. 36.

24  Kupchan and Trubowitz, "The Illusion of Liberal Internationalism's Revival," pp. 105–108.

25  Kwame Holman, "Midterm Elections Oust Several Moderate Republicans," *Online Newshour*, November 24, 2006, http://www.pbs.org/newshour/bb/ politics/july-dec06/gop_11-24.html.

26  Sabrina Tavernise and Robert Gebeloff, "Immigrants Make Paths to Suburbia, Not Cities," *New York Times*, December 15, 2010.

27  As of 2010, the richest one percent of Americans accounted for approximately twenty-four percent of all income earned; the top ten percent earned nearly fifty percent of income. By means of comparison, between the end of World War II and 1980, the richest ten percent of Americans earned around thirty-five percent of income. See Timothy Noah, "The Great Divergence," *Slate.com*, September 3, 2010, http://www.slate.com/ id/2266025/entry/2266026. For inequality rankings, see CIA, "The World Factbook: Ginni Index," https://www.cia.gov/library/publications/the- world factbook/rankorder/2172rank.html?countryName=United%20Sta tes&countryCode=us&regionCode=na&rank=42#us.

28  See Nolan McCarty, Keith T. Poole, and Howard Rosenthal, *Polarized America: The Dance of Ideology and Unequal Riches* (Cambridge: MIT Press, 2006).

29  See Kupchan and Trubowitz, "Dead Center," pp. 36–37; and Jennifer Rizzo, "Veterans in Congress at Lowest Level Since World War II," January 21, 2011, *CNN.com*, http://www.cnn.com/2011/US/01/20/congress.veterans/ index.html.

30  See Kupchan and Trubowitz, "Dead Center," p. 32.

31  On the impact of single-interest lobby groups and their deep-pocketed donors, see Jacob S. Hacker and Paul Pierson, *Off Center: The Republican Revolution and the Erosion of American Democracy* (New Haven: Yale University Press, 2005).

32  See David W. Rohde, *Parties and Leaders in the Postreform House* (Chicago: University of Chicago Press, 1991).

33   See Joe Pompeo, "CNN Just Clocked Its Worst Primetime Ratings in 10 Years Thanks to Eliot Spitzer and Larry King," *Business Insider*, October 12, 2010, http://www.businessinsider.com/cnn-clocks-its-worst-primetime-ratings-in-10-years-2010-10.

34   Walter Lippmann, *U.S. Foreign Policy: Shield of the Republic* (Boston: Little, Brown and Company, 1943), pp. 3–4.

35   Barack Obama, "Speech to the United Nations' General Assembly," September 23, 2009, http://www.nytimes.com/2009/09/24/us/politics/24prexy.text.html.

36   See Charles A. Kupchan, "Enemies into Friends: How the United States Can Court Its Adversaries," *Foreign Affairs*, Vol. 89, no. 2 (March/April 2010), pp. 120–34.

37   Kupchan and Trubowitz, "The Illusion of Liberal Internationalism's Revival," pp. 103–104.

38   Kupchan and Trubowitz, "Grand Strategy for a Divided America," pp. 73–76.

39   Pew Research Center, "America's Place in the World 2009," pp. 3, 12.

40   "Congress' Job Approval Rating Worst in Gallup History," *gallup.com*, December 15, 2010, http://www.gallup.com/poll/145238/congress-job-approval-rating-worst-gallup-history.aspx.

41   Michael Cooper and Megan Thee-Brenan, "Disapproval Rate for Congress at Record 82% after Debt Talks," *New York Times*, August 4, 2011.

42   For a notable exception, see Joseph Nye, "The Future of American Power," *Foreign Affairs*, Vol. 89, no. 6 (November/December 2010).

43   See Kupchan and Trubowitz, "Grand Strategy for a Divided America."

44   Julie Phelan and Gary Langer, "Assessment of Afghan War Sours," *ABC News*, December 16, 2010, http://abcnews.go.com/Politics/abc-news-washington-post-poll-exclusive-afghanistan-war/story?id=12404367.

45   Robert Putnam, *Bowling Alone: The Collapse and Revival of American Community* (New York: Simon & Schuster, 2000).

46   The Campaign for the Civic Mission of Schools seeks to increase civics education in U.S. schools. See http://www.civicmissionofschools.org/.

47   See FinAid, http://www.finaid.org/loans/forgiveness.phtml.

48   Michael Spence and Sandile Hlatshwayo, "The Evolving Structure of the American Economy and the Employment Challenge," Working Paper, Council on Foreign Relations, New York, March 2011, http://www.cfr.org/industrial-policy/evolving-structure-american-economy-employment-challenge/p24366, p. 4.

49   See "Facing the Challenge: The Lisbon Strategy for Growth and Employment," Report from the High Level Group chaired by Wim Kok, November 2004 (Luxembourg: Office for Official Publications of the European Communities, 2004), http://ec.europa.eu/research/evaluations/pdf/archive/fp6-evidence-base/evaluation_studies_and_reports/evalua-

tion_studies_and_reports_2004/the_lisbon_strategy_for_growth_and_employment__report_from_the_high_level_group.pdf.

50  See Emilia Istrate and Robert Puentes, "Investing for Success: Examining a Federal Capital Budget and a National Infrastructure Bank," The Brookings Institution, Metropolitan Infrastructure Initiative, no. 7, http://www.brookings.edu/reports/2009/1210_infrastructure_puentes.aspx. See also Bob Herbert, "The Master Key," *New York Times*, March 12, 2011; and Michael Porter, "Why America Needs an Economic Strategy," *Business Week*, October 30, 2008.

51  Spence and Hlatshwayo, "The Evolving Structure of the American Economy," pp. 36–37. See also Andrew Reamer, "The Federal Role in Encouraging Innovation: The 'I's' Have It," The Information Technology and Innovation Foundation, Innovation Policy Blog, December 17, 2010, http://www.innovationpolicy.org/the-federal-role-in-encouraging-innovation-th.

52  "Business, Science, Engineering and University Leaders Urge Tough Choices on the National Deficit," The Council on Competitiveness, March 31, 2011, http://www.compete.org/news/entry/1676/business-science-engineering-and-university-leaders-urge-tough-choices-on-the-national-deficit/.

53  For an example of diplomatic involvement in business deals, see Eric Lipton, Nicola Clark, and Andrew W. Lehren, "Diplomats Help Push Sales of Jetliners on the Global Market," *New York Times*, January 2, 2011.

54  Spence and Hlatshwayo, "The Evolving Structure of the American Economy," p. 37.

55  Steven Pearlstein, "China Is Following the Same Old Script—the One that Gives It All the Best Lines," *Washington Post*, January 19, 2011.

56  Paul Pierson, "Inequality and Its Casualties," *Democracy*, no. 20 (Spring 2011), p. 31.

57  Leslie Gelb, *Power Rules: How Common Sense Can Rescue American Foreign Policy* (New York: HarperCollins, 2009), p. 27.

58  See Morris Fiorina, Samuel Abrams, and Jeremy Pope, *Culture War: The Myth of a Polarized America* (Harlow: Longman, 2004), p. 8.

59  Fiorina, *Culture War*, pp. 214–19.

60  See, for example, The Key Research Center, "E-Democracy Development and Impact on Business (4)," http://www.thekeyresearch.org/krcblogde-tails.php?id=34.

61  See Matt Leighninger, *The Next Form of Democracy: How Expert Rule Is Giving Way to Shared Governance—and Why Politics Will Never Be the Same* (Nashville: Vanderbilt University Press, 2006).

62  See Kupchan and Trubowitz: "Grand Strategy for a Divided America," p. 83.

63  See Gelb, *Power Rules*, pp. 159–60.

64    Quentin Peel, "Germany to Overhaul Armed Forces," *Financial Times*, December 16, 2010; and International Institute for Strategic Studies, *The Military Balance 2010* (London: Routledge, 2010), pp. 31, 134.

65    Stockholm International Peace Research Institute, "Military Expenditure in Europe, 1988–2009," http://www.sipri.org/research/armaments/milex/resultoutput/regional/milex_europe; and IISS, *The Military Balance 2010*, pp. 426–63.

66    U.S. Department of Defense, Office of the Undersecretary (Comptroller), *Fiscal Year 2011 Budget Request: Overview*, February 2010, http://comptroller.defense.gov/defbudget/fy2011/fy2011_summary_tables_whole.pdf, p. 1; Linda Bilmes and Joseph Stiglitz, "The Iraq War Will Cost Us $3 Trillion, and Much More," *Washington Post*, March 9, 2008.

67    See Kupchan and Trubowitz: "Grand Strategy for a Divided America," pp. 80–83.

**CHAPTER SEVEN**

1    Indian Ministry of External Affairs, "Indian Foreign Service," http://www.mea.gov.in/mystart.php?id=5002; and U.S. Department of State, "Mission," http://careers.state.gov/learn/what-we-do/mission.

2    For a summary of such claims, see Kupchan, *The End of the American Era*, pp. 77–118.

3    Richard Ned Lebow, *Why Nations Fight: Past and Future Motives for War* (Cambridge: Cambridge University Press, 2011).

4    See Kupchan, *How Enemies Become Friends*.

5    George W. Bush, "President Bush's Second Inaugural Address," January 20, 2005, http://www.npr.org/templates/story/story.php?storyId=4460172.

6    Barack Obama, "Remarks by the President to the United Nations General Assembly," September 23, 2010, http://www.whitehouse.gov/the-press-office/2010/09/23/remarks-president-united-nations-general-assembly.

7    "Obama Speech Text: Middle East Has 'a Choice between Hate and Hope,'" *Los Angeles Times*, May 19, 2011.

8    Catherine Ashton, "Declaration by the High Representative on behalf of the European Union on the International Day of Democracy," September 15, 2010, http://www.eutrio.be/files/bveu/media/documents/09-15_International_Day_of_Democracy_CA_EN.pdf.

9    Robert Kagan, "End of Dreams, Return of History," pp. 18–19.

10    "From the Informal Meeting with Journalists after Vladimir Putin and the Italian Prime Minister Silvio Berlusconi Gave a Press Conference," President of Russia, August 9, 2005, http://archive.kremlin.ru/eng/text/speeches/2005/08/29/2134_type82915_93066.shtml.

11    "Transcript: John McCain's Foreign Policy Speech," *New York Times*, March 26, 2008.

12    The following discussion draws on Charles Kupchan and Adam Mount, "The Autonomy Rule," *Democracy: A Journal of Ideas*, no. 12 (Spring 2009).

13    Weber and Jentleson, *The End of Arrogance*, p. 105.

14    John Lewis Gaddis, "Ending Tyranny: The Past and Future of an Idea," *American Interest*, Vol. 4, no. 1 (September/October 2008), pp. 12–13.

15    See Kupchan and Mount, "The Autonomy Rule," pp. 15–16.

16    See, for example, Kofi Annan, "Two Concepts of Sovereignty," *The Economist*, September 16, 1999; U.S. Congress, Office of Technology Assessment, *Proliferation of Weapons of Mass Destruction: Assessing the Risks* OTA-ISC-599 (Washington, DC: U.S. Government Printing Office, August 1993), http://www.au.af.mil/au/awc/awcgate/ota/9341.pdf; John Agnew, "Sovereignty Regimes: Territoriality and State Authority in Contemporary World Politics," *Annals of the Association of American Geographers*, Vol. 95, no. 2 (June 2005); and "Nonstate Actors: Impact on International Relations and Implications for the United States," National Intelligence Council and Eurasia Group, Conference Report, August 2007, http://www.dni.gov/nic/confreports_nonstate_actors.html.

17    George W. Bush, "The President's News Conference with President Luiz Inácio Lula da Silva of Brazil in Sao Paulo," March 9, 2007, http://www.presidency.ucsb.edu/ws/index.php?pid=24571&st=&st1.

18    For a similar formulation, see Weber and Jentleson, *The End of Arrogance*, pp. 174–78.

19    Sewell Chan, "Poorer Nations Get Larger Role in World Bank," *New York Times*, April 26, 2010.

20    See Kupchan and Mount, "The Autonomy Rule," pp. 17–18.

21    On a global NATO, see James M. Goldgeier and Ivo Daalder, "Global NATO," *Foreign Affairs* Vol. 85, no. 5 (September/October 2006). On a League of Democracies, see chapter 5 above, note 120. For a critique of such proposals, see Charles A. Kupchan, "Minor League, Major Problems: The Case against a League of Democracies," *Foreign Affairs*, Vol. 80, no. 6 (November/December 2008).

22    See Kupchan and Mount, "The Autonomy Rule," pp. 18–20.

23    Elisa Gamberoni and Richard Newfarmer, "Trade Protection: Incipient but Worrisome Trends," World Bank Trade Note #37, March 2, 2009, http://siteresources.worldbank.org/NEWS/Resources/Trade_Note_37.pdf.

24    "China, Taiwan agree to more flights for Lunar New Year," *Agence France Presse*, December 30, 2010, http://news.asiaone.com/News/Latest%2BNews/Asia/Story/A1Story20101230-255643.html.

25    China defines the "first island chain" as extending south from Japan through the Ryuku Islands, Taiwan, the north coast of the Philippines and into the South China Sea. See James R. Holmes and Toshi Yoshihara, "When Comparing Navies, Measure Strength, Not Size," *Global Asia*, December 2010, http://www.globalasia.org/l.php?c=e347; "China Moving

toward Deploying Anti-carrier Missile," *Washington Post*, December 28, 2010; and Michael Wines and Edward Wong, "China's Push to Modernize Military Bears Fruit," *New York Times*, January 6, 2011.

26   See Kupchan, *How Enemies Become Friends*, pp. 73–111.

27   Chicago Council on Global Affairs, *Global Views 2010: Constrained Internationalism, Adapting to New Realities* (Chicago: Chicago Council on Global Affairs, 2010), http://www.thechicagocouncil.org/UserFiles/File/ POS_Topline%20Reports/POS%202010/Global%20Views%202010.pdf, p. 5.

# BIBLIOGRAPHY

Agnew, John. "Sovereignty Regimes: Territoriality and State Authority in Contemporary World Politics." *Annals of the Association of American Geographers* 95, no. 2 (June 2005): 437–461.

Ambrose, Stephen E., and Douglas G. Brinkley. *Rise to Globalism: American Foreign Policy Since 1938*. 8th ed. New York: Penguin Books, 1997.

Anderson, Benedict. *Imagined Communities: Reflections on the Origin and Spread of Nationalism*. New York: Verso, 1991.

Arnson, Cynthia J., and José Raúl Perales, eds. *The "New Left" and Democratic Governance in Latin America*. Washington, DC: Woodrow Wilson International Center for Scholars, 2007.

Ashton, Robert. *The English Civil War: Conservatism and Revolution, 1603–1649*. New York: W.W. Norton, 1979.

Aslund, Anders, and Andrew Kuchins. *The Russia Balance Sheet*. Washington, DC: Peterson Institute for International Economics/Center for International and Strategic Studies, 2009.

Barkey, Karen. *Empire of Difference: The Ottomans in Comparative Perspective*. Cambridge: Cambridge University Press, 2008.

Bates, Robert. *When Things Fell Apart: State Failure in Late-Century Africa*. Cambridge: Cambridge University Press, 2008.

Bayly, C.A. *The Birth of the Modern World: 1780–1914*. Oxford: Blackwell, 2004.

———. *Imperial Meridian: The British Empire and the World 1780–1830*. Harlow: Longman, 1989.

Bayrsch, Katinka. "A New Reality for the European Union." International Institutions and Global Governance Working Paper, Council on Foreign Relations, New York, NY, September 2010.

Berlin, Donald. "India in the Indian Ocean." *Naval War College Review* 59, no. 2 (Spring 2006): 58–89.

Bin Wong, R. *China Transformed: Historical Change and the Limits of European Experience*. Ithaca: Cornell University Press, 2000.

Bozeman, Adda. *Politics and Culture in International History*. Princeton: Princeton University Press, 1960.

Bratton, Michael, and Nicholas van de Walle. *Democratic Experiments in Africa: Regime Transitions in Comparative Perspective*. Cambridge: Cambridge University Press, 1997.

Braudel, Fernand. *The Wheels of Commerce: Civilization and Capitalism: 15th–18th Century*. New York: Harper & Row, 1982.

Britnell, Richard. "Town Life." In *A Social History of England 1200–1500*, edited by Rosemary Horrox and W. Mark Ormrod, 134–178. Cambridge: Cambridge University Press, 2006.

Brown, L. Carl. *Religion and the State: The Muslim Approach to Politics*. New York: Columbia University Press, 2000.

Brownlie, Ian. "The Expansion of International Society: The Consequences for the Law of Nations." In *The Expansion of International Society*, edited by Hedley Bull and Adam Watson, 357–369. Oxford: Clarendon Press, 1984.

Bull, Hedley. "The Revolt Against the West." In *The Expansion of International Society*, edited by Hedley Bull and Adam Watson, 217–228. Oxford: Clarendon Press, 1984.

Bull, Hedley, and Adam Watson, eds. *The Expansion of International Society*. Oxford: Clarendon Press, 1984.

Cameron, Euan. *The European Reformation*. New York: Oxford University Press, 1991.

Carlson, Eric. *Religion and the English People, 1500–1640: New Voices New Perspectives*. Kirksville: Thomas Jefferson University Press, 1998.

Castaneda, Jorge. "Latin America's Left Turn." *Foreign Affairs* 85, no. 3 (May/June 2006): 28–43.

Chang, Gordon. *The Coming Collapse of China*. New York: Random House, 2001.

Chaunu, Pierre. *The Reformation*. New York: St. Martin's Press, 1990.

Chicago Council on Global Affairs. *Global Views 2010: Constrained Internationalism, Adapting to New Realities*. Chicago: Chicago Council on Global Affairs, 2010.

Chollet, Derek, and James M. Goldgeier. *America Between the Wars: From 11/9 to 9/11*. New York: Public Affairs, 2008.

Church, Frederic C. *The Italian Reformers, 1534–1564*. New York: Columbia University Press, 1932.

Collinson, Patrick. *The Reformation: A History*. New York: Modern Library, 2004.

Council on Competitiveness. "Business, Science, Engineering and University Leaders Urge Tough Choices on the National Deficit." Washington, DC: Council on Competitiveness, 2011.

Daalder, Ivo. "The End of Atlanticism." *Survival* 45, no. 2 (Summer 2003): 147–166.

Daalder, Ivo, and James Lindsay. "Democracies of the World, Unite." *American Interest* 2, no. 3 (January/February 2007): 5–19.

Dale, Stephen. "India Under Mughal Rule." In *The New Cambridge History of Islam, Vol. 3: The Eastern Islamic World Eleventh to Eighteenth Centuries*, edited by David O. Morgan and Anthony Reid, 226–314. Cambridge: Cambridge University Press, 2010.

Davidson, Christopher M. "After Shaikh Zayed: The Politics of Succession in Abu Dhabi and the UAE." *Middle East Policy* 13, no. 1 (Spring 2006): 42–59.

———. *The United Arab Emirates: A Study in Survival.* Boulder, CO: Lynne Rienner, 2006.

de Krey, Gary. *Restoration and Revolution in Britain: Political Culture in the Era of Charles II and the Glorious Revolution.* New York: Palgrave Macmillian, 2007.

de Roover, Raymond. "The Account Books of Collard de Marke." *Bulletin of the Business Historical Society* 12, no. 3 (June 1938): 4–47.

Decalo, Samuel. "The Process, Prospects and Constraints of Democratization in Africa." *African Affairs* 91, no. 362 (January 1992): 7–35.

Desai, Meghnad. "India and China: An Essay in Comparative Political Economy." In *India's and China's Recent Experience with Reform and Growth*, edited by Wanda Tseng and David Cowen, 1–22. Basingstoke: Palgrave Macmillan, 2005.

Deudney, Daniel and G. John Ikenberry. "The Logic of the West." *World Policy Journal* 10, no. 4 (Winter 1993/94): 17–25.

Dewey, John. *Liberalism and Social Action.* New York: Prometheus Books, 1999.

Diamond, Larry. "The Rule of Law versus the Big Man." In *Democratization in Africa: Progress and Retreat*, edited by Larry Diamond and Marc F. Plattner, 47–58. Baltimore: The Johns Hopkins University Press, 1999.

Diamond, Larry, and Marc F. Plattner, eds. *Democritization in Africa: Progress and Retreat.* 2nd ed. Baltimore: Johns Hopkins University Press, 2010.

Dickson, Bruce. *Red Capitalists in China: The Party, Private Entrepreneurs, and the Prospects for Political Change.* Cambridge: Cambridge University Press, 2003.

Dix, Robert H. "Military Coups and Military Rule in Latin America." *Armed Forces and Society* 20, no. 3 (Spring 1994): 439–456.

Easterly, William, and Ross Levine. "Africa's Growth Tragedy: Policies and Ethnic Divisions." *Quarterly Journal of Economics* 112, no. 4 (November 1997): 1203–1250.

Economy, Elizabeth. *The River Runs Black: The Environmental Challenge to China's Future.* Ithaca: Cornell University Press, 2004.

Eisenstadt, Shmuel, ed. *Multiple Modernities.* Piscataway: Transaction Publishers, 2002.

Epstein, S. R., ed. *Town and Country in Europe 1300–1800.* Cambridge: Cambridge University Press, 2001.

Faroqhi, Suraiya. *The Ottoman Empire and the World Around It.* New York: I. B. Tauris, 2007.

Fiorina, Morris, Samuel Abrams, and Jeremy Pope. *Culture War: The Myth of a Polarized America*. White Plains: Longman, 2004.

Firpo, Massimo, and John Tedeschi. "The Italian Reformation and Juan de Valdes." *The Sixteenth Century Journal* 27, no. 2 (Summer 1996): 356–364.

Fitch, J. Samuel. *The Armed Forces and Democracy in Latin America*. Baltimore: Johns Hopkins University Press, 1998.

Friedman, Steven. "An Accidental Advance? South Africa's 2009 Elections." In *Democratization in Africa: Progress and Retreat*, edited by Larry Diamond and Marc F. Plattner, 265–279. Baltimore: The Johns Hopkins University Press, 1999.

Fukuyama, Francis. *The End of History and the Last Man*. New York: Free Press, 1992.

Gaddis, John Lewis. "Ending Tyranny: The Past and Future of an Idea." *American Interest* 4, no. 1 (September/October 2008): 6–15.

Gamberoni, Elisa, and Richard Newfarmer. "World Bank Trade Note #37: Trade Protection: Incipient but Worrisome Trends." Washington, DC: The World Bank (March 2, 2009).

Gat, Azar. *Victorious and Vulnerable: Why Democracy Won in the 20th Century and How It Is Still Imperiled*. Lanham: Rowman & Littlefield, 2010.

Gates, Robert M. "A Balanced Strategy: Reprogramming the Pentagon for a New Age." *Foreign Affairs* 88, no. 1 (January/February 2009): 11–17.

Gelb, Leslie. *Power Rules: How Common Sense Can Rescue American Foreign Policy*. New York: HarperCollins, 2009.

Giliomee, Hermann, James Myburgh, and Lawrence Schlemmer. "Dominant Party Rule, Opposition Parties and Minorities in South Africa." *Democratization* 8, no. 1 (Spring 2001): 161–182.

Gilley, Bruce. *China's Democratic Future: How It Will Happen and Where It Will Lead*. New York: Columbia University Press, 2004.

Goffman, Daniel. *The Ottoman Empire and Early Modern Europe*. Cambridge: Cambridge University Press, 2002.

Goldgeier, James M., and Ivo Daalder. "Global NATO." *Foreign Affairs* 85, no. 5 (September/October 2006): 105–113.

Goldstone, Jack. *Why Europe? The Rise of the West in World History, 1500–1850*. New York: McGraw-Hill, 2008.

Gong, Gerrit W. "China's Entry into International Society." In *The Expansion of International Society,* edited by Hedley Bull and Adam Watson, 171–183. Oxford: Clarendon Press, 1984.

Greengrass, Mark. *The French Reformation*. New York: Basil Blackwell, 1987.

Hacker, Jacob S., and Paul Pierson. *Off Center: The Republican Revolution and the Erosion of American Democracy*. New Haven: Yale University Press, 2005.

Hale, J. R. *Renaissance Europe, 1480–1520*. London: Wiley-Blackwell, 1992.

Halper, Stefan. *The Beijing Consensus: How China's Authoritarian Model Will Dominate the Twenty-First Century*. New York: Basic Books, 2010.

Hayek, Friedrich A. *The Road to Serfdom*. Chicago: University of Chicago Press, 2007.

Hedrick, Daniel R. *The Tools of Empire: Technology and European Imperialism in the Nineteenth Century*. New York: Oxford University Press, 1981.

Heindel, Richard. "Review of *The Private Papers of Senator Vandenberg*." *American Historical Review* 58, no. 2 (January 1953): 401–402.

Herbst, Jeffrey I. *States and Power in Africa: Comparative Lesson in Authority and Control*. Princeton: Princeton University Press, 2000.

Hiroshi, Kashiwagi. "On Rationalization and the National Lifestyle." In *Being Modern in Japan: Culture and Society from the 1910s to the 1930s*, edited by Elise Tipton and John Clark, 61–74. Honolulu: University of Hawaii Press, 2000.

Hoffman, Barak, and Lindsay Robinson. "Tanzania's Missing Opposition." In *Democratization in Africa: Progress and Retreat*, edited by Larry Diamond and Marc F. Plattner, 219–232. Baltimore: The Johns Hopkins University Press, 1999.

Holmes, James R., and Toshi Yoshihara. "When Comparing Navies, Measure Strength, Not Size." *Global Asia* 5, no. 4 (December 2010): 26-31.

Holt, Mack. *New Approaches to European History No. 8: The French Wars of Religion, 1562–1629*. Cambridge: Cambridge University Press, 1995.

Huntington, Samuel P. "How Countries Democratize." *Political Science Quarterly* 106, no. 4 (Winter 1991): 579–616.

Hurrell, Andrew. *On Global Order: Power, Values, and the Constitution of International Society*. Oxford: Oxford University Press, 2007.

Ikenberry, G. John. *After Victory: Institutions, Strategic Restraint, and the Rebuilding of Order after Major Wars*. Princeton: Princeton University Press, 2000.

———. "Liberal Internationalism 3.0: America and the Dilemmas of Liberal World Order." *Perspectives on Politics* 7, no. 1 (March 2009): 71–87.

———. *Liberal Leviathan: The Origins, Crisis, and Transformation of the American World Order*. Princeton: Princeton University Press, 2011.

———. "The Rise of China and the Future of the West." *Foreign Affairs* 87, no. 1 (January/February 2008): 23–37.

Ikenberry, G. John, and Anne-Marie Slaughter. "Forging a World of Liberty Under Law: U.S. National Security in the 21st Century." Princeton: The Princeton Project on National Security, 2006.

Inalcik, Halil. *The Ottoman Empire: The Classical Age 1300–1600*. New York: Praeger, 1976.

International Institute for Strategic Studies. *The Military Balance 2010*. London: Routledge, 2010.

Istrate, Emilia, and Robert Puentes. "Metropolitan Infrastructure Initiative, no. 7: Investing for Success: Examining a Federal Capital Budget and a National Infrastructure Bank." Washington, DC: The Brookings Institution, 2009.

Jacques, Martin. *When China Rules the World: The End of the Western World and the Birth of a New Global Order.* New York: Penguin, 2009.

Judt, Tony. *Postwar: A History of Europe Since 1945.* New York: Penguin Books, 2005.

Kaczmarczyk, Andrzej. "E-Democracy Development and Impact on Business (4)." Toronto: Key Research Center, 2010.

Kagan, Robert. "End of Dreams, Return of History." *Policy Review,* no. 144 (August/September 2007): 17–44.

———. *The Return of History and the End of Dreams.* New York: Knopf, 2008.

Kaufman, Robert. "Conceptual and Historical Perspectives." In *The "New Left" and Democratic Governance in Latin America,* edited by Cynthia J. Arnson and José Raúl Perales, 24–30. Washington, DC: Woodrow Wilson International Center for Scholars, 2007.

Keene, Edward. *Beyond the Anarchical Society: Grotius, Colonialism, and Order in World Politics.* Cambridge: Cambridge University Press, 2002.

Kennedy, Paul. *The Rise and Fall of British Naval Mastery.* London: Macmillan, 1983.

Khalifa, Ali Mohammed. *The United Arab Emirates: Unity in Fragmentation.* Boulder: Westview Press, 1979.

Khana, Parag. *Second World: How Emerging Powers Are Redefining Global Competition in the Twenty-first Century.* New York: Random House, 2008.

Kishlansky, Mark. *A Monarchy Transformed: Britain 1603–1714.* New York: Penguin, 1997.

Kissinger, Henry. "An End of Hubris." *The Economist.* November 19, 2008.

Kupchan, Charles, A. *The End of the American Era: U.S. Foreign Policy and the Geopolitics of the Twenty-first Century.* New York: Knopf, 2002.

———. "The End of the West." *The Atlantic Monthly* 290, no. 4 (November 2002): 42–44.

———. "Enemies into Friends: How the United States Can Court Its Adversaries." *Foreign Affairs* 89, no. 2 (March/April 2010): 120–134.

———. *How Enemies Become Friends: The Sources of Stable Peace.* Princeton: Princeton University Press, 2010.

———. "Minor League, Major Problems: The Case against a League of Democracies." *Foreign Affairs* 80, no. 6 (November/December 2008): 96–109.

———. "NATO's Final Frontier: Why Russia Should Join the Atlantic Alliance." *Foreign Affairs* 89, no. 3 (May/June 2010): 100–112.

Kupchan, Charles A., and Adam Mount. "The Autonomy Rule," *Democracy,* no. 12 (Spring 2009): 8–21.

Kupchan, Charles A., and Peter Trubowitz. "Dead Center: The Decline of Liberal Internationalism in the United States." *International Security* 32, no. 2 (Fall 2007): 7–44.

———. "Grand Strategy for a Divided America." *Foreign Affairs* 86, no. 4 (July/August 2007): 71–83.

———. "The Illusion of Liberal Internationalism's Revival." *International Security* 35, no. 1 (Summer 2010): 95–109.

Kuran, Timur. *The Long Divergence: How Islamic Law Held Back the Middle East.* Princeton: Princeton University Press, 2011.

Lebow, Richard Ned. *Why Nations Fight: Past and Future Motives for War.* Cambridge: Cambridge University Press, 2011.

Leighninger, Matt. *The Next Form of Democracy: How Expert Rule Is Giving Way to Shared Governance—and Why Politics Will Never Be the Same.* Nashville: Vanderbilt University Press, 2006.

Levin, Richard. "Top of the Class: The Rise of Asia's Universities." *Foreign Affairs* 89, no. 3 (May/June 2010): 63–75.

Lewis, Bernard. *Islam in History: Ideas, People, and Events in the Middle East.* Chicago: Open Court, 1993.

———. *Islam and the West.* New York: Oxford University Press, 1993.

Li, Nan, and Christopher Weuve. "China's Aircraft Carrier Ambitions: An Update." *Naval War College Review* 63, no. 1 (Winter 2010): 13–31.

Library of Congress, Federal Research Division. "Country Profile: Saudi Arabia." September 2006.

Lippmann, Walter. *U.S. Foreign Policy: Shield of the Republic.* Boston: Little, Brown and Company, 1943.

Lo, Ming-Cheng and Christopher Bettinger. "The Historical Emergence of a 'Familial Society' in Japan." *Theory and Society* 30, no. 2 (2001): 237–279.

Lockard, Craig A. *Societies, Networks, and Transitions: A Global History.* Vol. 2. 2nd ed. Boston: Wadsworth, 2011.

Luce, Edward. *In Spite of the Gods: The Strange Rise of Modern India.* New York: Random House, 2007.

Lynn, Martin. *Commerce and Economic Change in West Africa: The Palm Oil Trade in the Nineteenth Century.* Cambridge: Cambridge University Press, 1997.

MacCulloch, Diarmaid. *The Later Reformation in England, 1547–1603.* New York: Palgrave, 2001.

———. *The Reformation: A History.* New York: Penguin, 2003.

MacDonald, Scott, and Albert Gastmann. *A History of Credit and Power in the Western World.* New Brunswick: Transaction Publishers, 2004.

Mahbubani, Kishore. *The New Asian Hemisphere: The Irresistible Shift of Global Power to the East.* New York: Public Affairs, 2008.

Makeham, Karl. "Introduction." In *New Confucianism: A Critical Examination,* edited by John Makeham, 1–23. London: Palgrave, 2003.

Mandelbaum, Michael. *The Ideas That Conquered the World: Peace, Democracy, and Free Markets in the Twenty-First Century.* New York: Public Affairs, 2002.

Mann, Michael. *The Sources of Social Power: The Rise of Classes and Nation-States, 1760–1914.* Cambridge: Cambridge University Press, 1993.

Mbow, Penda. "Senegal: The Return of Personalism." In *Democratization in Africa: Progress and Retreat,* edited by Larry Diamond and Marc F. Plattner, 152–165. Baltimore: The Johns Hopkins University Press, 1999.

McCarty, Nolan, Keith T. Poole, and Howard Rosenthal. *Polarized America: The Dance of Ideology and Unequal Riches.* Cambridge: MIT Press, 2006.

McNeill, John R., and William H. McNeill. *The Human Web: A Bird's-Eye View of World History.* New York: Norton, 2003.

McNeill, William H. *History of Western Civilization: A Handbook.* Chicago: University of Chicago Press, 1969.

———. *The Rise of the West: A History of the Human Community.* Chicago: University of Chicago Press, 1963.

Menchi, Silvana Seidel. "Italy." In *The Reformation in National Context,* edited by Robert W. Scribner, Roy Porter, and Mikuláš Teich, 181–201. Cambridge: Cambridge University Press, 1994.

Meredith, Martin. *The Fate of Africa: From the Hopes of Freedom to the Heart of Despair.* New York: Public Affairs, 2005.

Milward, Alan. *The Reconstruction of Western Europe, 1945–51.* Berkeley: University of California Press, 1984.

Montgomery, John. *Forced to Be Free: The Artificial Revolution in Germany and Japan.* Chicago: University of Chicago Press, 1957.

Morris, Ian. *Why the West Rules—For Now: The Patterns of History, and What They Reveal about the Future.* New York: Farrar, Straus and Giroux, 2010.

Mwenda, Andrew. "Personalizing Power in Uganda." In *Democratization in Africa: Progress and Retreat,* edited by Larry Diamond and Marc F. Plattner, 233–247. Baltimore: The Johns Hopkins University Press, 1999.

Naff, Thomas. "The Ottoman Empire and the European States System." In *The Expansion of International Society,* edited by Hedley Bull and Adam Watson, 143–169. Oxford: Clarendon Press, 1984.

Nasr, Vali. *The Shia Revival: How Conflicts within Islam Will Shape the Future.* New York: W.W. Norton, 2006.

National Intelligence Council and Eurasia Group. "Conference Report: Nonstate Actors: Impact on International Relations and Implications for the United States." Washington, DC: National Intelligence Council and Eurasia Group, 2007.

Newman, Gerald, ed. *Britain in the Hanoverian Age, 1714–1837: An Encyclopedia.* London: Routledge, 1997.

Nexon, Daniel. *The Struggle for Power in Early Modern Europe: Religious Conflict, Dynastic Empires, and International Change.* Princeton: Princeton University Press, 2009.

Nye, Joseph. "The Future of American Power." *Foreign Affairs* 89, no. 6 (November/December 2010): 2–12.

Office of Naval Intelligence. "The People's Liberation Army Navy: A Modern Navy with Chinese Characteristics." Washington, DC: Office of Naval Intelligence, 2009.

O'Neill, Jim, and Anna Stupnystka. "Global Economics Paper No: 192: The Long-Term Outlook for the BRICs and N-11 Post Crisis." New York: Goldman Sachs Global Economics, Commodities and Strategic Research, 2009.

O'Rourke, Ronald. "China Naval Modernization: Implications for U.S. Navy Capabilities—Background and Issues for Congress." Washington, DC: Congressional Research Service (April 9, 2010).

Osterhammel, Jürgen, and Niels Petersson. *Globalization: A Short History.* Translated by Dona Geyer. Princeton: Princeton University Press, 2005.

Owen, John. *The Clash of Ideas in World Politics: Transnational Networks, States, and Regime Change, 1510–2010.* Princeton: Princeton University Press, 2010.

Polayni, Karl. *The Great Transformation.* Boston: Beacon Press, 2001.

Patrick, Stewart. *The Best Laid Plans: The Origins of American Multilateralism and the Dawn of the Cold War.* Lanham: Rowman & Littlefield, 2009.

Pei, Minxin. *China's Trapped Transition: The Limits of Developmental Autocracy.* Cambridge: Harvard University Press, 2006.

Perry, Marvin, Myrna Chase, Margaret C. Jacob, James R. Jacob, and Theodore H. Van Laue. *Western Civilization: Ideas, Politics, and Society*, 9th ed. Boston: Houghton Mifflin Harcourt, 2009.

Peterson, Willard J. "Introduction: New Order for the Old Order." In *The Cambridge History of China.* Vol. 9, Part One: *The Ch'ing Empire to 1800*, edited by Willard J. Peterson, 1–8. Cambridge: Cambridge University Press, 2002.

Pew Research Center for the People and the Press. "America's Place in the World 2009: An Investigation of Public and Leadership Opinion about International Affairs." Washington: DC: The Pew Research Center, 2009.

Pew Research Center's Global Attitudes Project. "Most Embrace a Role for Islam in Politics: Muslim Publics Divided on Hamas and Hezbollah." Washington, DC: The Pew Research Center (December 2, 2010).

———. "Muslim Disappointment: Obama More Popular Abroad Than at Home, Global Image of U.S. Continues to Benefit." Washington, DC: The Pew Research Center, 2010.

Philpott, Daniel. *Revolutions in Sovereignty: How Ideas Shaped Modern International Relations.* Princeton: Princeton University Press, 2001.

Pierson, Paul. "Inequality and Its Casualties." *Democracy*, no. 20 (Spring 2011): 27–32.

Pincus, Steven. *1688: The First Modern Revolution.* New Haven: Yale University Press, 2009.

Pion-Berlin, David. "Military Autonomy and Emerging Democracies in South America." *Comparative Politics* 25, no. 1 (October 1992): 83–102.

Pomeranz, Kenneth. *The Great Divergence: China, Europe, and the Making of the Modern World Economy.* Princeton: Princeton University Press, 2000.

Porter, Bernard. *The Lion's Share: A Short History of British Imperialism, 1850–2004.* 4th ed. Harlow: Longman, 2004.

Posner, Daniel, and Daniel Young. "The Institutionalization of Political Power in Africa." In *Democratization in Africa: Progress and Retreat,* edited by Larry Diamond and Marc F. Plattner, 59–72. Baltimore: The Johns Hopkins University Press, 1999.

Pounds, Norman. *The Medieval City.* Westport: Greenwood Press, 2005.

Prempeh, H. Kwasi. "Presidents Untamed." In *Democratization in Africa: Progress and Retreat,* edited by Larry Diamond and Marc F. Plattner, 18–32. Baltimore: The Johns Hopkins University Press, 1999.

Prestwich, Menna. "Calvinism in France, 1559–1629." In *International Calvinism, 1541–1715,* edited by Menna Prestwich, 71–107. Oxford: Clarendon Press, 1985.

Price, Roger. *A Concise History of France.* 2nd ed. Cambridge: Cambridge University Press, 2005.

Putnam, Robert. *Bowling Alone: The Collapse and Revival of American Community.* New York: Simon & Schuster, 2000.

Quataert, Donald. *The Ottoman Empire, 1700–1922.* New York: Cambridge University Press, 2005.

Ramadan, Tariq. *Islam, the West and the Challenges of Modernity.* Leicester: The Islamic Foundation, 2009.

Ramazani, R.K. *The Gulf Cooperation Council: Record and Analysis.* Charlottesville: University of Virginia Press, 1988.

Ramusack, Barbara N. *The Indian Princes and Their States.* Cambridge: Cambridge University Press, 2004.

Reamer, Andrew. "Putting America to Work: The Essential Role of Federal Labor Market Statistics." Washington, DC: The Brookings Institution, 2010.

Reid, Michael. *Forgotten Continent: The Battle for Latin America's Soul.* New Haven: Yale University Press, 2007.

Richards, John F. *The Mughal Empire.* Cambridge: Cambridge University Press, 1996.

Roberts, Kenneth, Leslie Bethness, and René Antonio Mayorga. "Conceptual and Historical Perspectives." In *The "New Left" and Democratic Governance in Latin America,* edited by Cynthia J. Arnson and José Raúl Perales, 10–23. Washington, DC: Woodrow Wilson International Center for Scholars, 2007.

Rohde, David W. *Parties and Leaders in the Postreform House.* Chicago: University of Chicago Press, 1991.

Rossabi, Morris. "The 'Decline' of the Central Asian Caravan Trade." In *The Rise of Merchant Empires: Long Distance Trade in the Early Modern World, 1350–1750*, edited by James D. Tracy, 351–370. New York: Cambridge University Press, 1993.

Roy, Olivier. *Globalized Islam: The Search for a New Ummah*. New York: Columbia University Press, 2006.

———. *Secularism Confronts Islam*. Translated by George Holoch. New York: Columbia University Press, 2007.

Rubio, Luis, and Jeffrey Davidow. "Mexico's Disputed Election." *Foreign Affairs* 85, no. 5 (September 2006): 75–85.

Salmon, J.H.M. *Society in Crisis: France in the Sixteenth Century*, New York: St. Martin's Press, 1975.

Saniel, Josefa M. "The Mobilization of Traditional Values in the Modernization of Japan." In *Religion and Progress in Modern Asia*, edited by Robert Bellah, 124–129. New York: The Free Press, 1965.

Scott, David. *China and the International System, 1840–1949: Power, Presence, and Perceptions in a Century of Humiliation*. Albany: State University of New York, 2008.

———. "India's Drive for a 'Blue Water' Navy." *Journal of Military and Strategic Studies* 10, no. 2 (Winter 2007–2008): 1–42.

Sen, Amartya. *Development as Freedom*. New York: Anchor Books, 2000.

Shambaugh, David. *China's Communist Party: Atrophy and Adaptation*. Washington, DC: Woodrow Wilson Center Press, 2008.

Shirk, Susan. *China: Fragile Superpower*. Oxford: Oxford University Press, 2007.

Southern, Neil. "Political Opposition and the Challenges of a Dominant Party System: The Democratic Alliance in South Africa." *Journal of Contemporary African Studies* 29, no. 3 (July 2011): 281–298.

Spear, Percival. *The Oxford History of Modern India, 1740–1975*. 2nd ed. New Delhi: Oxford University Press, 1978.

Spence, Michael, and Sandile Hlatshwayo. "The Evolving Structure of the American Economy and the Employment Challenge." Maurice R. Greenberg Center for Geoeconomic Studies Working Paper, Council on Foreign Relations, New York, NY, March 2011.

Spruyt, Hendrik. *The Sovereign State and Its Competitors*. Princeton: Princeton University Press, 1994.

Steinfeld, Edward S. *Playing Our Game: Why China's Economic Rise Doesn't Threaten the West*. Oxford: Oxford University Press, 2010.

Suberu, Rotimi. "Nigeria's Muddled Elections." In *Democratization in Africa: Progress and Retreat*, edited by Larry Diamond and Marc F. Plattner, 121–136. Baltimore: The Johns Hopkins University Press, 1999.

Sweig, Julia. *Friendly Fire: Losing Friends and Making Enemies in the Anti-American Century*. New York: Public Affairs, 2006.

Terrill, Ross. *The New Chinese Empire*. New South Wales: University of New South Wales Press, 2003.

Tilly, Charles. "War-Making and State-Making as Organized Crime." In *Bringing the State Back In*, edited by Peter Evans, Dietrich Rueschemeyer, and Theda Skocpol, 169–191. Cambridge: Cambridge University Press, 1985.

Totman, Conrad. *Early Modern Japan*. Los Angeles: University of California Press, 1995.

Tsai, Kellee S. *Capitalism without Democracy: The Private Sector in Contemporary China*. Ithaca: Cornell University Press, 2007.

U.S. Congress, Office of Technology Assessment. *Proliferation of Weapons of Mass Destruction: Assessing the Risks*. OTA-ISC-599. Washington, DC: U.S. Government Printing Office, 1993.

U.S. Department of Defense, Office of the Undersecretary (Comptroller). *Fiscal Year 2011 Budget Request: Overview*. Washington, DC: U.S. Department of Defense, 2010.

van de Walle, Nicolas. "Presidentialism and Clientelism in Africa's Emerging Party Systems." *The Journal of Modern African Studies* 41, no. 2 (June 2003): 297–321.

Walter, Carl, and Fraser Howie. *Red Capitalism: The Fragile Financial Foundation of China's Extraordinary Rise*. Singapore: John Wiley & Sons, 2011.

Watson, Adam. "European International Society and Its Expansion." In *The Expansion of International Society*, edited by Hedley Bull and Adam Watson, 13–32. Oxford: Clarendon Press, 1984.

———. *The Evolution of International Society: A Comparative Historical Analysis*. London: Routledge, 1992.

Weber, Steven, and Bruce Jentleson. *The End of Arrogance: America in the Global Competition of Ideas*. Cambridge: Harvard University Press, 2010.

The White House. *National Security Strategy of the United States*. Washington, DC: The White House, 2010.

Wilson, Dominic, and Anna Stupnytska. "Global Economics Paper No. 153: The N-11: More Than an Acronym." New York: Goldman Sachs Economic Research, 2007.

Wilson, Peter. *The Thirty Years War: Europe's Tragedy*. Cambridge: Harvard University Press, 2009.

Wittfogel, Karl. *Oriental Despotism: A Comparative Study of Total Power*. New Haven: Yale University Press, 1957.

Wolpert, Stanley A. *India*. 3rd ed. Berkeley: University of California Press, 2005.

———. *A New History of India*. 8th ed. New York: Oxford University Press, 2009.

Zakaria, Fareed. *The Post-American World*. New York: Norton, 2008.

# INDEX